RODIN

AT THE MUSÉE RODIN

AT THE MUSÉE RODIN

RODIN

Jacques Vilain
Director of the Musée Rodin
General Curator of French Heritage

Claudie Judrin
Head Curator of Drawings and the Collection

Antoinette Le Normand-Romain
Head Curator of Sculpture

Alain Beausire
Archivist and Librarian

Hélène Pinet
In charge of photograph collections

Hélène Marraud
Research assistant to the Head Curator of Sculpture

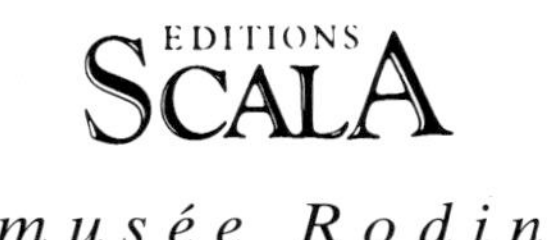

musée Rodin

© 1996 Éditions Scala
26 rue de Charonne, 75011 Paris
All rights reserved

Translated from French by Judith Hayward
Copy edited by Maggie Doyle
Design : Jérôme Faucheux
Cover design : Jean-Pierre Jauneau

Distributed by CDE - Sodis

All the works reproduced are by Auguste Rodin unless the name of another artist is given.
All form part of the collection of the Musée Rodin except where another provenance is specified.
The measurements given in the captions are in centimetres.

TABLE OF CONTENTS

Foreword

Rodin took up residence in the Hôtel Biron, a magnificent eighteenth-century town house and one of the jewels of the French *rocaille* style, in 1908. Emptied of its paintings, panelling and ironwork by the previous occupants, the very straitlaced Dames du Sacré-Coeur de Jésus, the house at that time looked desolate, an impression reinforced by a number of added buildings. However, the garden in its abandoned state had a certain charm, and Rilke commented: "My dear friend, you should see this fine building and the room I have been living in since this morning. Its three bays provide a prodigious view of an abandoned garden where every so often you can see unsuspecting rabbits hopping through the trellis work like on early tapestries." Rodin installed his Greco-Roman marbles there along with some of his monumental sculptures such as *The Walking Man* or *Jean d'Aire*.

During his time there Rodin associated with a number of artists, including not only Rainer Maria Rilke but Cocteau, Matisse and the dancer Isadora Duncan. At the beginning of the twentieth, century at the age of 68, he seemed like a patriarch beside these young artists, all in their different ways representing modernity. Rodin fell in love with the place and formed the project of donating all his collections to the State so that they could be installed at the Hôtel Biron, so transforming it into a Rodin museum, just like the Villa des Brillants which he owned at Meudon. The negotiations were protracted and difficult, but came to a successful conclusion; the acceptance of the three donations by a vote in Parliament was officially confirmed by publication in *Le Journal Officiel de la République Française* on 24 December 1916. However, Rodin died on 17 November 1917 and was not able to see the opening of the museum he had so much wanted.

Only once the huge task of arranging, classifying, inventorying and making photographic records had recently been completed was it possible to gauge the vastness and variety of Rodin's bequest. The Musée Rodin does not consist solely of the marbles and bronzes on view; to give some idea of its scope, there are over 6000 works in plaster, more than 6000 of the photographs passionately hoarded by the artist, including the famous series of 84 shots by Steichen, over 7800 drawings, over 7000 items from his own collection – mainly Greco-Roman antiquities but also paintings by Monet, Renoir or Van Gogh – not forgetting a library and a huge archive containing tens of thousands of exhibits. Adhering to a revealing pattern of behaviour aimed at preparing his own posterity, Rodin kept everything: the letters he received, his rough drafts, his bills... From the 1880s he subscribed to the press cuttings agency *Je Lis Tout* which has since become the *Argus de la Presse*; this is how we now come to have press cuttings about him dating back over more than 110 years.

As can be seen, this donation is an inexhaustible resource for research students and specialists. It is from this base that the story of Rodin's life and work in all its diversity and complexity can be constructed little by little.

This book is the first to take account of the whole collection and we feel sure that the public who are not familiar with the museum "backstage" will be surprised to discover what treasures we have in store.

It is often said that a museum that fails to add to its collections is a dying museum. The imposing iconography illustrating this book demonstrates that the opposite is true of our museum, and seventeen of the works illustrated are among the many that have been acquired by the museum since 1980. Through these purchases but also through its catalogues, inventories or publications, and exhibitions both at the museum and abroad, the Musée Rodin demonstrates an undeniable vitality, a vitality that we hope to share with you through this book.

JACQUES VILAIN
Director of the Musée Rodin
General Curator of French Heritage

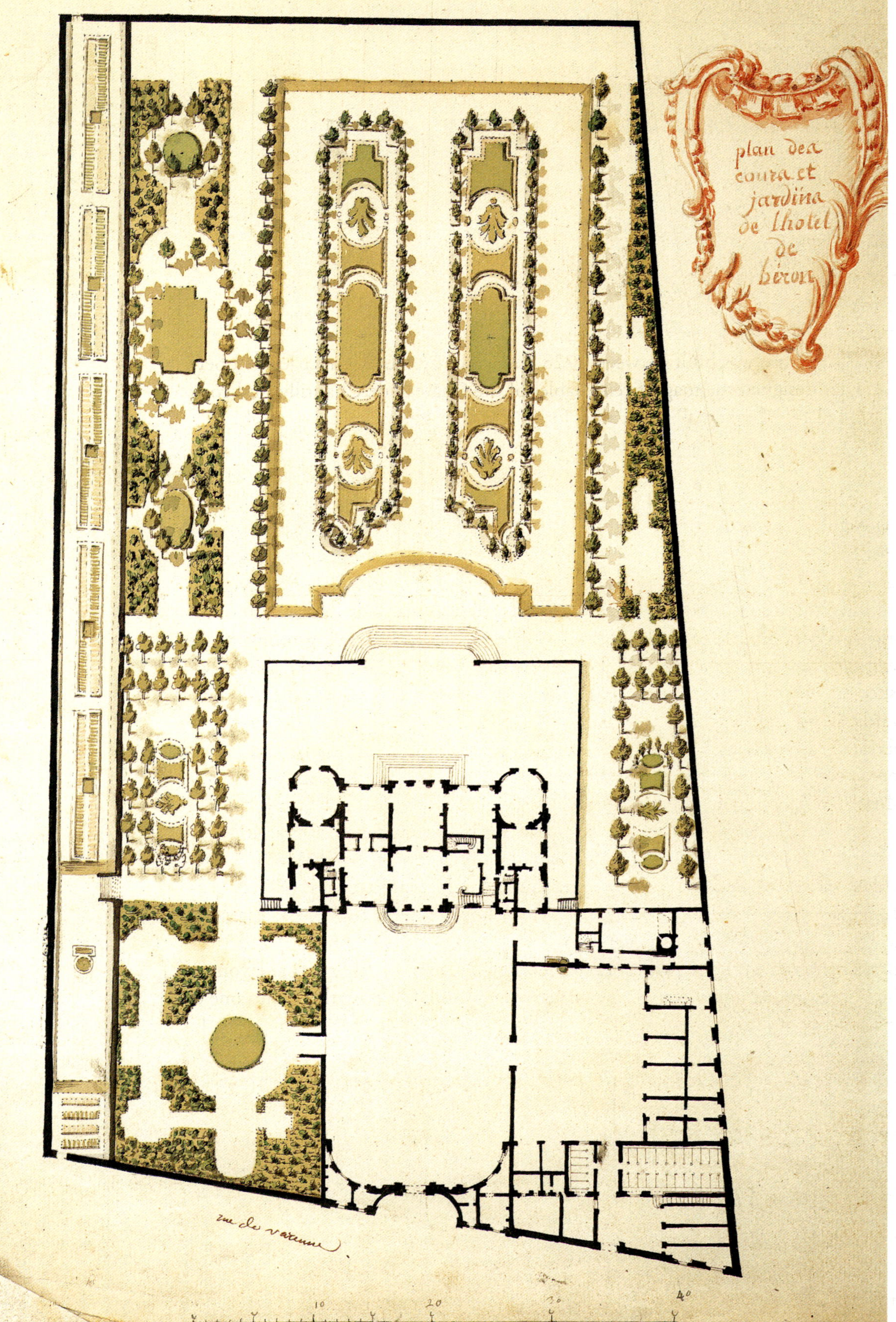
plan des
cours et
jardins
de lhotel
de
biron
rue de varenne
10
20
30
40

From the Hôtel Biron to the Musée Rodin

Jacques Vilain

The Hôtel Biron stands below the dome of the Invalides at 77 rue de Varenne. It is not located between a courtyard and a garden like most of the large houses in the Faubourg Saint-Germain, but is detached like a real château, surrounded by three hectares (7.4 acres) of grounds.

The house was built between 1728 and 1730 by the architect Jean Aubert, who later designed the magnificent stables of the Château de Chantilly, and commissioned by Abraham Peyrenc de Moras, a wig-maker who had made his fortune through speculating in paper money. Although Peyrenc de Moras was one of the *nouveaux riches*, he demonstrated unerring good taste, calling on Aubert who created one of the masterpieces of *rocaille* architecture in this house. The beauty of the façades, the south pediment and the masks above the windows is equalled by the refinement of the internal decoration, particularly the skilfully carved panelling in the suite of five interconnecting rooms overlooking the grounds to the south. Fortunately the museum was able to buy back much of the original decor after World War II, the panelling of the oval drawing-rooms to the east and west in particular. François Lemoyne, First Painter to the King, was asked to supply the painted decor, sixteen medallions or overdoors; shortly afterwards he was to undertake the decoration of the ceiling of the *salon d'Hercule* at Versailles. Recently the museum was able to buy back three overdoors and restore them to their original positions, while a fourth which has been deposited at the Musée Rodin by Nancy museum has been installed in the Camille Claudel room.

As we can see, the house in 1730 was notable for its magnificence and refinement. However, Peyrenc de Moras did not enjoy it long as he died in 1732; his widow subsequently rented it out to the duchesse du Maine, Louis XIV's daughter-in-law, until her death in 1753. The property was then sold to the maréchal de Biron, who had distinguished himself at the Battle of Fontenoy, and from then on it bore his name. Biron made very few changes to the internal layout of the house, but he completely transformed the grounds, turning them into one of finest parks in Paris, commented on by all the guides of the period. In 1782 the comte and comtesse du Nord - actually the future Tsar Paul I who was travelling incognito using this pseudonym - visited the Hôtel Biron: "Their Imperial Highnesses studied the garden which is one of the wonders of Paris, admiring the beauty of the flowers and the variety of the borders. They walked among the flower beds and the shrubberies, marvelling at the boldness and elegance of the trellis work forming gateways, arcades, grottoes, domes, Chinese pavilions..."

When the maréchal de Biron died in 1788 the estate passed to his nephew, the duc de Lauzun; despite the fact that he had been a hero in the American War of Independence and commanded the Revolutionary Army of the Rhine, he was guillotined in 1793. The property was rented out to people who organized public balls and started on its downward spiral, the magnificent flower beds making way

After Jean-François Blondel
Plan of the Courts and Gardens of the Hôtel Biron,
after 1752
Pen and water colour with traces of graphite on cream paper. 45.2 x 29.4
Acquired in 1995
Inv. D.7791

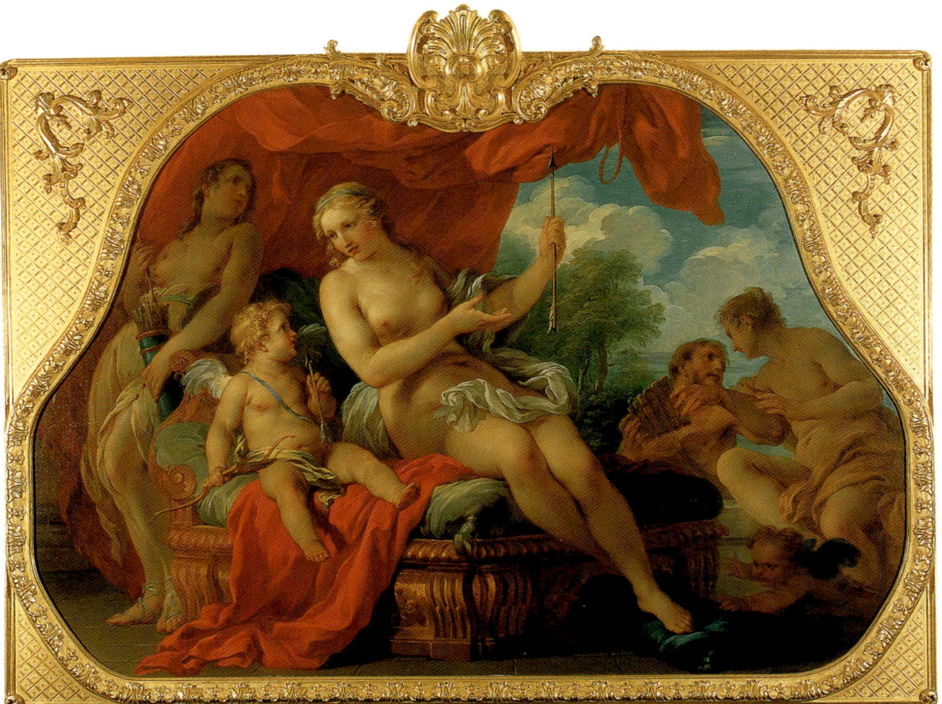

François Lemoyne
(1688-1737)
Venus and the Graces Showing Cupid the Ardour of his Arrows,
*c.*1728
Canvas. 109 x 164
Acquired in 1987
Inv. P.7681

for a fairground. However during the Consulate and the Empire the house reverted to its original purpose housing the Papal legate, and then the Russian ambassador.

The house still belonged to the duchesse de Béthune-Charost and its future was destined to be in line with the devout duchess's religious principles. In 1820 it was handed over to the Société du Sacré-Coeur de Jésus, founded in 1804 by Mother Sophie Barat and devoted to the education of young girls of aristocratic and noble birth. Life there was hard and austere; Marie Dagoult, the Egeria of Franz Liszt, described the daily routine of the boarders who got up at 6 a.m., lived with no heating and washed in cold water. Banishing all luxury from the house, the Mother Superior Sophie Barat had all superfluous elements such as panelling, mirrors, iron work and paintings removed. Some time later in 1875-1876 the chapel was built by the architect Lisch - it is now used as a temporary exhibition room. This was the blackest period in the history of the Hôtel Biron, and when it was confiscated in 1905 as a result of the application of the law separating Church and State property, it looked no more than an empty shell surrounded by derelict grounds.

Although the intention was that it should be demolished, it meanwhile served as a temporary home to an impressive number of artists: Jean Cocteau, Henri Matisse, the actor de Max, Isadora Duncan who had her dancing school in a building standing in the *cour d'honneur* that has now been demolished, as well as Rodin who on Rainer Maria Rilke's advice took up residence in the suite of south-facing drawing-rooms in 1908. Although he carried on living and working at the Villa des Brillants in Meudon, Rodin was enchanted by the beauty of the house and the wild charm of the grounds. He assembled his works there, covering the walls with his drawings and filling the park with his Greek and Roman antiquities; he received a number of distinguished guests there under the eagle eye of the redoubtable duchesse de Choiseul.

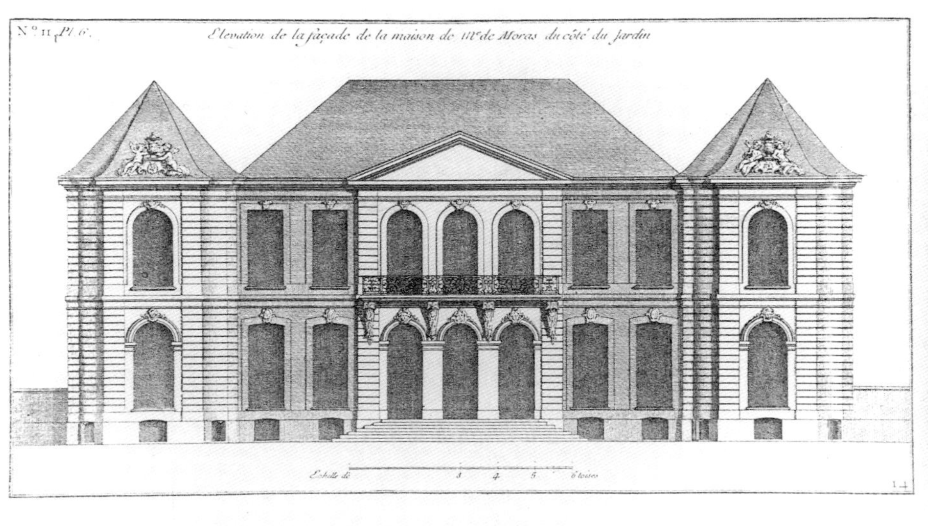

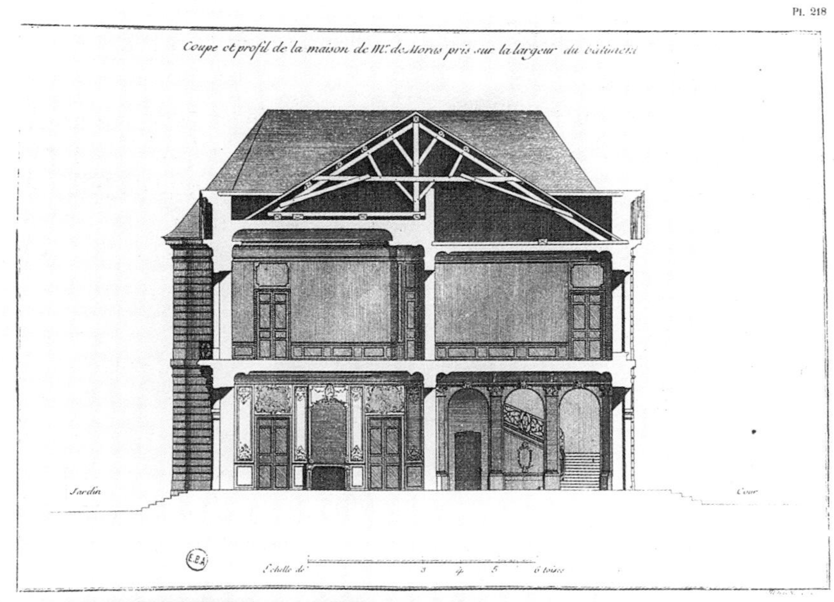

Jean-François Blondel
(1683-1756)
Elevation of the Garden Façade of Madame de Moras's House,
Book 2, Plate 6

Cross-section and Profile of Madame de Moras's House
Book 2, Plate 7
L'Architecture Française,
Paris, 1752

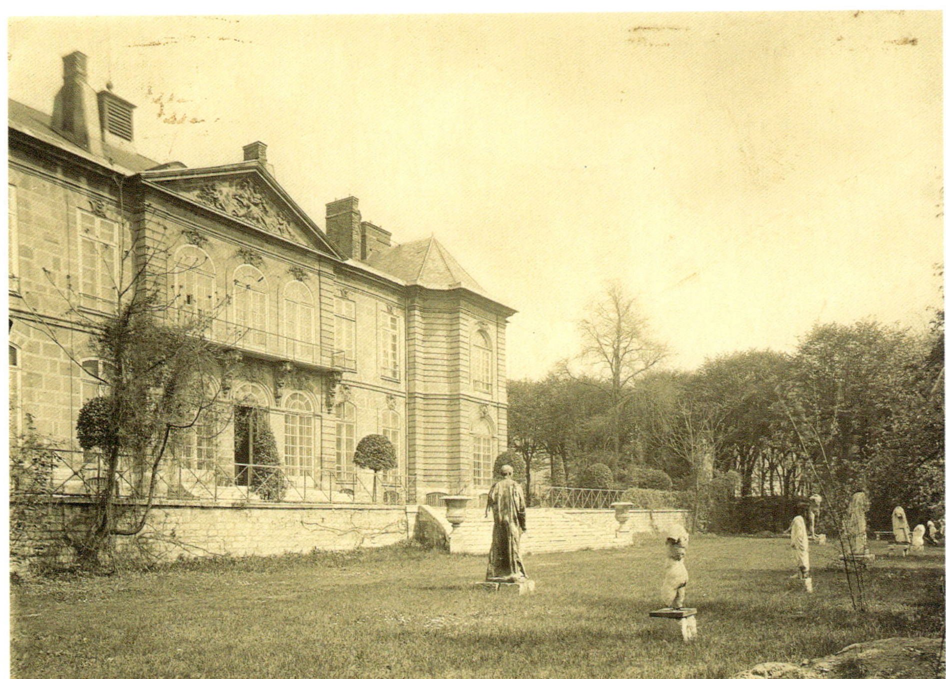

Charles Berthelomier
Hôtel Biron Viewed from the Garden,
*c.*1912
Gelatin silver print. 12.4 x 16.8
Rodin donation, 1916
Inv. Ph.6019

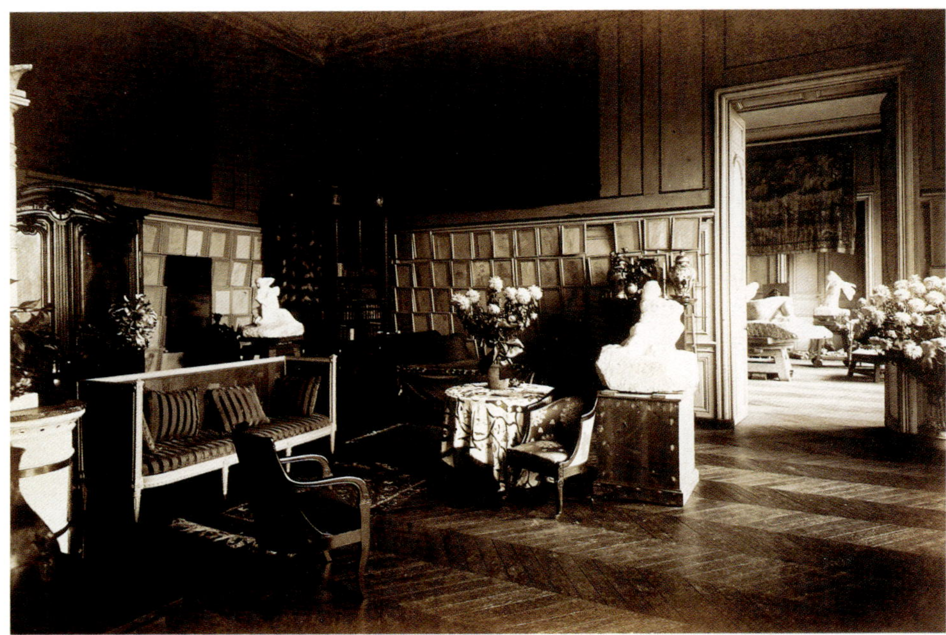

Henri Manuel
View of a Room in the Hôtel Biron,
*c.*1914
Silver print. 15.2 x 22.3
Rodin donation, 1916
Inv. Ph.1382

In 1911 the State bought the property, with the south part lopped off and assigned to the Lycée Victor Duruy, while Rodin hatched the plan of handing over everything he had collected to the State on condition that a museum was devoted to him at the Hôtel Biron. Claude Monet, Octave Mirbeau, Raymond Poincaré, Georges Clemenceau and Étienne Clémentel were among those supporting the scheme, but it was still difficult to bring to a successful conclusion because even at that period the sculptor's art was still so little understood, or even regarded as the work of the devil. The three donations were approved by a vote in Parliament and made official on 24 December 1916, with Rodin giving the State all his collections, his photographs and archives, as well as all his work -

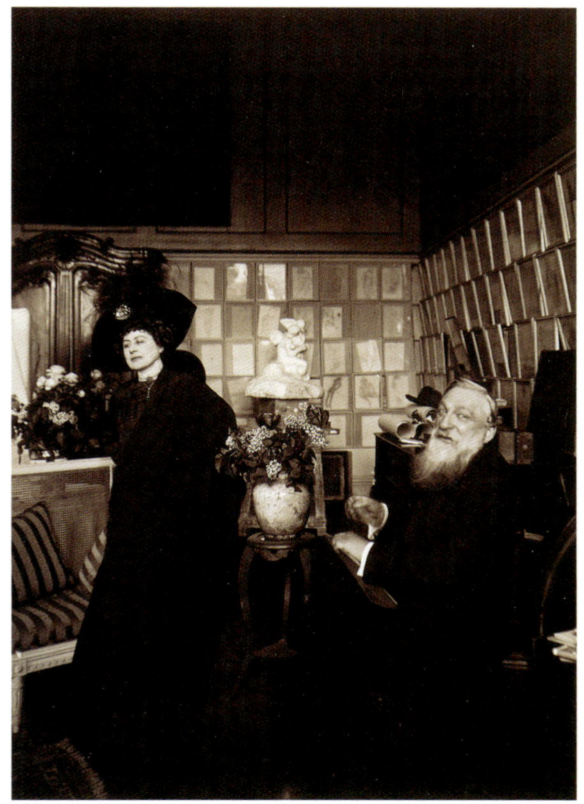

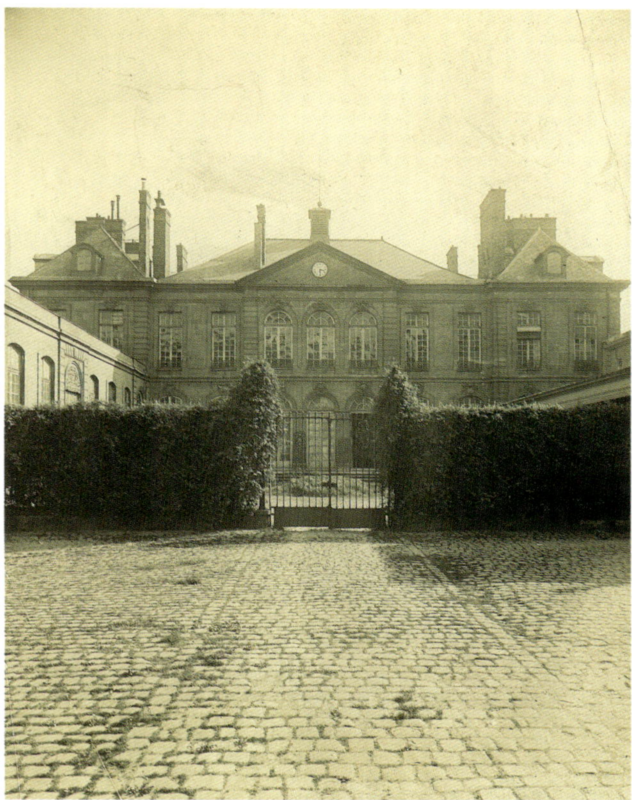

sculptures and drawings - along with the proprietary rights that went with it. As Rodin died on 17 November 1917 he did not see the materialization of his final dream, the opening of his own museum, which took place in 1919.

As a Public Administrative Establishment under the aegis of the Ministry of Culture, the Musée Rodin is endowed with a legal personality and is independent with regard to its income and expenditure. With an average of 600,000 visitors a year, it is one of the most popular museums in France, coming after the Louvre, Versailles and the Musée d'Orsay, but ahead of the Orangerie and the Picasso museum. This obviously reflects the renown and notoriety of Rodin's work. It also reflects the special charm of the site and its grounds, the whole southern part of which was remodelled in 1993, but also of the building housing the Master's works and collections. Everything comes from Rodin, including the chairs, armchairs or sofas where visitors are free to sit down. The Musée Rodin does not set out to reconstitute a period, which would in any case be impossible, but it offers the unique charm of an artist's home where it is pleasant to stroll at leisure. It is this special quality that characterizes the museum and makes it stand out against the backdrop of other French museums.

Henri Manuel
Rodin and the Duchesse de Choiseul at the Hôtel Biron, *c.*1910
Silver print. 21.5 x 15.5
Rodin donation, 1916
Inv. Ph.863

Cl. Lemery
Hôtel Biron Viewed from the Court, *c.*1912
Silver print. 20.9 x 16.6
Acquired in 1995
Inv. Ph.9025

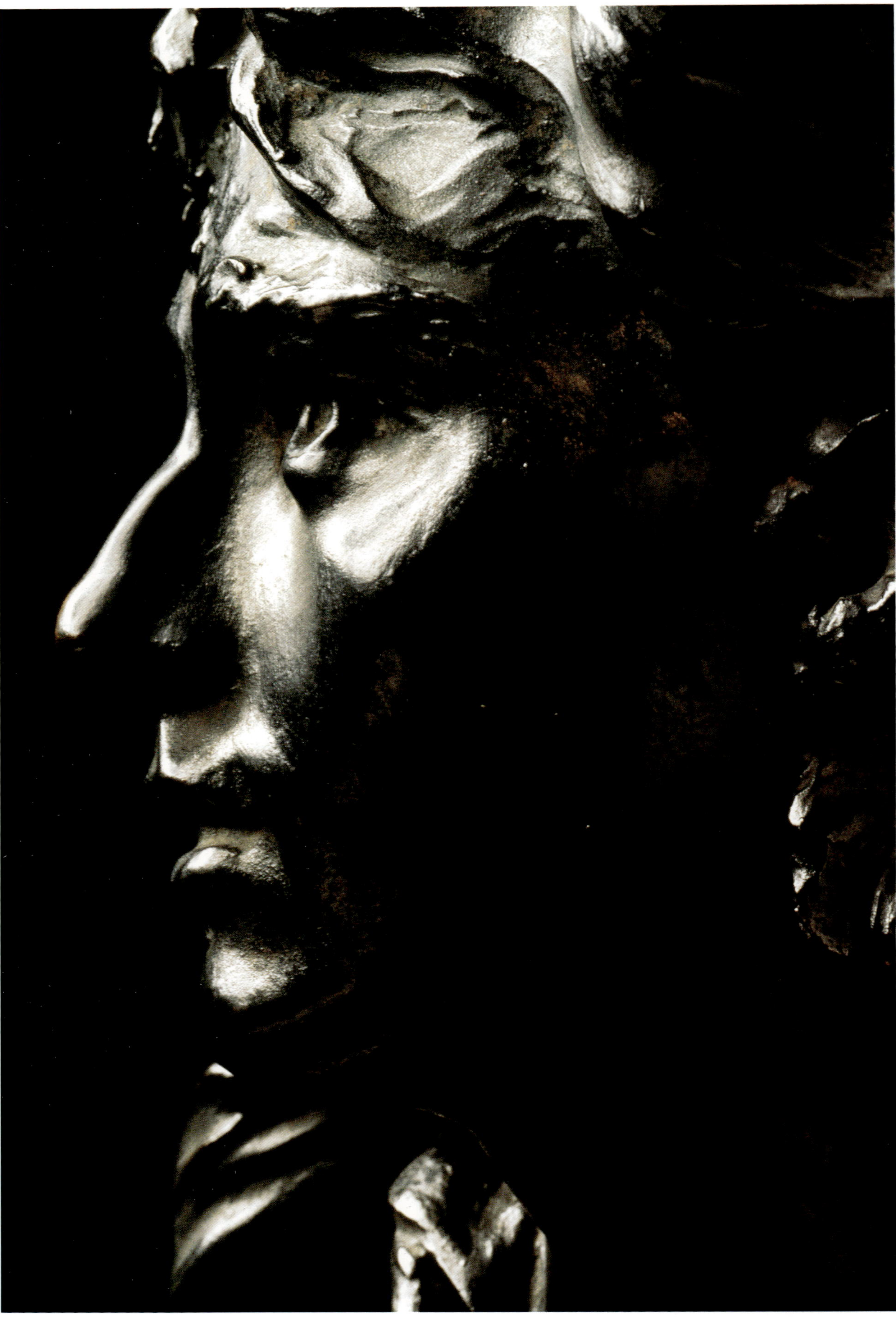

Youth, training, time in Brussels

Hélène Marraud

Auguste was fourteen years old when he went to the Ecole Spéciale de Dessin et Mathématiques, the future Ecole des Arts Décoratifs, known as the Petite Ecole, in 1854. From Lecoq de Boisbaudran he learnt how to draw from memory and he studied the great masters at the Louvre. After three unsuccessful applications to study at the Ecole des Beaux-Arts he worked for ornamentalists and then for Carrier-Belleuse (1864-1872) and this enabled him to earn his living and acquire tremendous skill. Rodin himself said: "In the workshop of a decorator and ornamentalist you carry out work which has some responsibility attached to it as it meets a need, and this makes your hand alert. Thus you learn to see quickly what has to be done, to determine the means of guaranteeing good handiwork, not to get bogged down in detail, in short to do what is necessary (...) you learn to have a high regard for work."

The modeller Constant, whom he met at the start of his career in a decoration workshop, opened his eyes to the skill of relief, an aspect of the work which was to affect Rodin's oeuvre profoundly: "Watching me one day as I modelled a capital decorated with foliage in the clay he said to me, 'Rodin, you're going about it the wrong way. All the leaves are shown flat. That's why they don't look real. Why don't you make some with the tips pointing towards you so that when you look at them you get a sense of depth.' I followed his advice and was amazed by the results I achieved."

He carried out his first personal pieces of sculpture, the portraits of his father *Jean-Baptiste Rodin* (1860), that of *Père Eymard* (1863), the founder of the Order of the Pères du Saint-Sacrement which he had entered for a time after the death of his sister Maria, and *The Man with the Broken Nose* (1864) while following courses given by Barye at the Museum d'Histoire Naturelle. It was at this time that he met Rose Beuret, his lifelong companion, by whom he had a son two years later.

In February 1871 after the war was over he rejoined Carrier-Belleuse in Brussels, collaborated in some decorative work (at the Bourse and the Palais des Académies, the Caryatids) and went into partnership with the sculptor Van Rasbourgh in 1873.

Rodin made some decorative busts, such as *Suzon* and *Dosia*, editions of which were cast in bronze and distributed widely, small trifles such as *Venus and Cupid* and portraits, works of a more personal nature, such as *Doctor Thiriar* and *De Vigne*. He was close to artists such as Dillens or Constantin Meunier and took part in several exhibitions within Belgium and abroad in the Belgian section (London, 1872-73; Vienna, 1873; Philadelphia, 1876). He then went to Italy (from the end of 1875 until March 1876), to Florence in particular, where he discovered Michelangelo with great excitement; in 1877 he produced *The Age of Bronze*, a work that was decisive for his future.

Rodin loved Belgium, its countryside – "Dear forest of Groenendaël!... That may be where I found my wild muse" – and its painters, Rubens in particular, after whom he made a great many studies.

Mignon (detail),
*c.*1870
Bronze, cast by Alexis Rudier.
41 x 31 x 27
Rodin donation, 1916
Inv. S.973

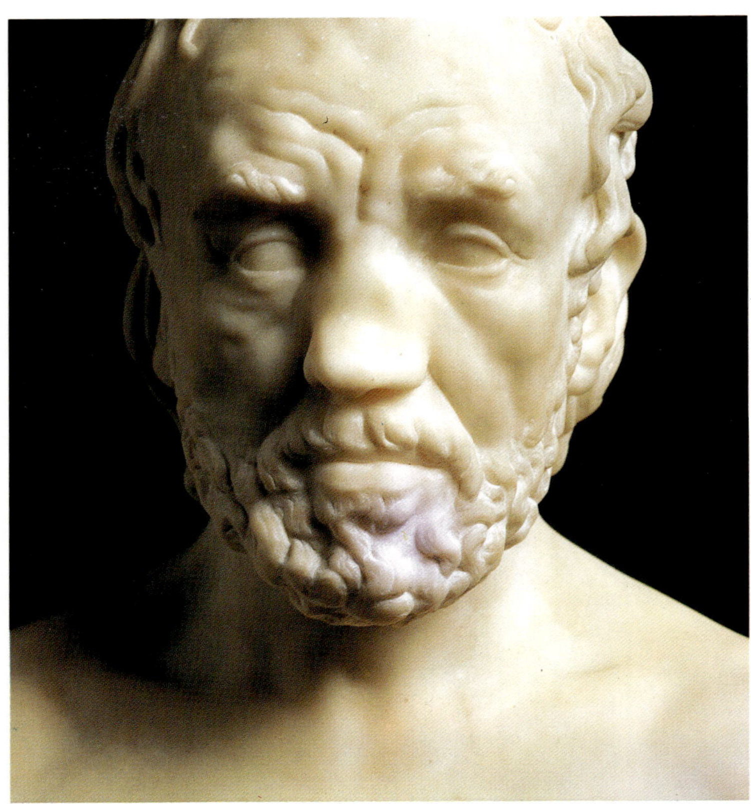

The Man with the Broken Nose,
1865
Marble executed by Léon Fourquet.
44.8 x 41.5 x 23.9
Exhibited at 1875 Salon
Rodin donation, 1916
Inv. S.974

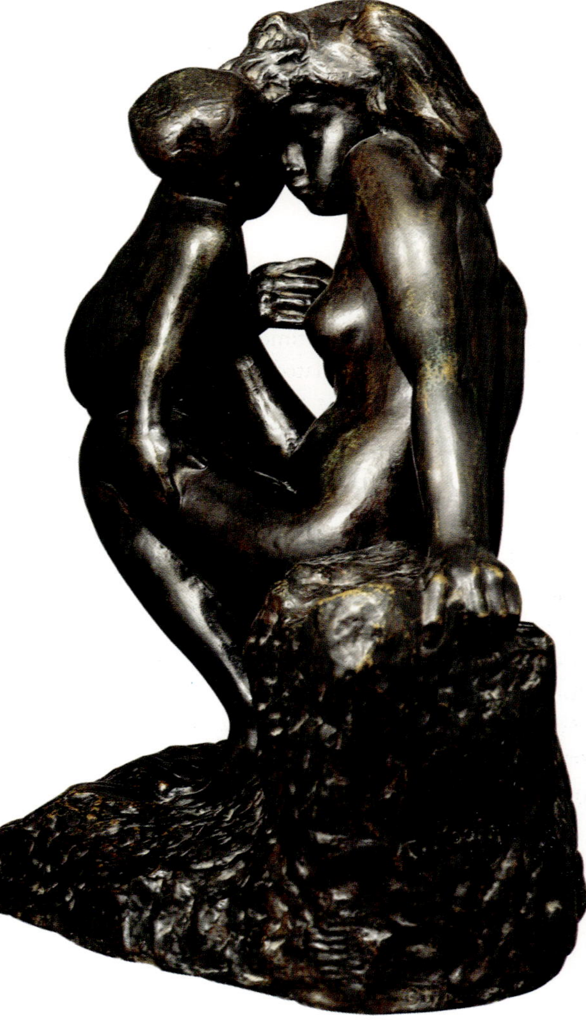

The Young Mother,
1885
Bronze, cast by Georges Rudier.
39 x 36.9 x 25.5
Cast for the Museum's collections in 1956
Inv. S.977

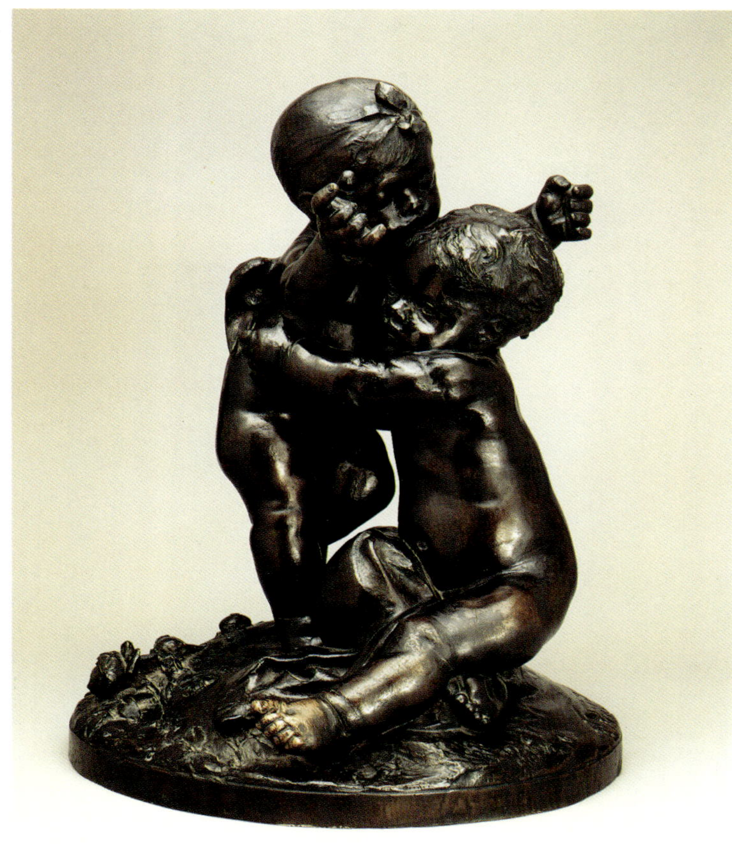

The Idyll of Ixelles,
1885
Bronze. 53 x 41 x 41.5
Acquired in 1956
Inv. S.978

Young Woman in the Floral Hat,
*c.*1865
Terra cotta (on small marble pedestal).
69 x 34 x 29
Acquired between 1944 and 1959
Inv. S.1056

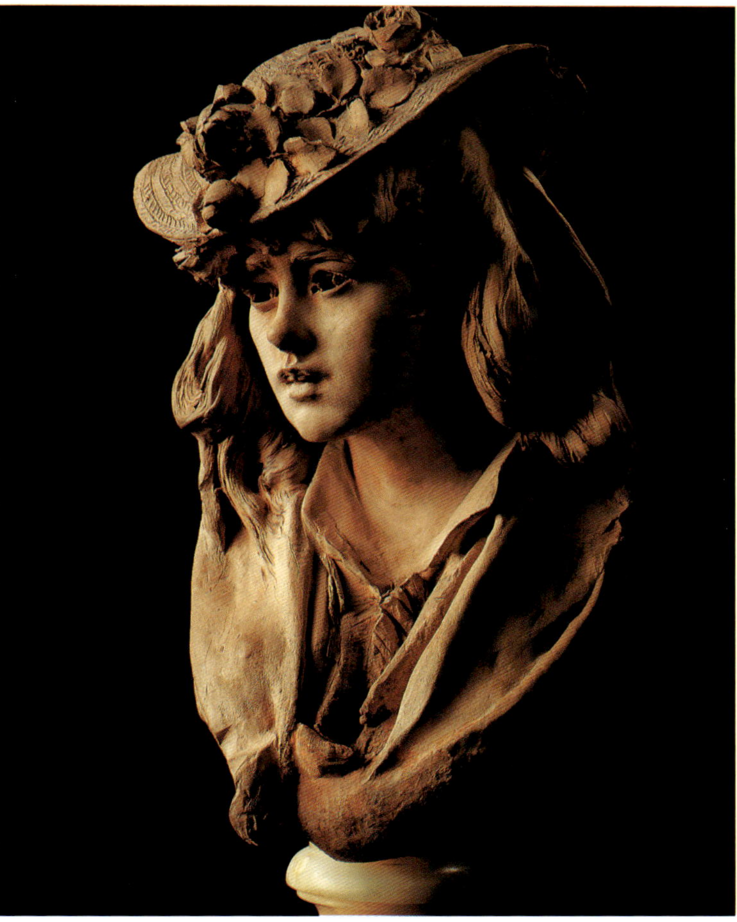

The Man with the Broken Nose is a striking work refused by the 1865 Salon in Paris, then exhibited for the first time in Brussels in 1872 before being translated into marble; it clear-sightedly reveals the features of "Bibi", an odd-job man working in the Saint-Marcel district.

The Young Woman in the Floral Hat on the other hand conjures up all the decorative grace beloved by the Second Empire.

Mignon, named after one of Goethe's heroines, is a true portrait where the powerful temperament of the model, Rose Beuret, shows through.

The Young Mother and *The Idyll of Ixelles* were sculpted a little later in the pleasing style Rodin learnt from Carrier-Belleuse.

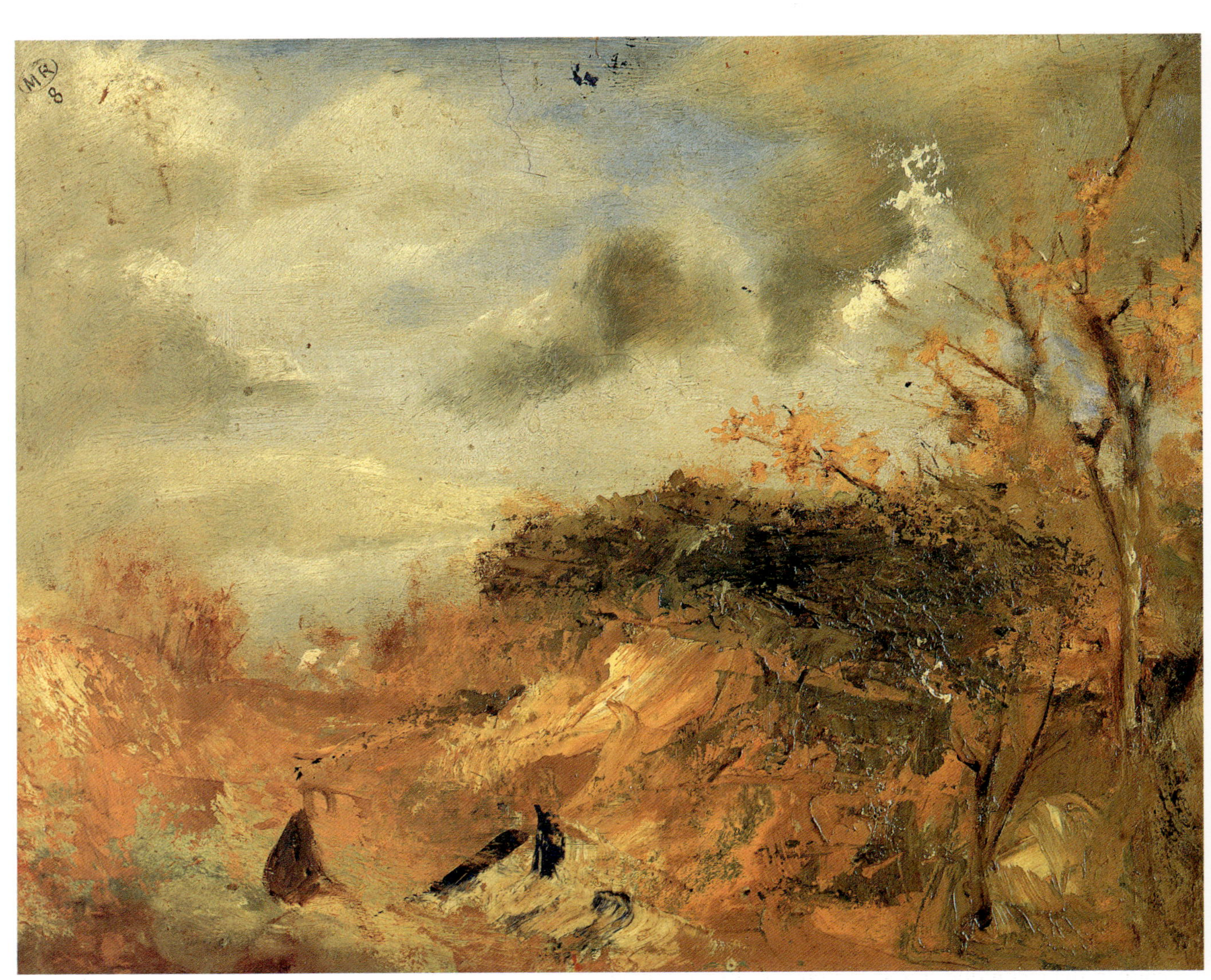

Rodin as painter and engraver

Claudie Judrin

Rodin painted before he sculpted and throughout his youth seemed to hesitate between the two disciplines. His original liking for drawing encouraged him to try oils. He must have learnt human anatomy at the Petite Ecole in the rue de l'Ecole-de-Médecine. The nudes used in the studios were his first models *c.*1855. Then there were portraits including those of family and friends: Rodin's father *Jean-Baptiste*, one of his friends *Abel Poulain* and *Mme Rodin.* He even did a *Self-portrait* later on when he was between thirty and forty years old. In his painting he was not much drawn to animals as a subject, except for a *Horse* which he saw at the Saint-Marcel market when he was in digs at 96 rue Lebrun in 1864.

Is there any means of learning how to paint without copying! In Belgium where Rodin took refuge after the Franco-Prussian War of 1870 he took great pleasure in copying Rubens paintings such as the *Crucifixion* after the *Coup de Lance* at Antwerp museum. The Forest of Soignes near Brussels was a favourite resort between 1871 and 1877. Working from nature he produced many small landscape compositions glued onto cardboard, very free in their inspiration, reminiscent in style of the Lyons landscapist Auguste Ravier, a precursor of Impressionism, discreet in their appeal but not devoid of boldness.

On his return from Belgium Rodin found himself obliged to take on decorative work at the Sèvres porcelain factory. At the same period the etcher Alphonse Legros, who had taken refuge in London, taught him how to use drypoint on copper, the technique closest to drawing. Rodin joined Legros in England in 1881 and a plate engraved on either side by the two men shows how closely they worked together. Rodin's *Cupids Leading the World* is matched by a scored-through, probably unique study of a *Woman's Head* by Legros. A woman, cupids and centaurs all form part of the familiar repertory of the creator of *The Gates of Hell.* Whether he was working as a sculptor, a ceramicist, a graphic artist or an engraver, the themes were the same.

The success of his busts and his total mastery of drypoint prompted Rodin to engrave after his sculptures. He did not scruple to "assemble profiles" on a single copper plate, placing a three-quarter view of the writer Henri Becque alongside his two profiles. Rather than effacing his experiments he juxtaposed them, so profiting from his second thoughts. The *Three-quarter View of Victor Hugo* is the finest example of this.

Small Sand Pit in the Forest of Soignes,
between 1871 and 1877
Oil on cloth-backed paper. 28 x 36.5
Rodin donation, 1916
Inv. P.7218

Three-quarter View of Victor Hugo,
1885
Drypoint, 2nd state. 22.6 x 17.7 (plate)
Rodin donation, 1916
Inv. Gr.29

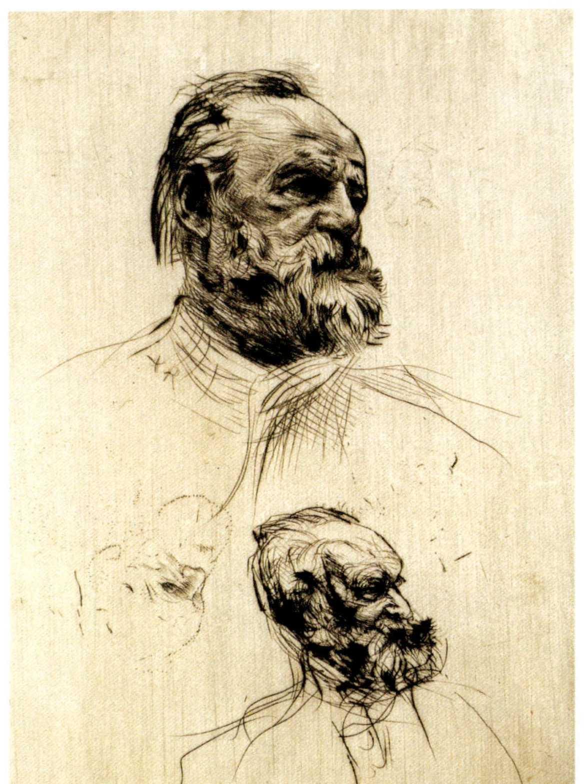

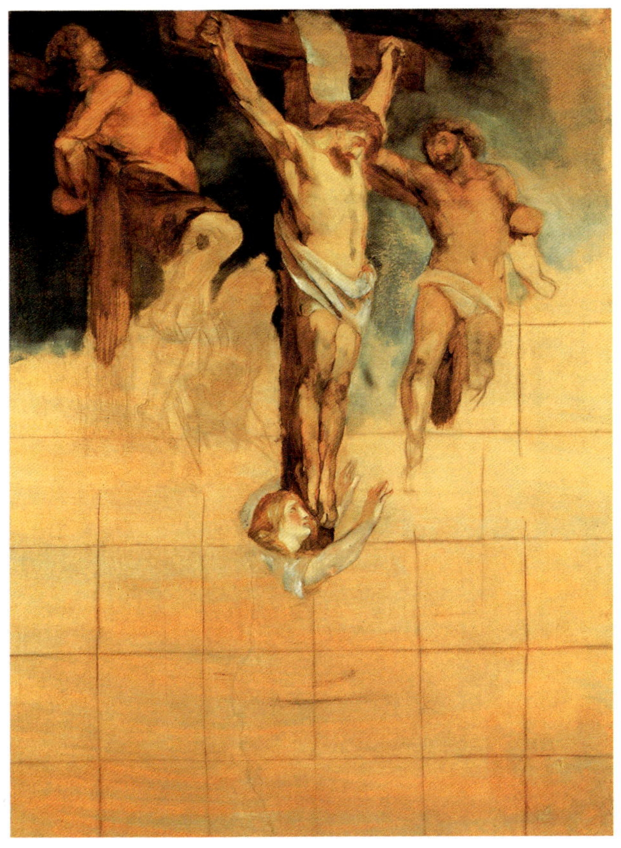

Crucifixion: Copy after Rubens' Coup de Lance *at the Royal Museum of Antwerp,*
between 1871-1877
Oil on cloth-backed paper. 105 x 78
Rodin donation, 1916
Inv. P.7244

The Horse,
*c.*1864?
Oil on cloth-backed paper. 31.3 x 40.7
Rodin donation, 1916
Inv. P.7241

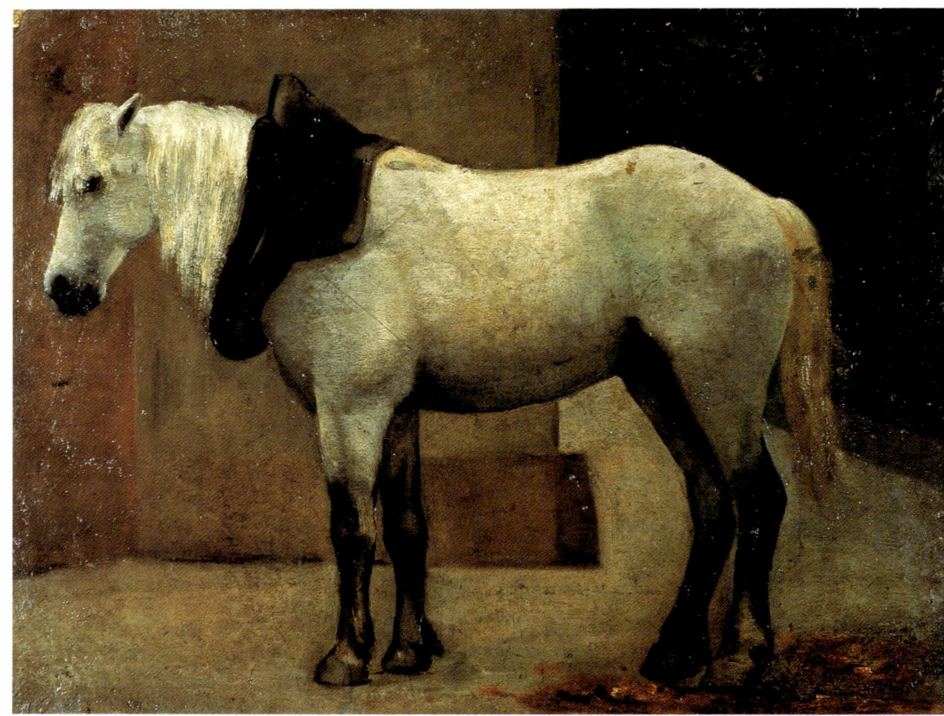

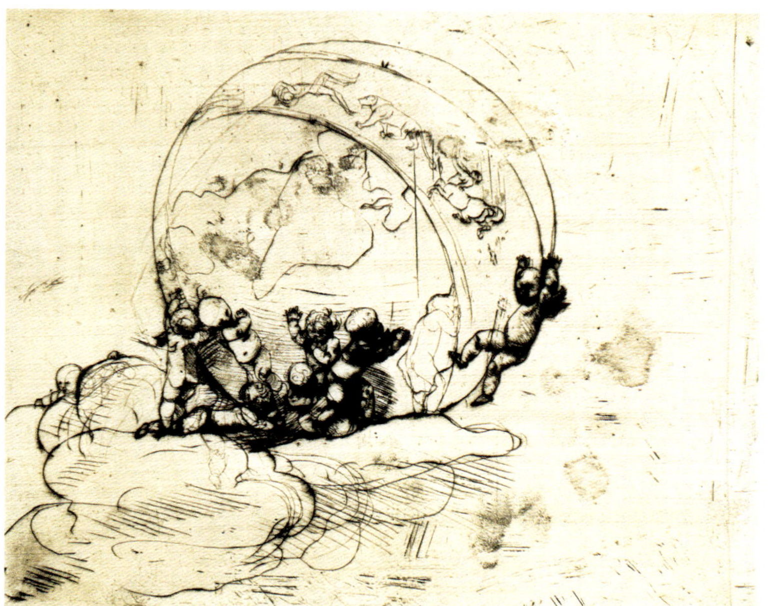

Les Amours Conduisant le Monde,
1881
Drypoint, 2nd state. 20 x 25 (plate)
Rodin donation, 1916
Inv. Gr.1

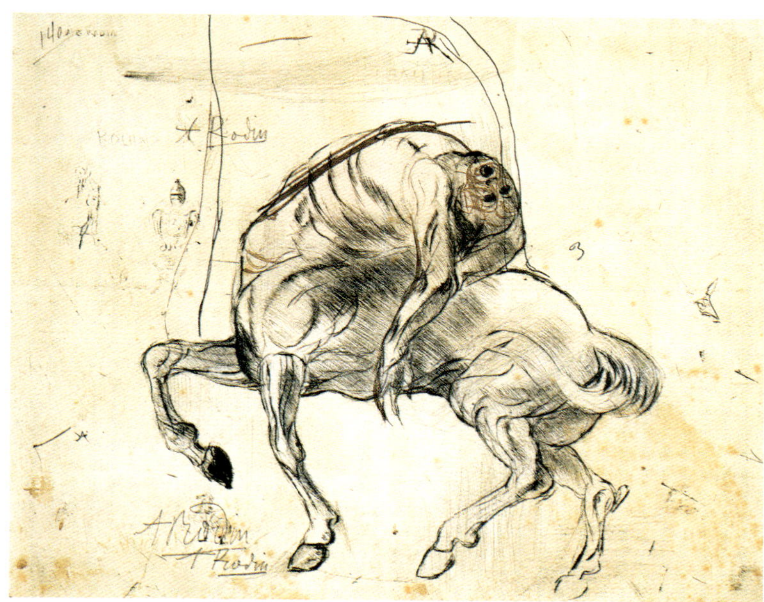

Dying Centaur
Drypoint retouched in pen and brown ink. 18.2 x 22.7
Acquired in 1992
Inv. G.7757

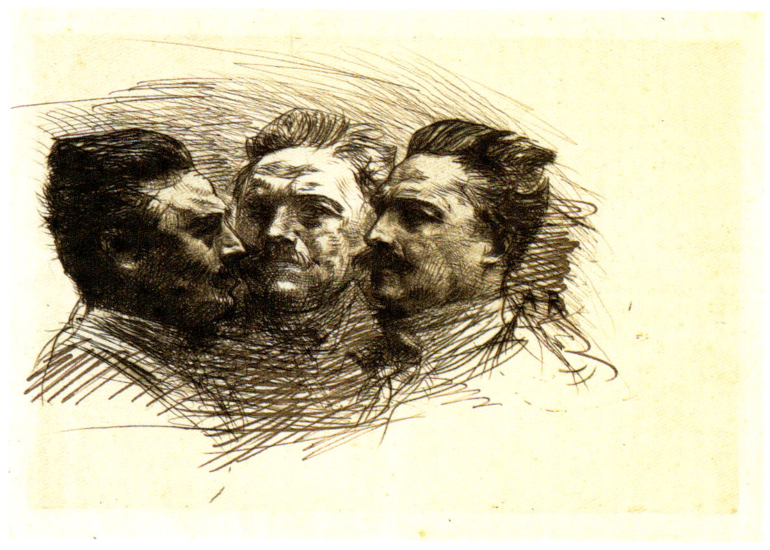

Henri Becque,
1883
Drypoint, 1st state. Retouched in pen and black ink. 15.7 x 20.3 (plate)
Acquired in 1991
Inv. G.7751

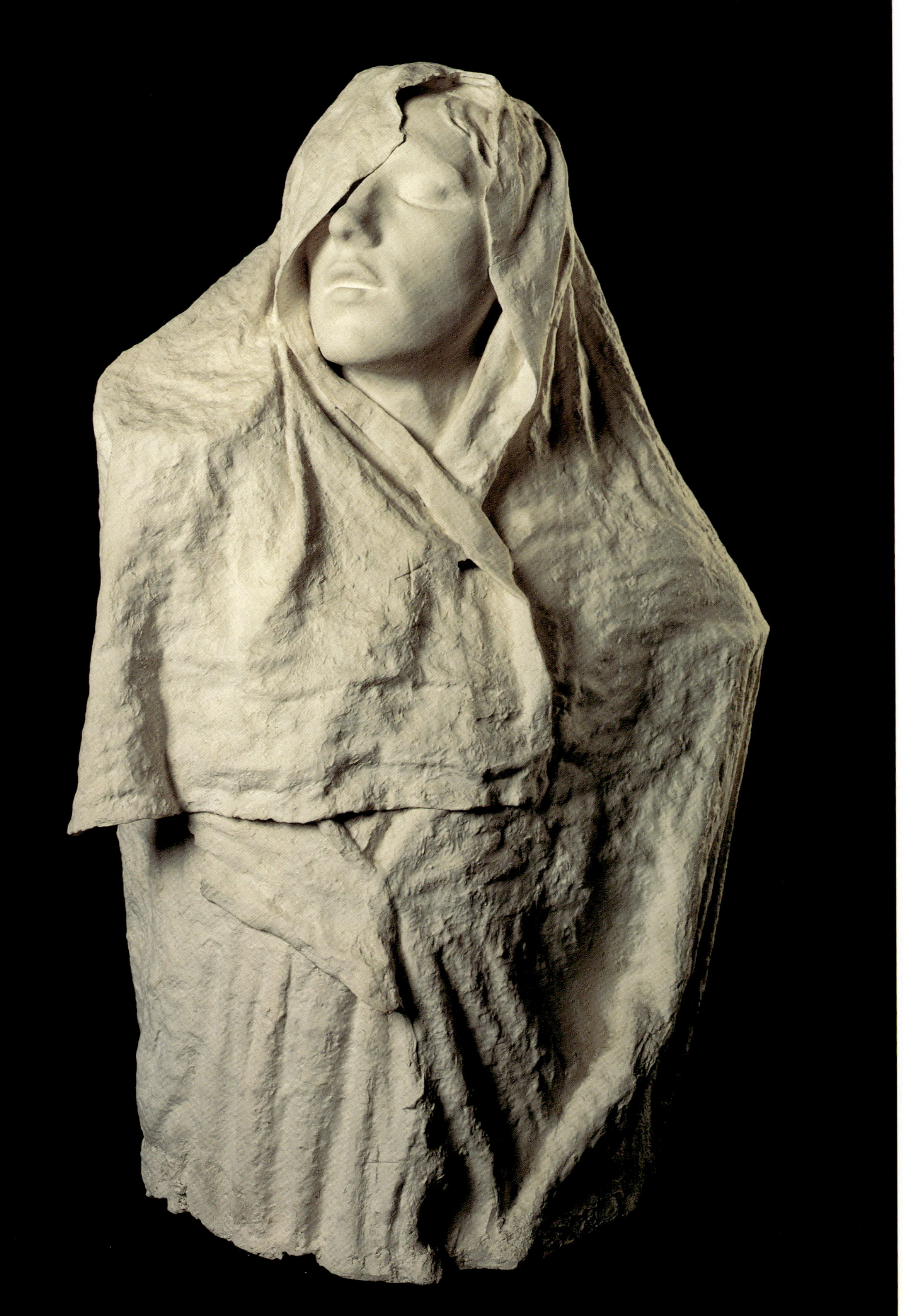

Return to Paris

Hélène Marraud

"During the long years that elapsed between the mask of *The Man with the Broken Nose* and this statue of *Early Man* many silent changes had taken place within Rodin. (...) *The Man with the Broken Nose* had revealed how Rodin could follow a path of his own using a face as a vehicle, *The Age of Bronze* demonstrated his absolute command over the body. (...) It was a nude great as life" (Rilke).

Enriched by his experience in Belgium and his journey to Italy, Rodin returned to Paris in the autumn of 1877. The uproar caused by the scandal surrounding *The Age of Bronze* - accusations were made that it was cast directly from the model, a young Belgian soldier called Auguste Neyt - preceded him. The figure had been exhibited at the Cercle Artistique of Brussels in January 1877 and was favourably received in spite of initial suspicions that it had been cast from life; the examining jury of the Paris Salon echoed the suspicion, and in May when it went on show to the public a heated argument ensued.

With this work Rodin asserted his total mastery of the human body, allying powerful relief to his technique of working from profiles: "Rodin always regarded accessories as pointless. His *Age of Bronze* which was initially called *Vanquished* – with the roughing chisel wielded to simulate a wound on the forehead – was initially supported on a lance. Rodin thought that this superfluous stick prevented the profiles from being seen and removed it" (Chéruy). After stripping first *The Age of Bronze* then *St John the Baptist* of their respective attributes, the lance and the cross, Rodin accorded the gesture implied its full power. *The Age of Bronze* which "points to the birth of the gesture in Rodin's work. That gesture which grows and gradually attains such grandeur and power" already heralds the figure of *St John the Baptist*, exhibited at the 1880 Salon. "He walks. He walks as if the whole expanse of the world were within him and as if he were distributing it through his footsteps. He walks" (Rilke, 1903).

Rodin established himself gradually, at the same time as carrying out various decorative assignments, work designed to earn some money and carried out for other people. He was continuing the type of experience he had had with Carrier-Belleuse in Brussels. It was in this context that he asked to play a part in decorating the Palais du Trocadéro, built to designs by Davioud and Bourdais for the 1878 Exposition Universelle, obtaining the commission to provide two mascarons for the fountain representing *Fair Weather* and *Foul Weather*. The following year he went to the Sèvres porcelain factory – employed on an occasional rather than a permanent basis – to rejoin Carrier-Belleuse who had been artistic director there since 1875. He stayed on there until 1882, producing several items in ceramics (*Vase of the Elements*, *Saigon Vase*, etc.). He also took part in the external decoration of the new Hôtel de Ville in Paris and the figure of *D'Alembert* commissioned from him in 1880 can still be seen in the niche on the

The Age of Bronze, Draped Torso
Plaster. 78 x 49.5 x 31
Rodin donation, 1916
Inv. S.3179

St John the Baptist with the Cross
Pencil and black ink drawing. 32.3 x 22.4
Harvard University, Cambridge (Mass.)
Grenville L. Winthrop bequest

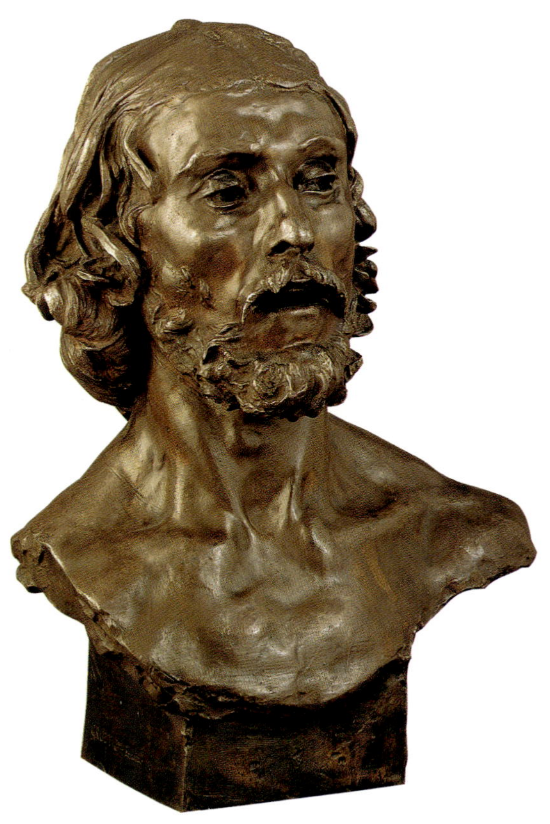

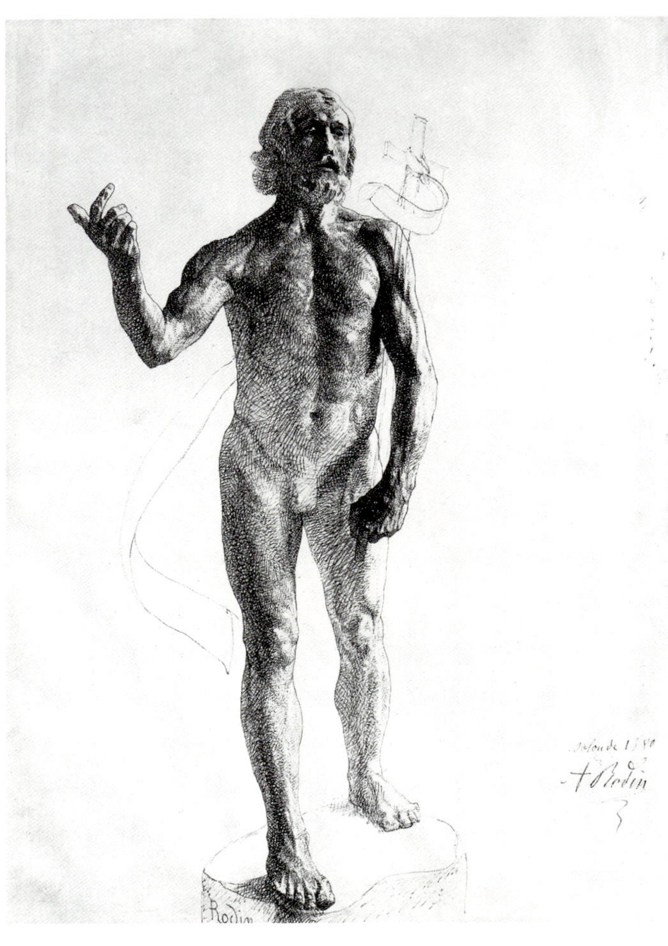

St John the Baptist, Bust,
1879
Bronze, cast by Gruet 1880.
54.6 x 38.5 x 26.4
Acquired in 1995
Inv. S.6670

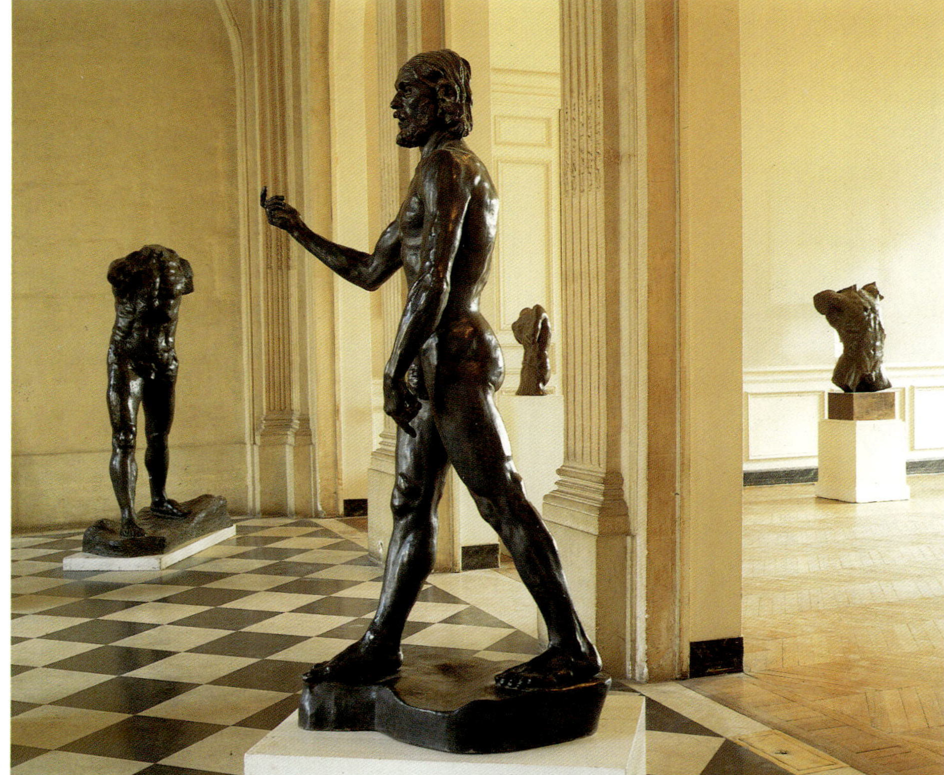

St John the Baptist,
1880
Bronze, cast by Alexis Rudier.
203 x 71.7 x 119.5
Rodin donation, 1916
Inv. S.999

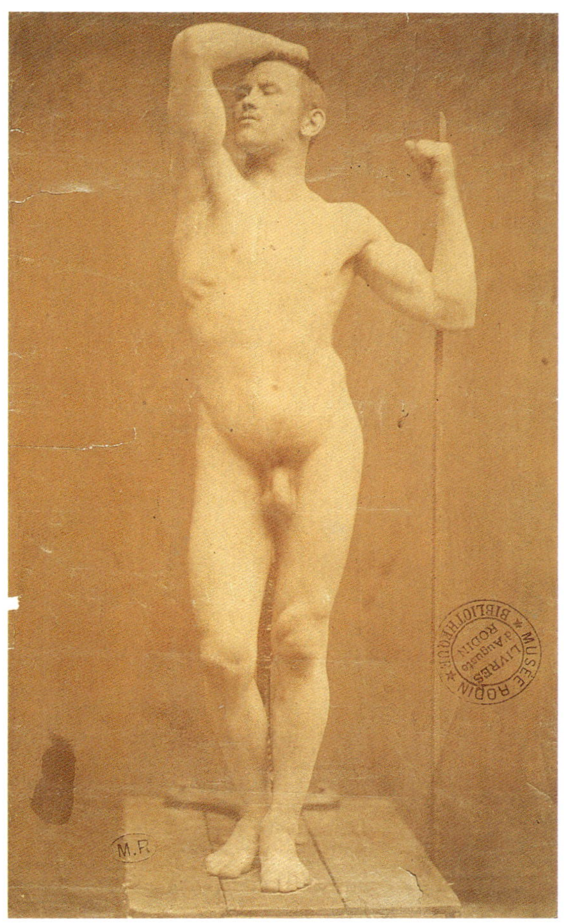

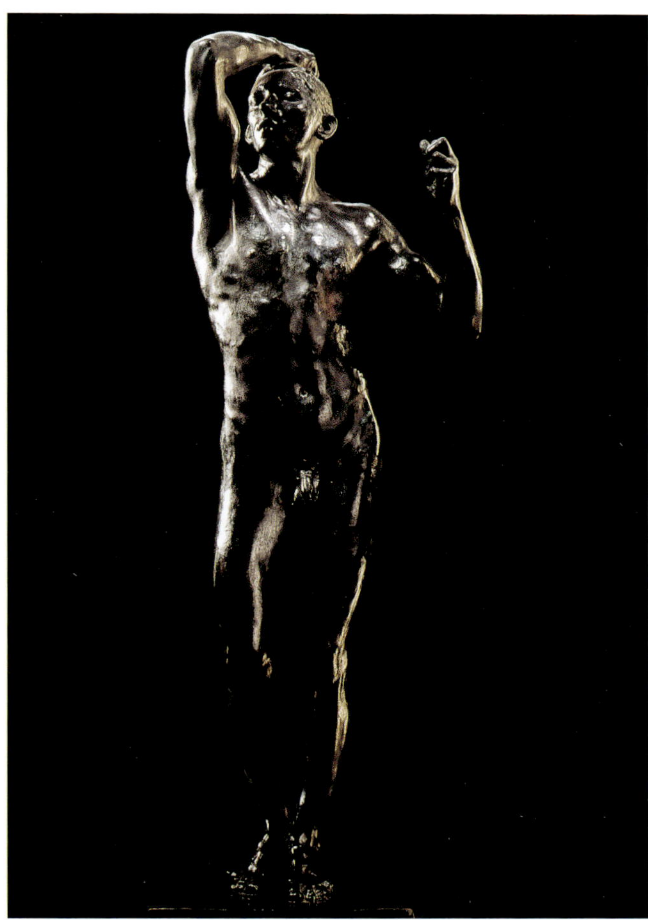

Gaudenzio Marconi
(1842-after 1885)
Auguste Neyt, Front View,
1877
Albumen print. 24 x 14.8
Rodin donation, 1916
Inv. Ph.270

The Age of Bronze,
1877
Bronze, cast by Alexis Rudier.
180.5 x 68.5 x 54.5
Rodin donation, 1916
Inv. S.986

first floor, at the right-hand corner of the façade. Finally during the summer of 1879 Rodin went to Nice, summoned there by the sculptor Cordier who was responsible for the decoration of the Villa Neptune on the Promenade des Anglais. He executed two figures, "two caryatids with the appearance of graceful young tritons" supporting a large bay "directly overlooking the sea" (J. Cladel).

Rodin's admiration for Michelangelo and the "lesson" he had learnt from him while staying in Florence were more clearly demonstrated *c.*1879-1880. Writing to Rose in 1876 he confided: "...I have roughed out some sketches in the evening at home not after his works but after all the scaffoldings and systems that I build in my imagination to understand him; and you know, I feel I am managing to give them the look, that nameless something, that only he can give."

The works produced at that period demonstrate this. *The Defence* or *The Call to Arms*, a proposal for an "allegorical monument representing the defence of Paris in 1870" intended for the Rond-point de Courbevoie, depicts a naked wounded soldier reminiscent of the Christ in Michelangelo's *Pietà* in the Duomo in Florence. A winged spirit supports him, its furious expression, horizontally outstretched arms and clenched fists recalling Rude's *La Marseillaise*. But this group "must have appeared too violent, too vibrant. There has been so little progress since Rude's *La Marseillaise* which also shouts out with all its strength" (Rodin, 1917). The monument was enlarged to twice the original size in 1912, then taken up again and enlarged yet again between 1917 and 1919 for a Dutch

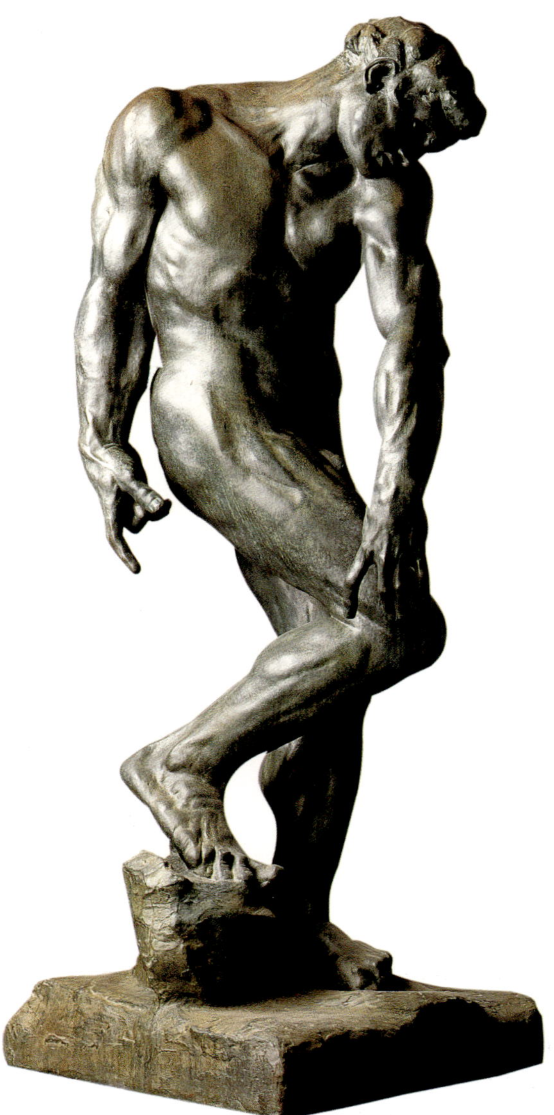

Adam,
1881
Bronze, cast by Susse. 197 x 76 x 77
Cast for the Museum's collections in 1972
Inv. S.1303

Rodin took part in many competitions which were the means for any artist to earn his living. In 1879 he carried out two projects, one to commemorate *The Defence* of Paris during the Franco-Prussian War of 1870, the other being a bust of the Republic known as *Bellona* intended to adorn the new town hall of the 13th arrondissement. But neither won a prize, as their tortured, passionate conception, close to Michelangelo, meant that the artist's work was not at all in keeping with the tastes of his contemporaries. With *The Creation of Man* or *Adam* Rodin again showed how directly his work was descended from Antiquity and the Renaissance.

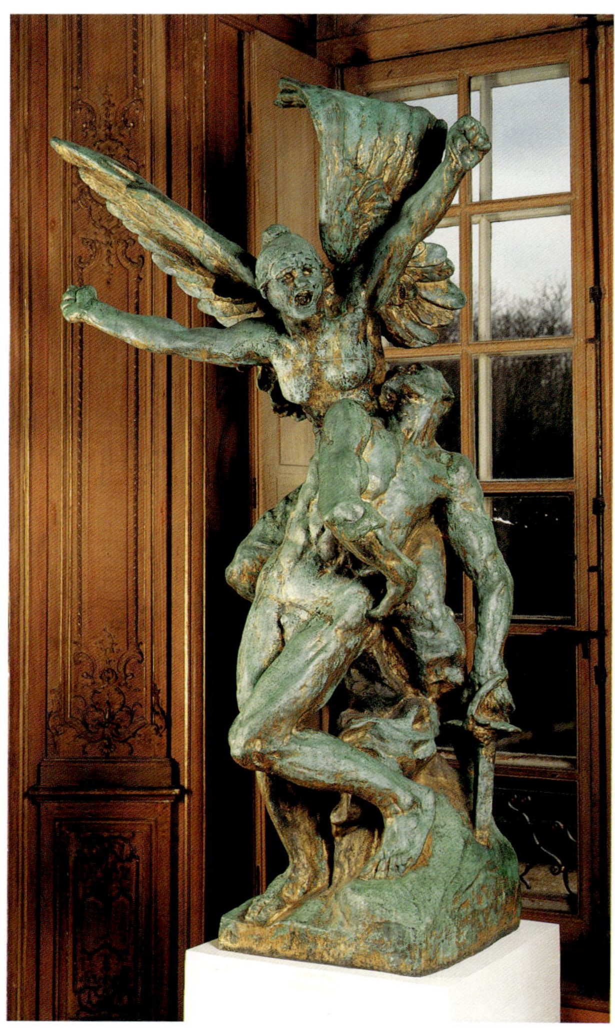

The Defence,
1879
Enlargement to twice original size carried out in 1912
Gilded bronze, cast by Alexis Rudier.
230 x 116 x 84.5
Gift from Rudier in 1921 or 1922
Inv. S.1301

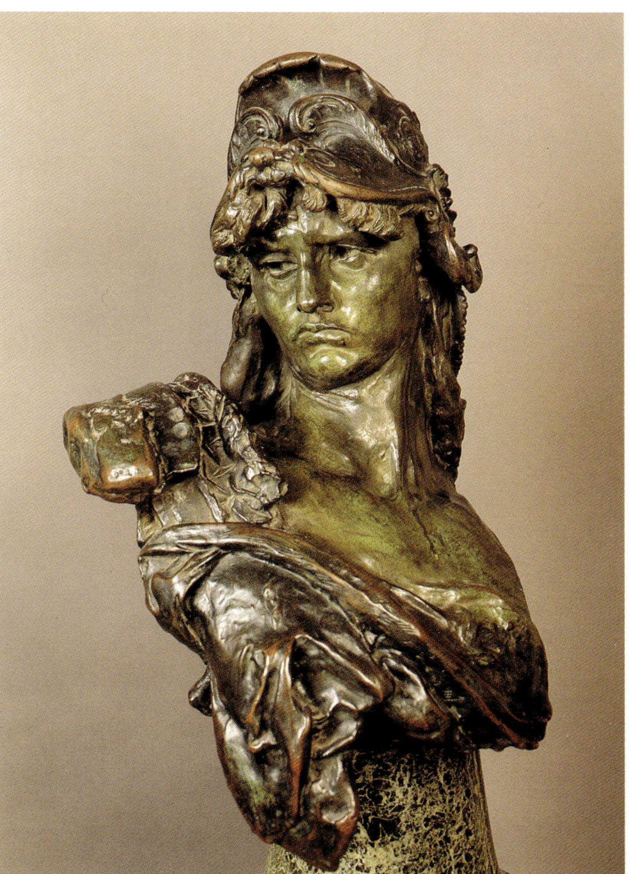

Bellona,
1879
Bronze, cast by Alexis Rudier.
103 x 52 x 43 (with small pedestal)
Rudier bequest, 1957
Inv. S.476

committee which presented it to Verdun. The bust of *Bellona* – which must have been inspired by Rose Beuret in a temper – as the image of the Republic, wearing a Greek helmet rather than the traditional Phrygian bonnet on her head, demonstrates the strong, powerful character which was shocking at the period. With his right arm pointing towards the ground in a gesture reminiscent of Michelangelo's painting of the *Creation of Man* on the ceiling of the Sistine Chapel, *Adam*, though standing free of the material in comparison with Michelangelo's *Captives*, adopts a similar attitude. The *contrapposto* movement animating the figure cannot fail to bring to mind Rodin's comments when confronted by the works of the great Renaissance master, "two main directions only. The legs on our side, the torso on the opposite side. This gives great power to the attitude".

"What a sorrow it is to see my figure which can help my future which is slow in coming for I am 36 years old, what a sorrow it is to see it rejected because of a withering suspicion," Rodin wrote in April 1877 regarding his *Age of Bronze*. The period between 1877 when his return to Paris was marred by the scandal surrounding *The Age of Bronze* and 1880 when the State bought the plaster figure, commissioned a casting of it and entrusted the sculptor with the project for *The Gates of Hell* proved to be a turning-point. This period typified by work done to earn a living along with personal work, struggles in conjunction with some recognition, was at last to open up the way for Rodin's own future, his work and his career.

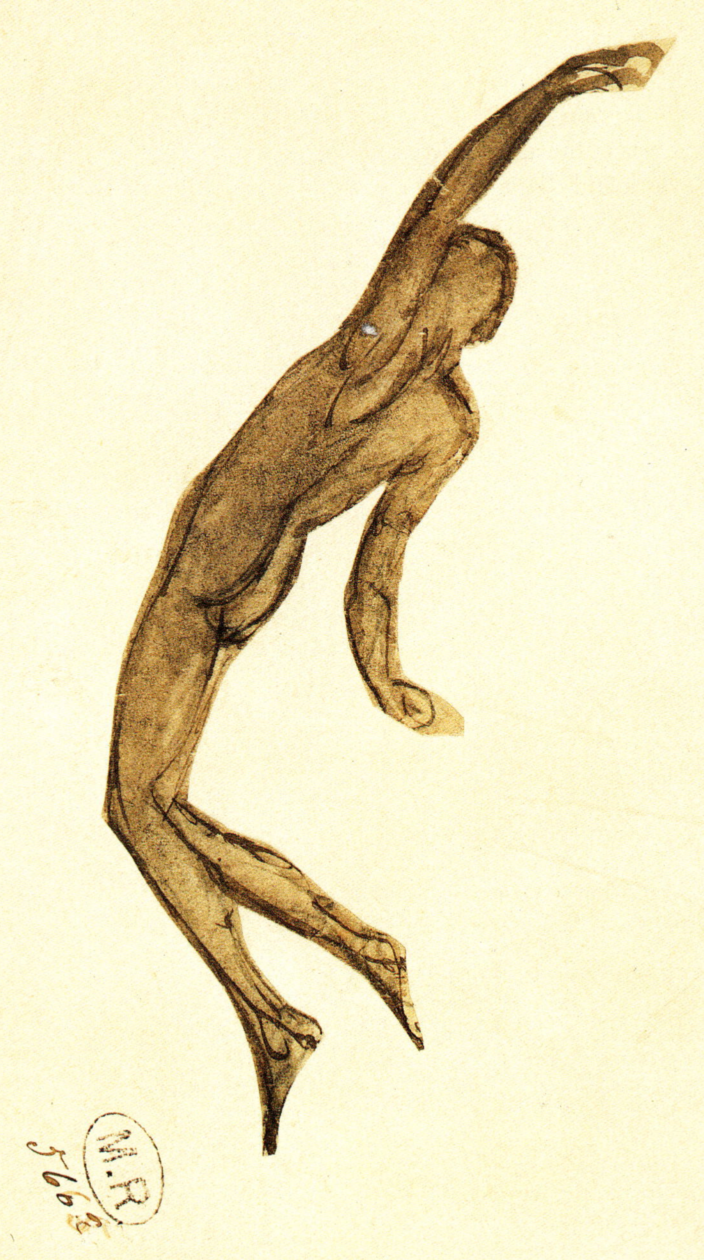
M.R

Drawings and Dante's *Inferno*

Claudie Judrin

In Rodin's mind there was no distinction between Dante the poet and Dante the thinker. From his time at the Petite Ecole Dante had formed part of his reading matter, becoming his bedside book in a translation by Rivarol on his return from Italy in 1875; but it was at the age of forty that *The Gates of Hell* influenced the direction of his life's work and *The Divine Comedy* took over his inspiration.

For a whole year, no doubt 1883, he lived only on Dante and with Dante, making drawings of the eight circles of his *Inferno*. Such familiarity with a fourteenth-century writer is hard to imagine in our day.

The drawings he made from the book are much more faithful to the letter of the text than the sculptures in *The Gates of Hell*. He used a hundred or so to make an album published by Goupil, Manzi et Joyant in 1897; the preface was written by Octave Mirbeau and the work was financed by Maurice Fenaille, a rich patron of the arts. This publication marks the end of a stage for Rodin as a graphic artist, bringing the dark period of his imagination to a close; it contains a few anonymous shades, but canto after canto we witness a true descent into hell.

After crossing the Acheron Rodin is happier to linger on the Circle of Love where Minos sits in judgment with doomed couples such as Francesca da Rimini and Paolo Malatesta appearing before him. The sculpture *The Kiss* was inspired by the embraces drawn here. Next we move on to the misers and wastrels. After setting out under the guidance of the ferryman Phlegias, Dante meets the Medusa who turns those who gaze on her into stone, and Virgil spares the poet this sight calling out to him: "If Medusa saw you, you would no longer live." In Canto XII the men of violence and the centaurs reign supreme, and Rodin is often tempted to draw them. Appalled by the tortures reserved for those who have blasphemed, Dante sits astride the monster Geryon to go down to the cheats and frauds. Seducers such as Interminelli di Lucca are plunged into filth. In Canto XXVII the Count of Urbino, Guido di Montefeltre, is condemned to torture by fire for having practised deceit. In the following circle, the sectarians are conjured up by means of Mohammed with his intestines hanging out. Canto XXXIII was to be illustrated at length by Rodin through the tragic story of Ugolino punished for treason, reduced to devouring his sons before dying of hunger in Pisa. Step by step, drawing after drawing, Rodin follows the stages of his death throes which take place over a week. After witnessing human decadence, step by step, Dante with Rodin following in his wake sees souls rising towards the semi-obscurity of Purgatory before reaching the full light of Paradise, always less tempting for an artist.

This complicity with the Florentine poet penetrated Rodin to such an extent that he made Dante's ideas his own. Dante's *Inferno* is Rodin's, and Rodin's is in turn ours.

Demon in Space,
*c.*1880
Pen and Indian ink wash on cut-out art paper. 13 x 3.8
Rodin donation, 1916
Inv. D.5665

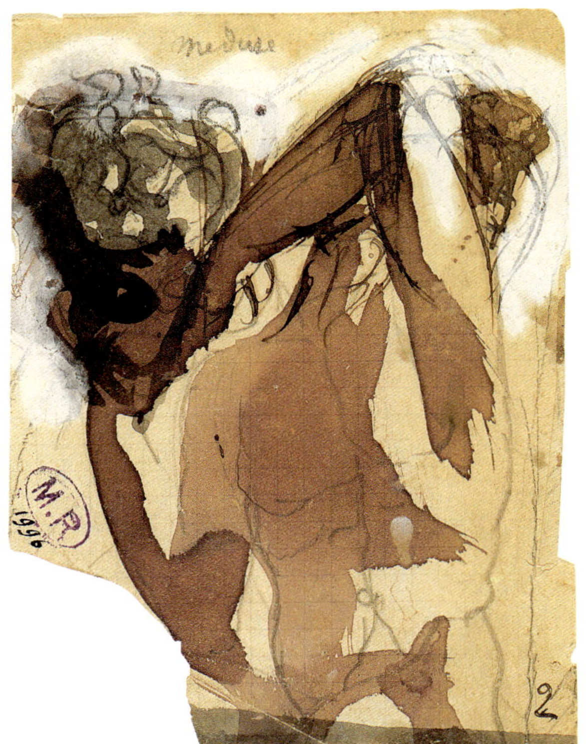

Medusa,
*c.*1880
Graphite, pen, ink washes and gouache on paper. 10.9 x 8.2
Rodin donation, 1916
Inv. D.1996

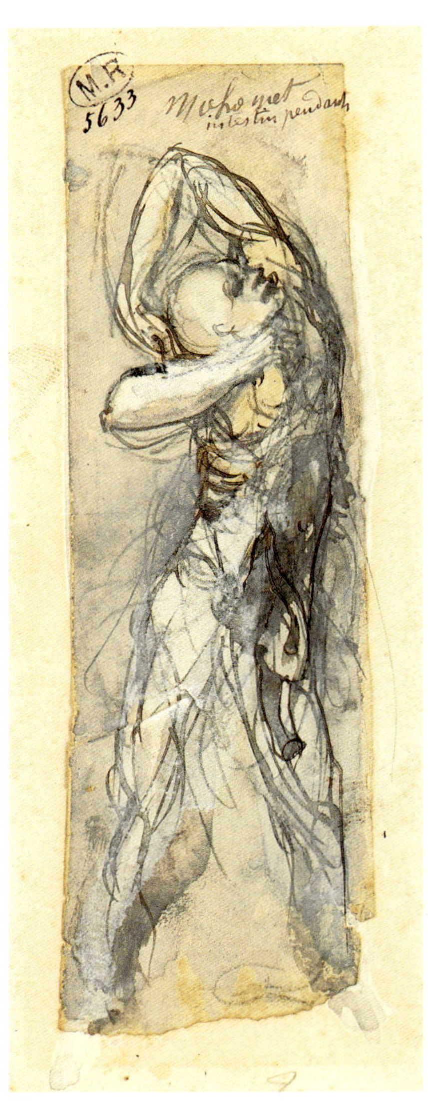

Mohammed with his Entrails Hanging out,
*c.*1880
Graphite, pen, ink washes and gouache on paper glued onto cardboard. 17 x 5.2
Rodin donation, 1916
Inv. D.5633

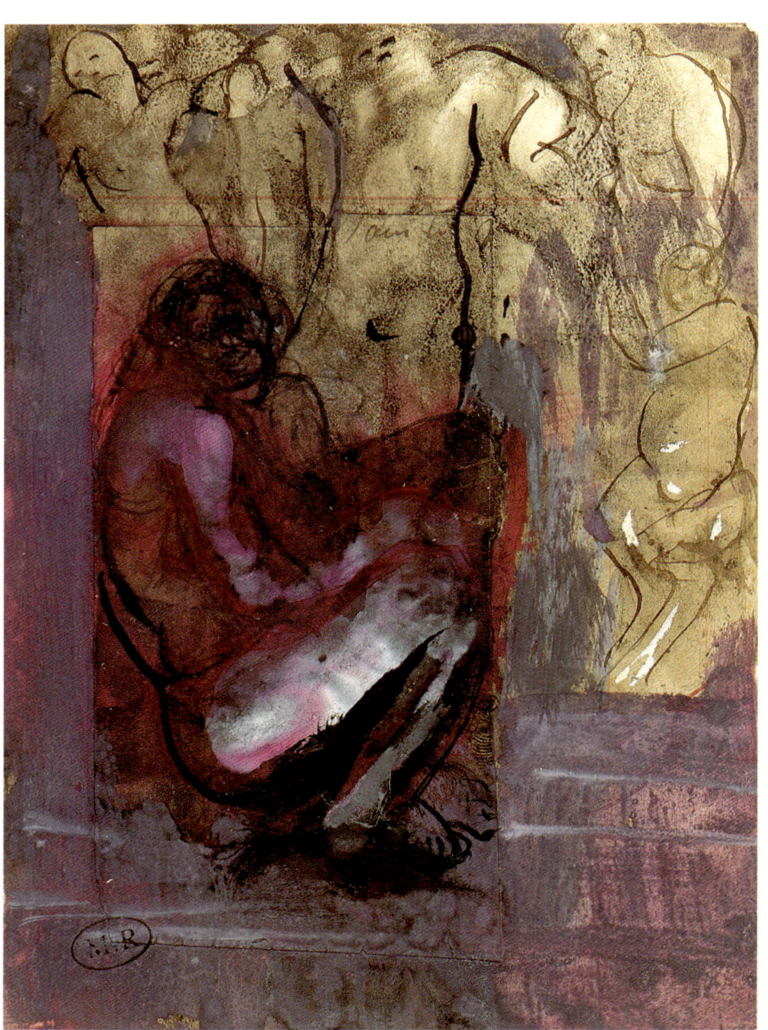

Dans la M...,
*c.*1880
Graphite, pen, ink washes and gouache on paper. 18.2 x 13.6
Acquired in 1929
Inv. D. 7616

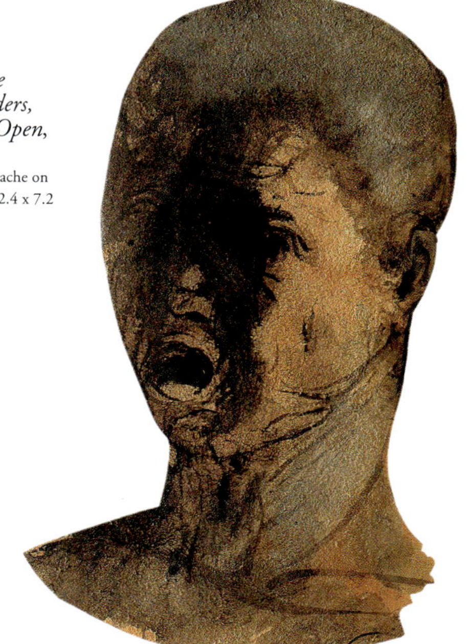

Man's Head Seen to the Beginning of his Shoulders, with the Mouth Wide Open,
*c.*1880
Graphite, pen, ink wash, and gouache on paper, cut out and stuck down. 12.4 x 7.2
Acquired in 1991
Inv. D.7745

The 7000 or so drawings held by the Musée Rodin which are fated to be kept hidden away inside boxes because of their fragility are shown to the public in rotation for three months at a time in a small room devoted to them on the ground floor of the Hôtel Biron. Light, which is the great enemy of works on paper, is kept at a low level in line with international conservation standards.

The Circle of Love,
*c.*1880
Graphite, pen, sepia ink wash and gouache on paper. 19.5 x 15.1
Acquired in 1992
Inv. D.7756

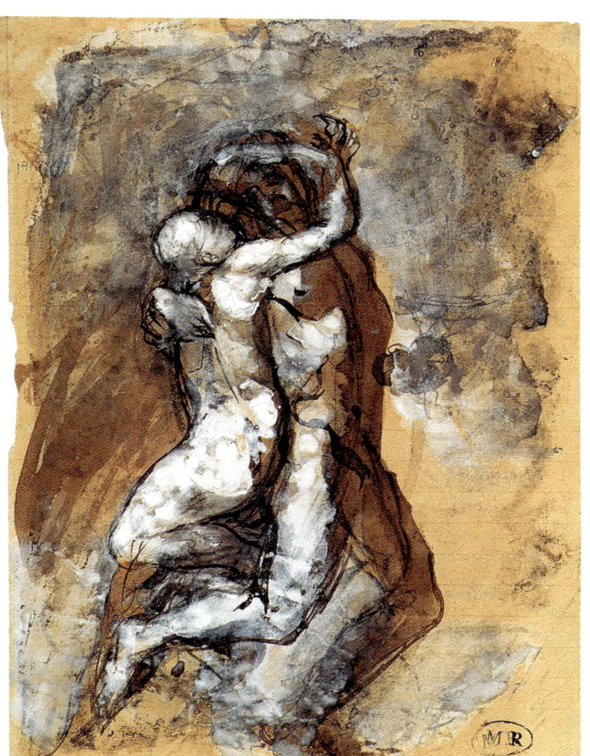

Ugolino Surrounded by Three Children,
*c.*1880
Graphite, pen and inks, and gouache on paper. 17.3 x 13.7
Acquired in 1929
Inv. D.7627

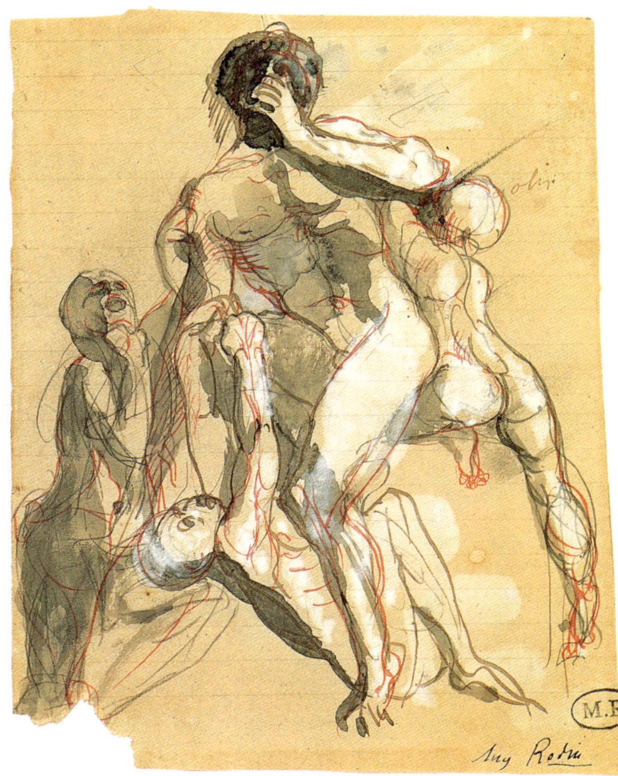

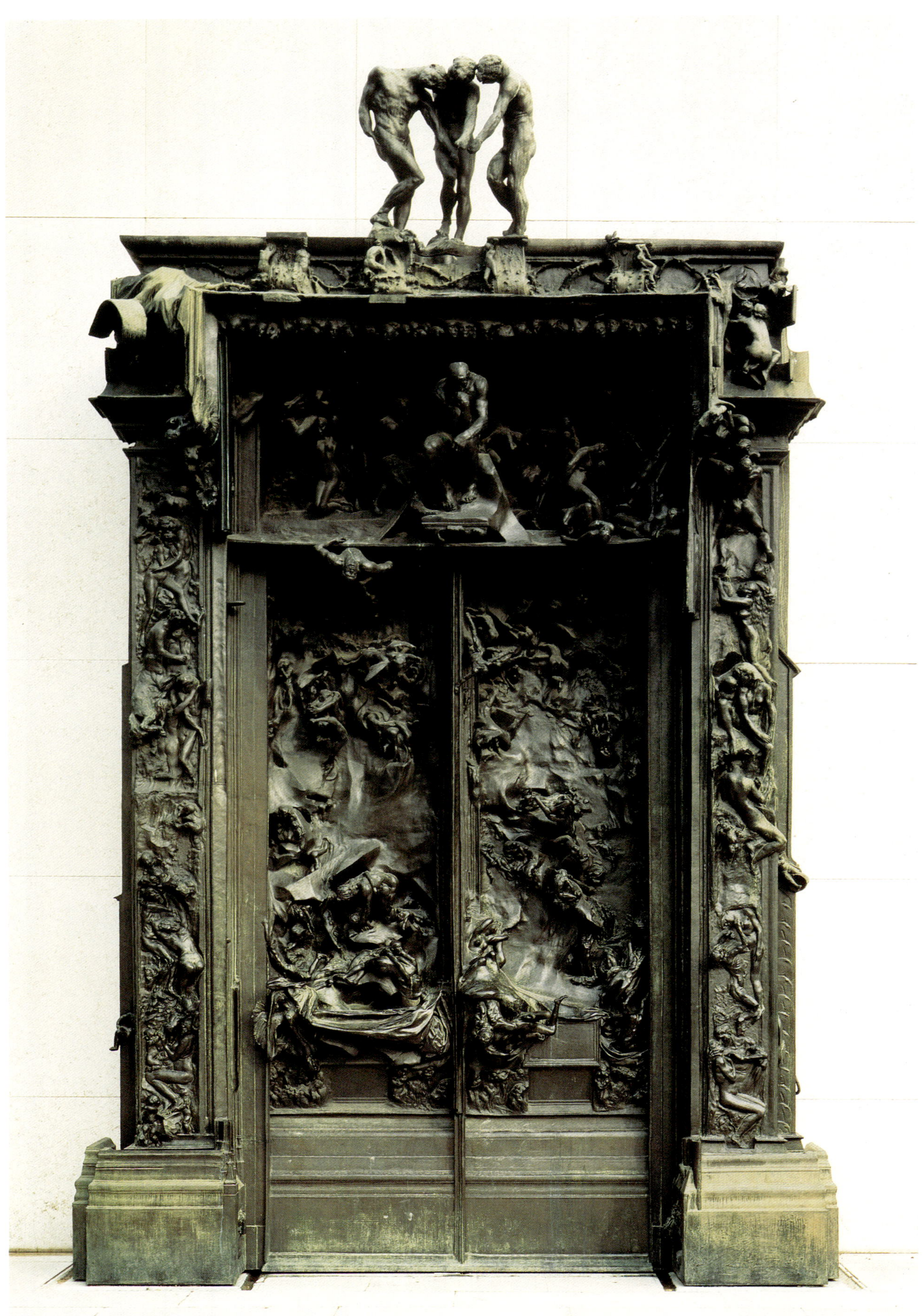

The Gates of Hell

Antoinette Le Normand-Romain

Described by Champsaur as "a poem with over five hundred characters... conveying Dante's book with a striking novelty of concept, even for those who do not know it," *The Gates of Hell* accompanied Rodin throughout his career: from 1880 to 1917 it stood in his studio. After fervently using it as a vehicle to express his admiration for Gothic architecture and Renaissance sculpture, for Dante and Baudelaire, and even his boundless love for nature, he gave himself time for reflection and the outcome was the elimination of all the figures; for by 1895 the richness of the *Gates* was such that like the movement of the sea they could continue to develop only by retreating.

By a decree dated 16 August 1880, Rodin had been awarded the commission for a doorway intended for a museum of decorative arts then being planned. The door was to be decorated with bas-reliefs inspired by Dante's *Divine Comedy*, a subject no doubt suggested by Rodin himself in view of his long-standing admiration for Dante. He enthusiastically threw himself into the huge task, creating a door over six metres in height comprising dozens of small figures in the round. As was the normal practice of the directorate of the Beaux-Arts, along with the commission he was allocated a studio at the Dépôt des Marbres, and payment was made in stages after the progress of the work had been inspected.

The stage payments demonstrate that the work made rapid progress. Rodin's first idea had been to divide the doors into panels, as on Ghiberti's *Gate of Paradise* on the Baptistery in Florence, but by the second maquette he had done away with any divisions between the panels, and retaining only the darkest part of Dante's poem, the *Inferno*, he reinterpreted it in the light of Baudelaire. A multitude of figures flooded into the subjacent structure; they were modelled independently of one another, tried out on the panels represented by a wooden frame, then set aside.

By 1884 Rodin felt sufficiently sure of himself to spend money on casting. Even so the model, which must have been set up at the end of 1885 or the beginning of 1886, did not satisfy him and he adjusted it over and over again, as his inspiration dictated, until *c.*1895, by which date it seems that *The Gates* had reached their final state. As was only natural he decided to exhibit the piece in 1900. But when the exhibition opened on 1 June those visitors who had been fortunate enough to see the plaster cast at the Dépôt des Marbres discovered a new and very surprising work, as the figures had disappeared. As he had done in the case of *The Age of Bronze* where the lance was eliminated or for *The Three Shades* where the hands were cut off, Rodin stripped his *Gates* of everything that made them too immediately comprehensible. It would also seem that his concept of relief had evolved over the twenty-year period and he found the contrast between the hollows and the projections too marked: "The door is too full of holes," he told Léonce Bénédite.

The Gates of Hell,
1880-1890/95
Bronze after the plaster set up by Bénédicte in 1917, cast by Alexis Rudier
1928 . 635 x 400 x 35
Installed in 1938
Inv. S.1304

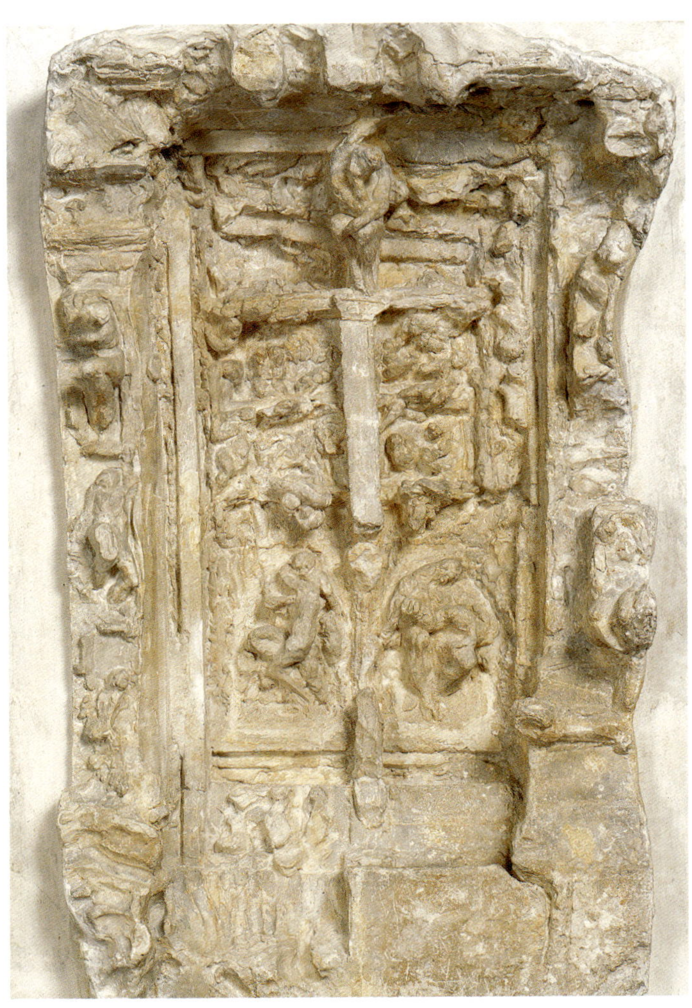

Third Maquette for The Gates of Hell,
1880
Plaster. 111.5 x 75 x 30
Rodin donation, 1916
Inv. S.1189

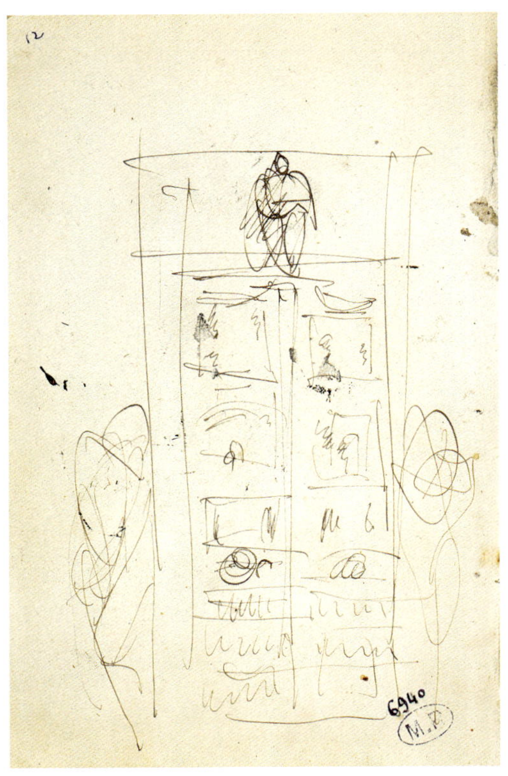

Proposal for the Gates of Hell with the Thinker, Adam and Eve,
*c.*1880
Pen and sepia ink. 16.5 x 11.2
Rodin donation, 1916
Notebook 46.
Inv. D.6940

After the exhibition closed, *The Gates* went back to the Dépôt des Marbres before being moved to Meudon, where they are now on show, still incomplete. At the beginning of 1917, however, Bénédite had two other plaster casts made which included all the figures: one served as a model for the first bronze casts (Philadelphia, Paris, Tokyo) made between 1925 and 1930; the other has been lodged with the Musée d'Orsay.

Apart from *The Thinker,* who is Dante himself contemplating his work, the groups of *Ugolino and his Children* and *Paolo and Francesca,* the characters on *The Gates* cannot be identified. The names ascribed to them today were given to them at a later stage, mainly by the writers forming part of the master's entourage who enjoyed suggesting titles to him; moreover these could vary over a period of time. Rodin was not interested by the subject or the anecdote; he was trying to conjure up the despair of the damned, of those whose vices, particularly illicit love, had taken them into the abyss. And here again it was not a question of describing despair by means of literary or religious references, but simply of describing it in the most direct manner possible, i.e. the most physical: in Rodin's words, "The body is a casting bearing the imprint of the passions." These "furiously, desperately intertwined" (Frémine, 1889) couples, these figures modelled in their hundreds after live models, the Abruzzezi sisters in particular, surprised those who saw them because of the realism of their attitudes which appeared as daring as they were novel, passion being expressed in them in a direct

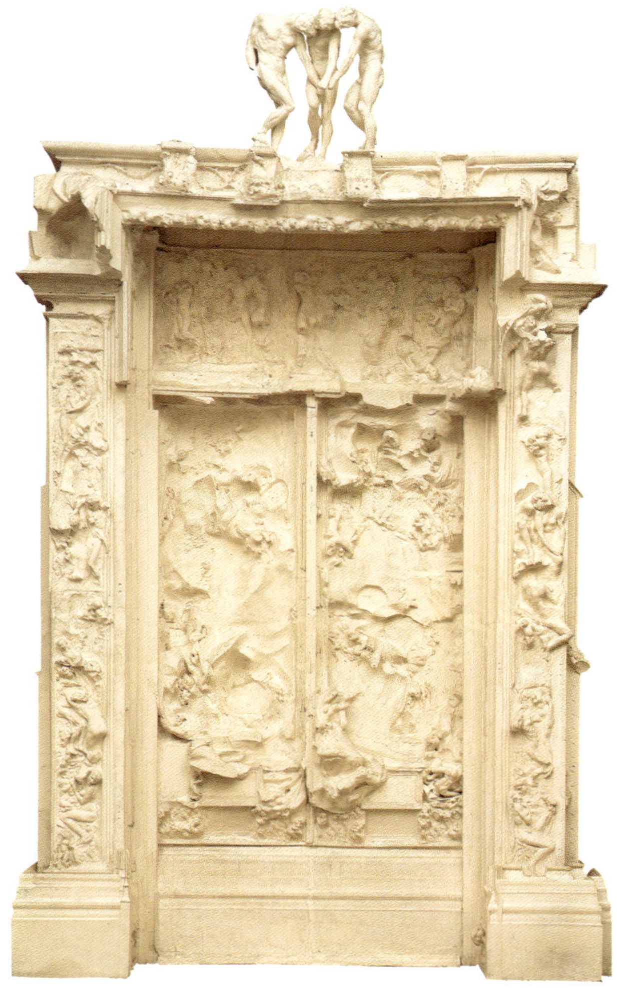

The Gates of Hell,
1900
Exhibited at Meudon
Plaster. 520 x 388 x 97,3
Rodin donation, 1916
Inv. S.2000

Writing in 1886 Félicien Champsaur was the first to mention the *Shades* pointing from the top of the *Gates* to Dante's famous phrase: "Laciate ogni speranza voi ch'entrate" [Abandon all hope you who enter here]. The *Shade* was derived from *Adam* who was to be placed at the foot of *The Gates*, but Rodin had the astonishing idea of grouping together three identical figures, so as to heighten the expressivity: then he dispensed with the inscription and cut off the three right hands. The *Shade* was enlarged in that state, but after 1902 Rodin asked the Czech sculptor Maratka who was then working for him to remake the hand.

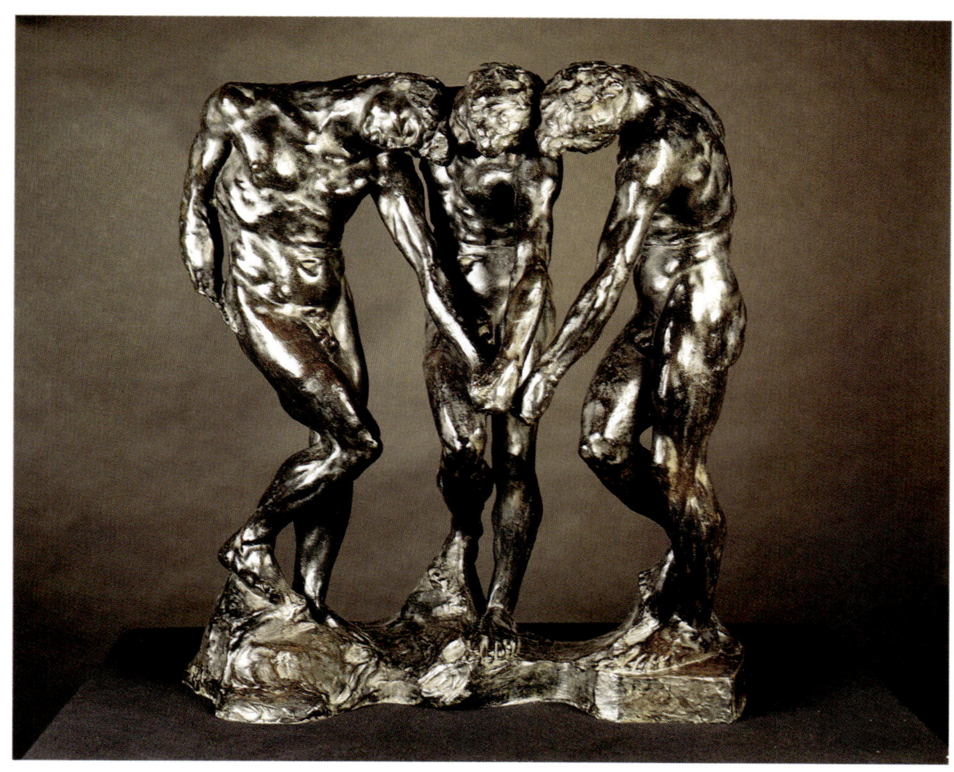

The Three Shades,
before 1886
Bronze, cast by Alexis Rudier after 1902.
96.6 x 92 x 54.1
Rodin donation, 1916
Inv. S.1191

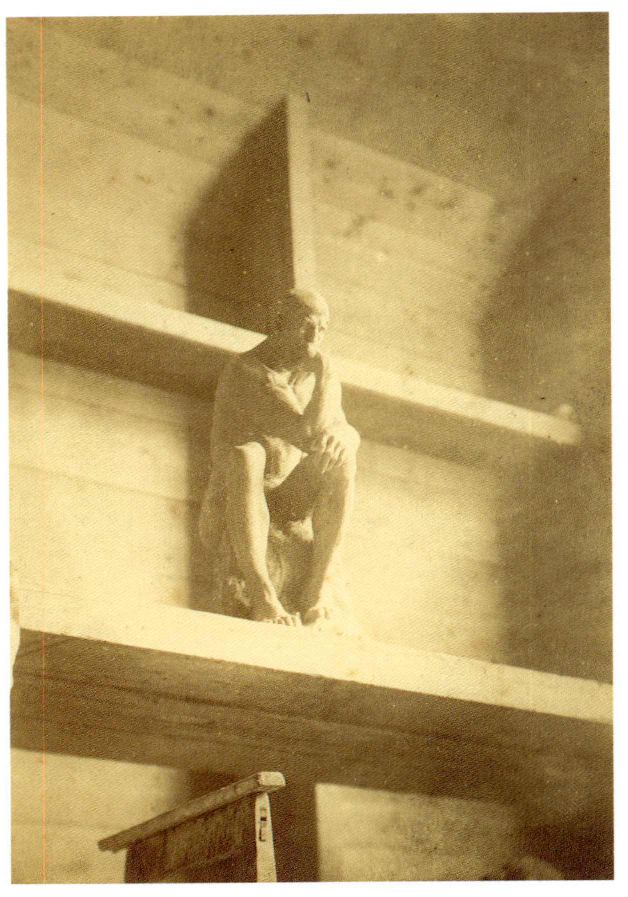

Like *The Kiss*, *The Thinker*, who is none other than Dante, was on *The Gates* from 1880. An invaluable photograph then shows it on the wooden mock-up of the door in the studio at the Dépôt des Marbres, which enabled Rodin to try out the small groups modelled for the panels. But very soon the groups too began to have an independent life: so *The Thinker* was exhibited in its original size at Copenhagen in 1888. The large version (1903), a bronze of which was installed in front of the Panthéon in 1906 while another was placed on Rodin's tomb at Meudon, shows the monumentality and power of the figure to advantage.

Victor Pannelier
(1840-after 1904)
or Charles Bodmer
(1809-1893)
The Thinker (in Clay) in the Mock-up of the Gates,
*c.*1881-1882
Gelatin silver print. 14.5 x 10
Rodin donation, 1916
Inv. Ph.289

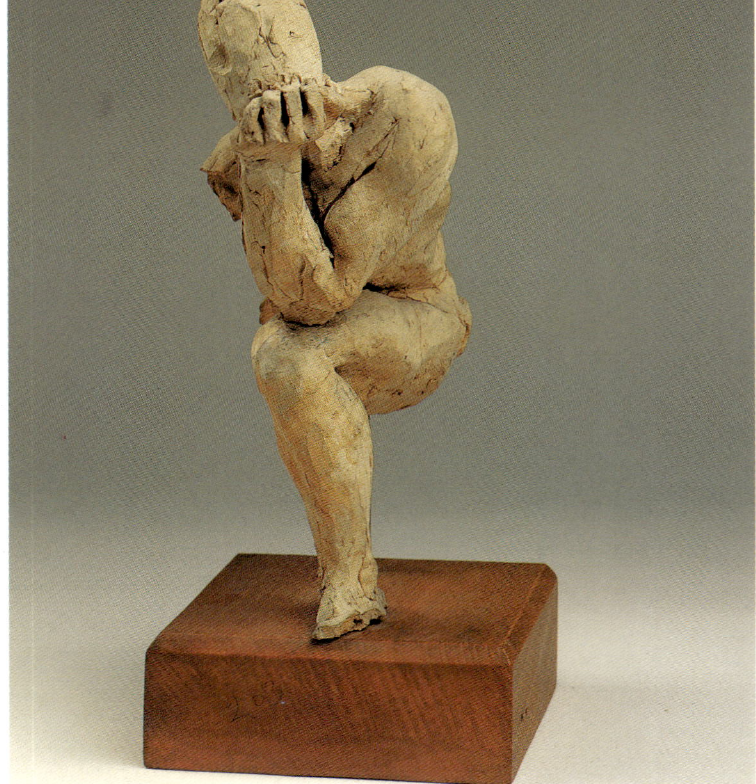

The Thinker,
*c.*1880
Terra cotta sketch. 24.5 x 19.8 x 9.9
Rodin donation, 1916
Inv. S.1168

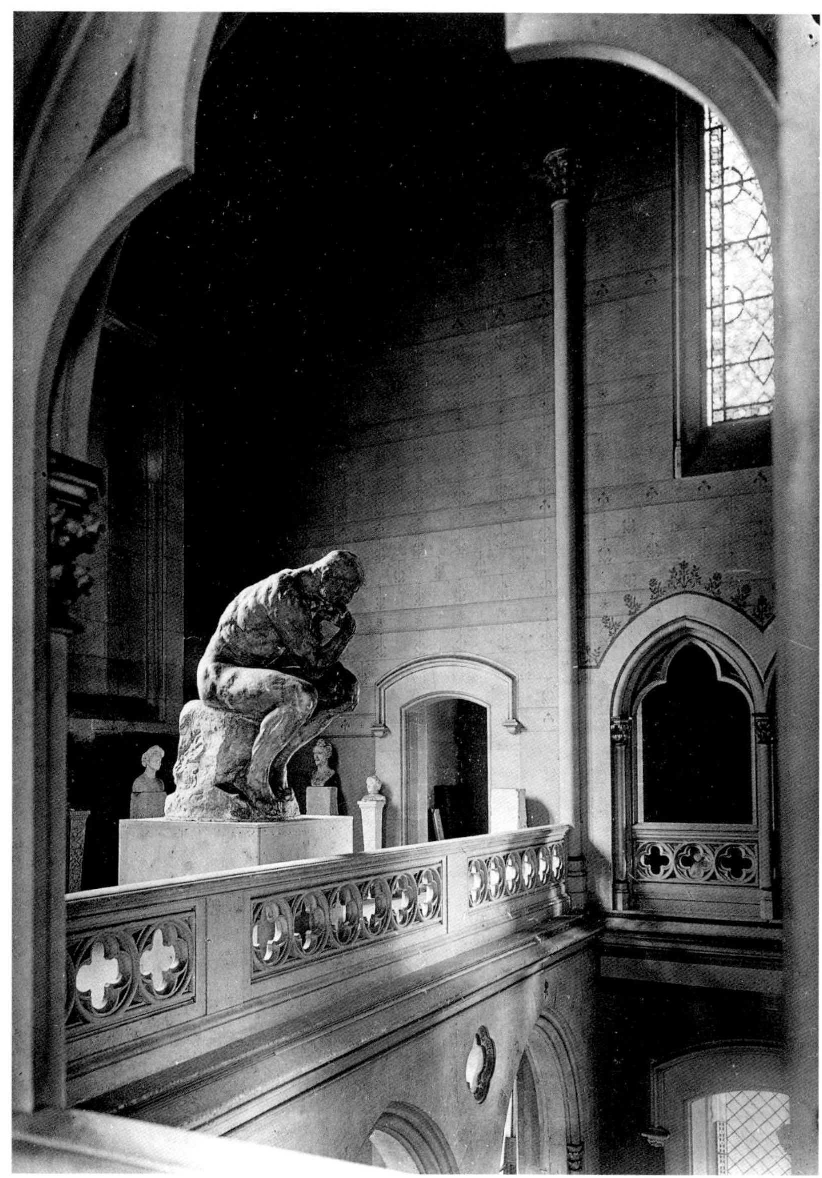

Charles Berthelomier
The Great Thinker in the Chapel at the Hôtel Biron,
*c.*1934
17 x 12.1
Gelatin silver print.
Inv. Ph.1974

manner "through bones, muscles, nerves, the whole organism, with the whole body contributing to the intensity of the rendering" (Guillemot, 1889). What sculptor before Rodin would have had the idea of indicating despair by a figure holding her foot, with the leg raised to the level of the head?

"Monsieur Rodin's work," the Beaux-Arts inspector had recognized as early as January 1883, "is interesting in the extreme. This young sculptor has a truly amazing originality and tortured power of expression. Behind the energy of the attitudes, the vehemence of the poses so evocative of movement, he conceals his disdain, or rather his indifference, for the coldly sculptural style. Monsieur Rodin is haunted by Michelangelesque visions. He may astonish the viewer, he will never leave him indifferent" (*Rapport* of 23 January 1883). Mirbeau, Champsaur and those who had access to Rodin's studio were also struck by this work: "Earthly misery is expressed in this work with its very personal imaginative view,

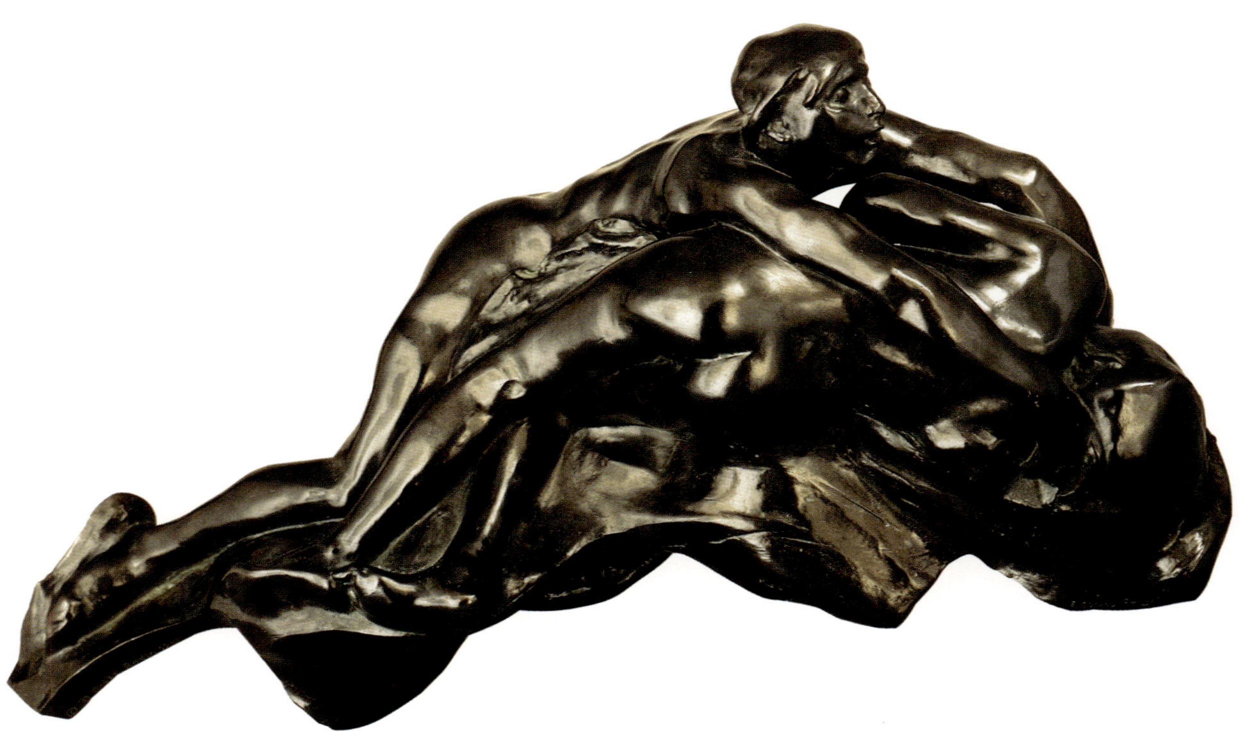

Paolo and Francesca,
*c.*1886?
Bronze, cast by E. Godard.
29.3 x 60.7 x 28.4
Cast for the Museum's collections in 1988
Inv. S.5841

Fugit Amor,
before 1887
Marble. 51 x 72 x 38.9
Previously Peytel Collection
Acquired in 1963
Inv. S.1154

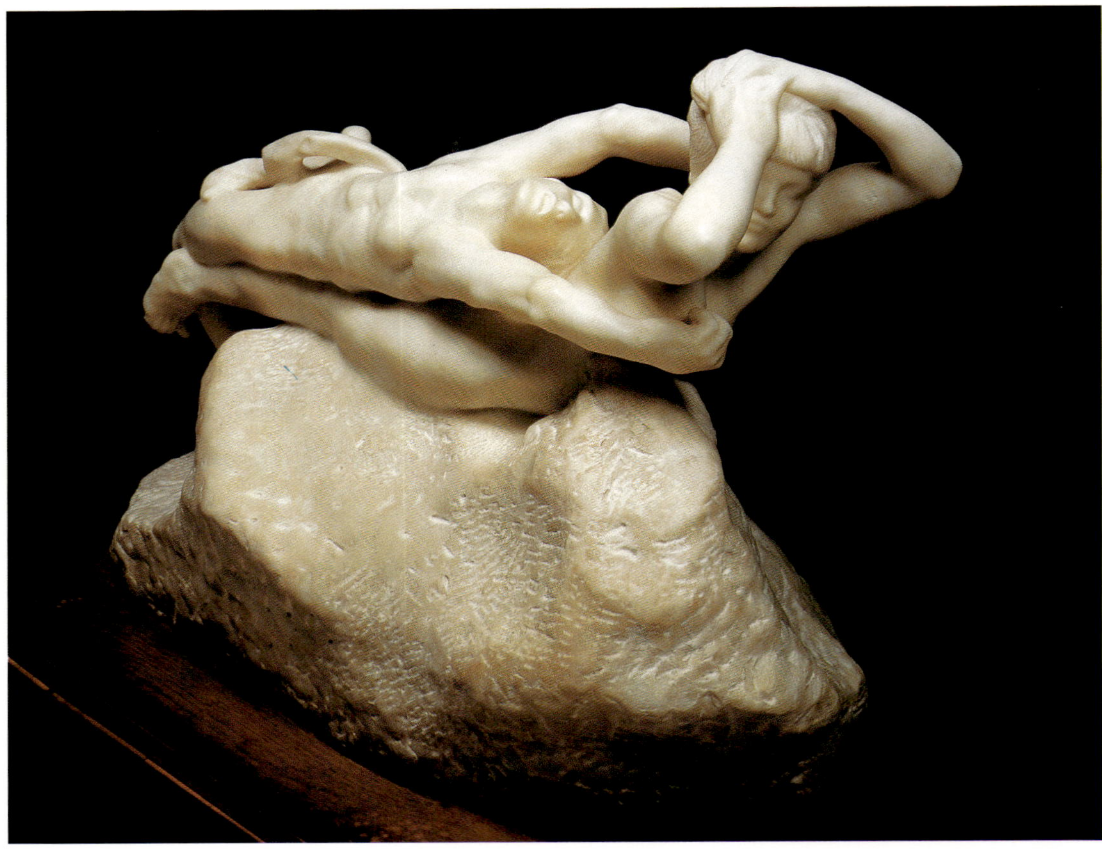

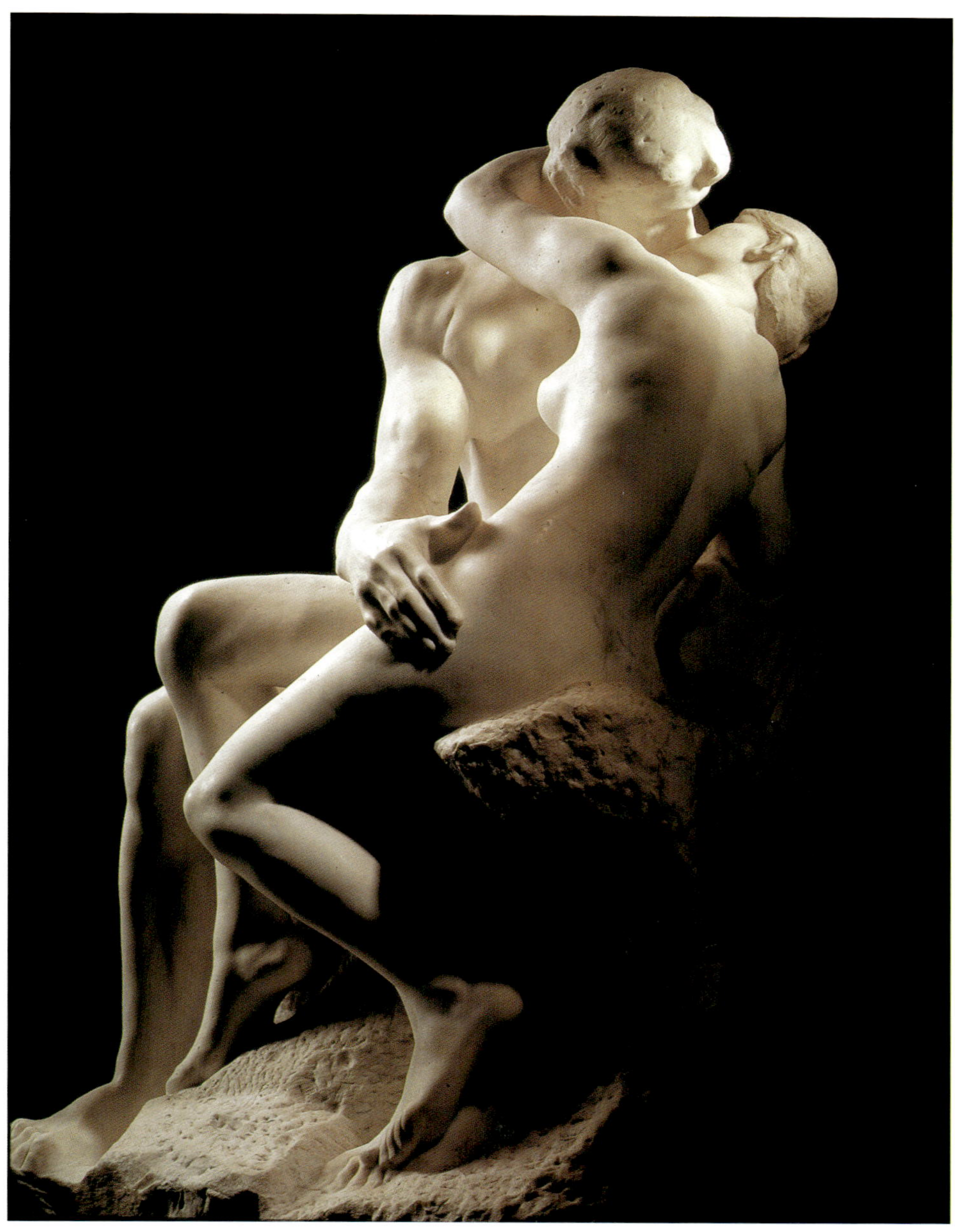

The Kiss,
1888-1889
Marble executed by Jean Turcan.
183.6 x 110.5 x 118.3
Commissioned by the State in 1888,
exhibited at the 1898 Salon de la Société
Nationale des Beaux-Arts,
delivered in 1898
Musée du Luxembourg
Deposited by the Musée du Luxembourg,
1919
Inv. S.1002

The famous couple Paolo Malatesta and Francesca da Rimini made their appearance in the third maquette of *The Gates* and remained there until 1886 when the group was removed because it conjured up a state of pure happiness at odds with the composition as a whole. Once it had become autonomous the group was given the title *The Kiss* and after being commissioned by the State it was doubled in size and carved in marble. It was exhibited in 1898 and was extremely successful, as evidenced by countless bronze castings. Paolo and Francesca nonetheless remained present on *The Gates of Hell*, albeit in different form: floating in the wind as they were described by Dante in the last circle of *The Inferno.*

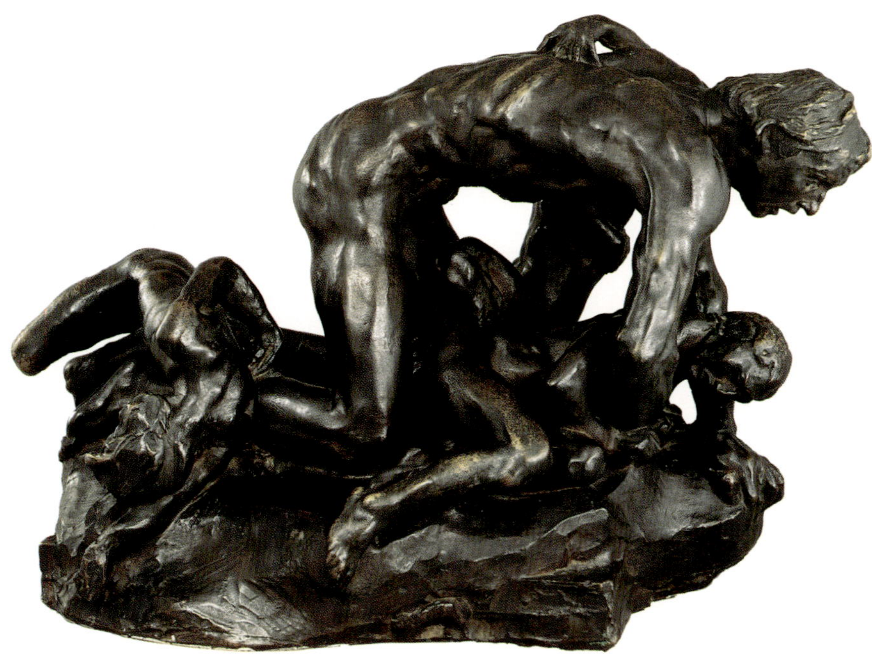

Ugolino,
*c.*1881-1882
Bronze. 41 x 61.5 x 41
Rodin donation, 1916
Inv. S.1146

Ugolino, a Pisan tyrant defeated and condemned to die of hunger along with his children whom he ultimately ate, made his appearance on *The Gates of Hell* at a very early stage. Initially he was seated, like Carpeaux's *Ugolino* (Musée d'Orsay) of which Rodin owned a reduced version, but Rodin was always seeking the expressivity of bodies above all else, and opted for a Ugolino crouching over the bodies of his dead or dying children. The group was enlarged after 1900, fragment by fragment as enlargements were habitually made, and recomposed in a slightly different way.

Ugolino
Enlargement, 1901-1904
Bronze, cast by Eugène Rudier.
133.5 x 140 x 194
Cast for the Museum's collections
*c.*1925
Inv. S.1427

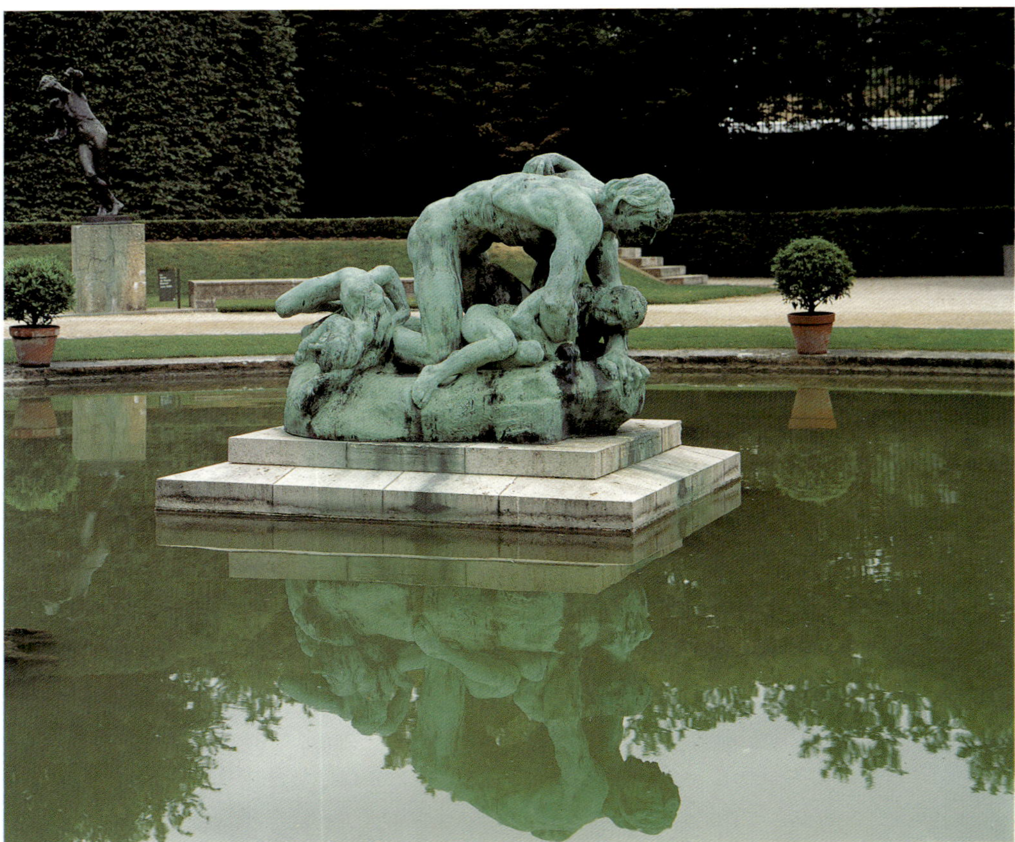

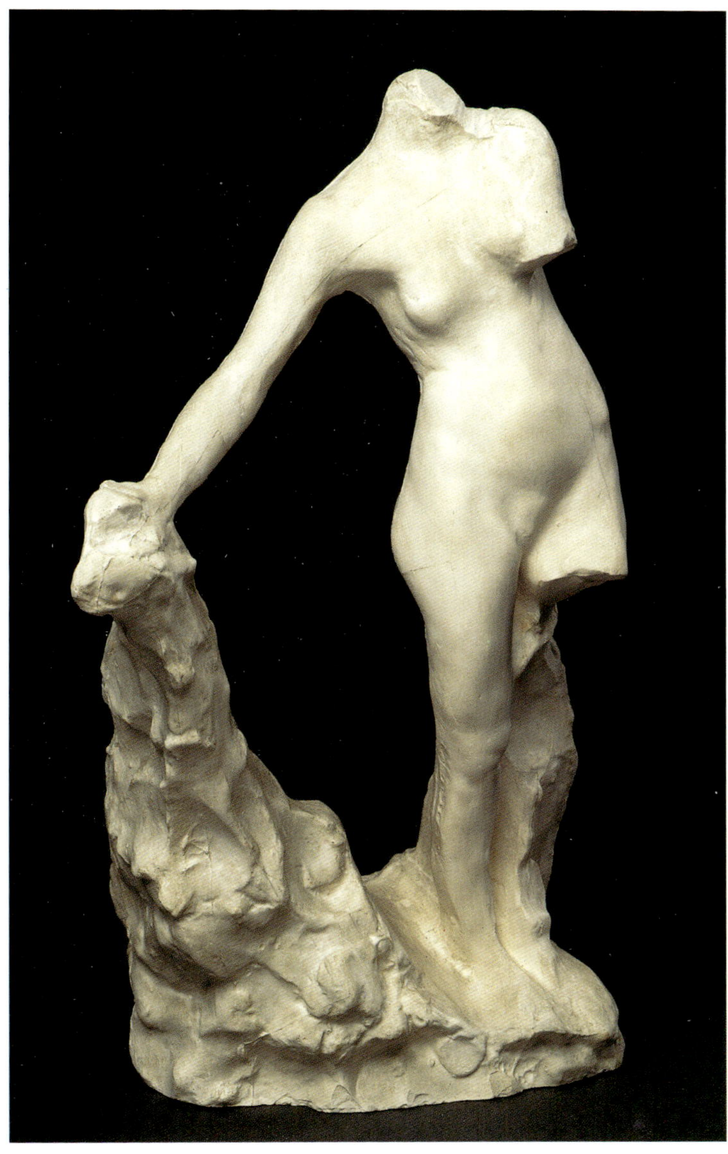

Study for Galatea,
1889?
Plaster. 28.2 x 18.4 x 12.2
Rodin donation, 1916
Inv. S.1179

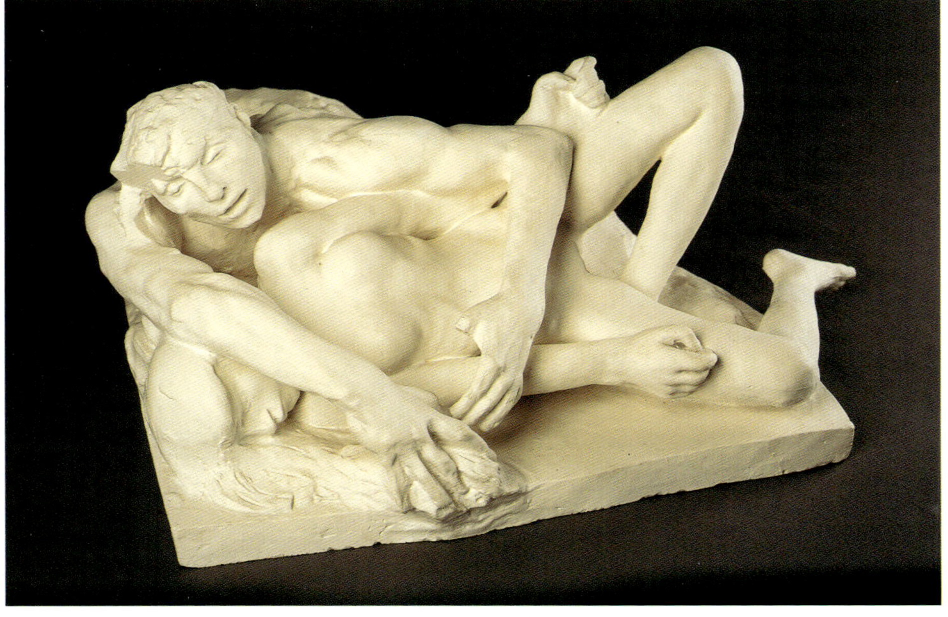

Avarice and Lust
*c.*1887
Plaster. 22.5 x 53.5 x 46
Rodin donation, 1916
Inv. S.7

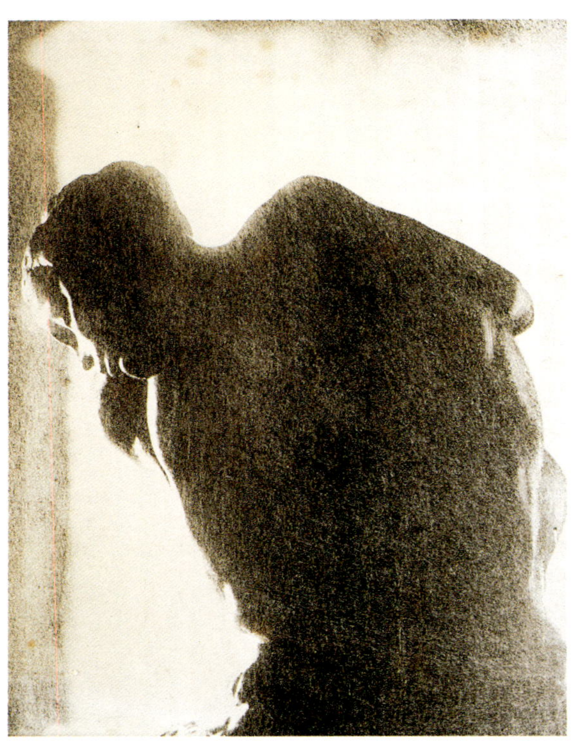

Charles Bodmer
(1809-1893)
The Crouching Woman
(in clay),
*c.*1881-1882
Albumen print. 16.6 x 11.7
Rodin donation, 1916
Inv. Ph.297

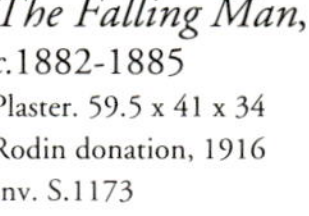

The Falling Man,
*c.*1882-1885
Plaster. 59.5 x 41 x 34
Rodin donation, 1916
Inv. S.1173

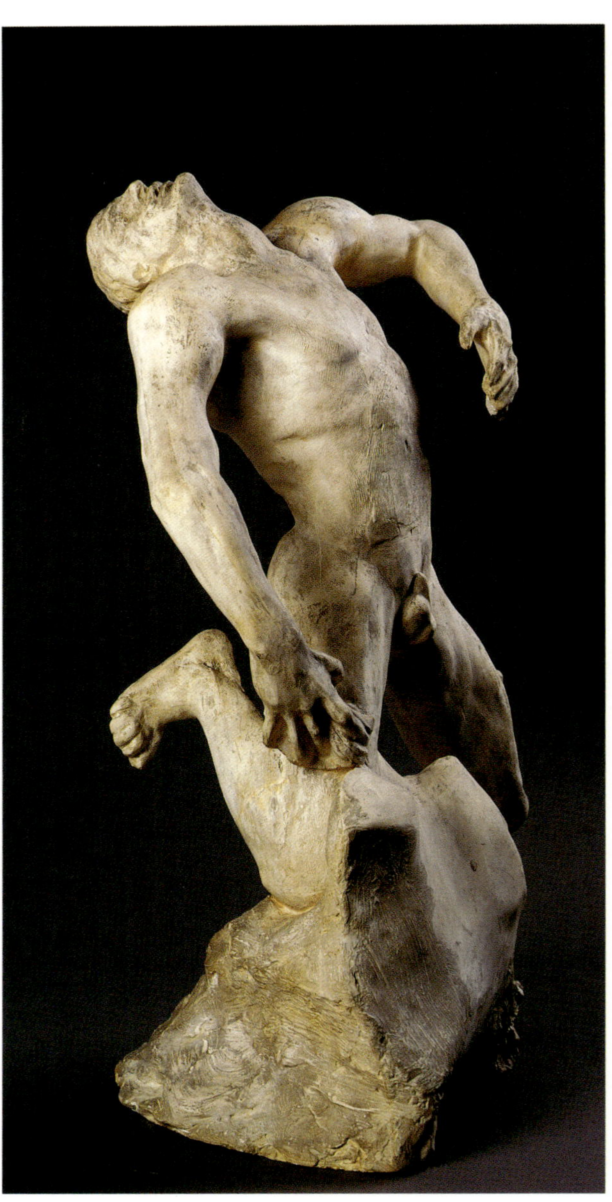

its grandeur which moves the viewer momentarily, then obsesses him" (Champsaur). Nobody hitherto had dared go so far, and while very few people had seen *The Gates of Hell* in the studio before 1900, a wider public had become aware of it thanks to exhibitions, at the Galerie Petit in particular, where Rodin had shown his small groups since the 1880s. The way in which he had modelled these freely, trying them in *The Gates* then removing them, resulted in their having a life of their own, whether or not they were retained for the final version.

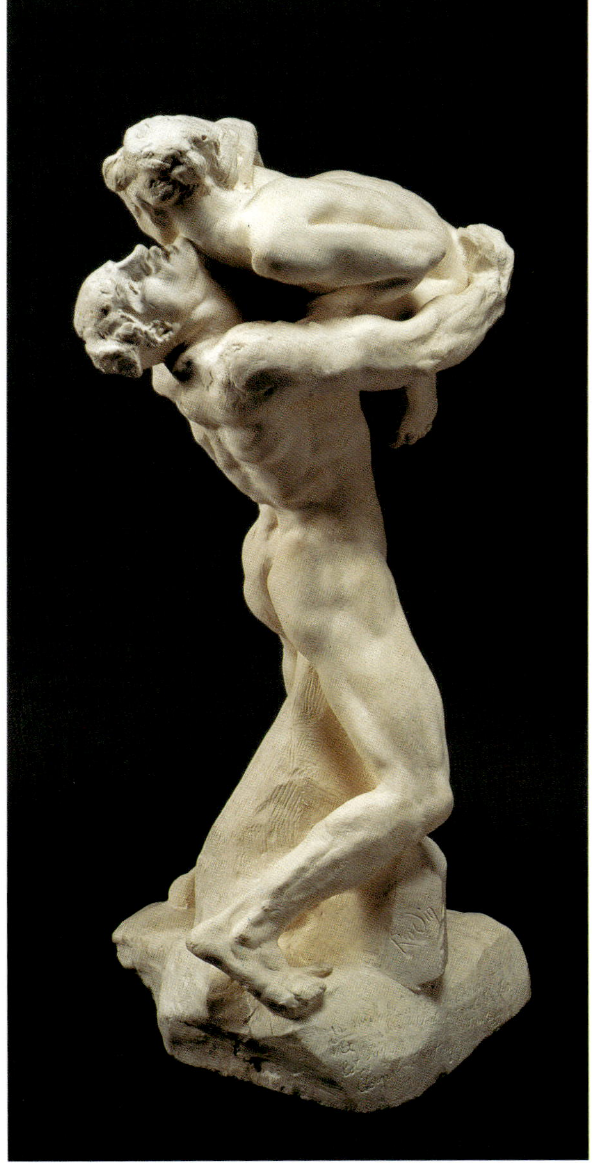

I am Beautiful,
before 1886
Plaster. 69.8 x 33.2 x 34.5
Rodin donation, 1916
Inv. S.1292

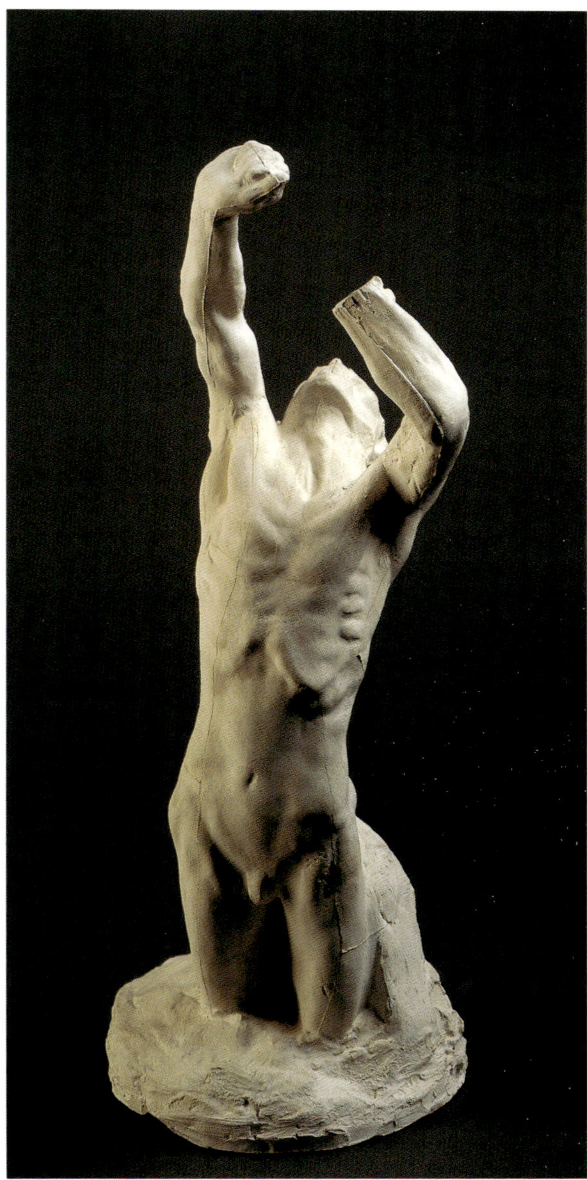

The Despairing Adolescent,
*c.*1882
Plaster. 41.4 x 19.2 x 17.9
Rodin donation, 1916
Inv. S.1176

Rodin gave the figures in *The Gates of Hell* an independent existence at a very early stage, and also very quickly thought of assembling them: in 1886 he exhibited a group made up from *The Falling Man* and *The Crouching Woman* which was later given the title *I am Beautiful* as a tribute to Baudelaire's poem, "Je suis belle, ô mortels, comme un rêve de pierre...". This group was inserted in *The Gates* at the top of the right-hand pilaster, not far from the two isolated figures: *The Crouching Woman*, also exhibited in 1886, mingling with the figures of the damned on the lintel, while her companion is clinging on to the edge of the same lintel.

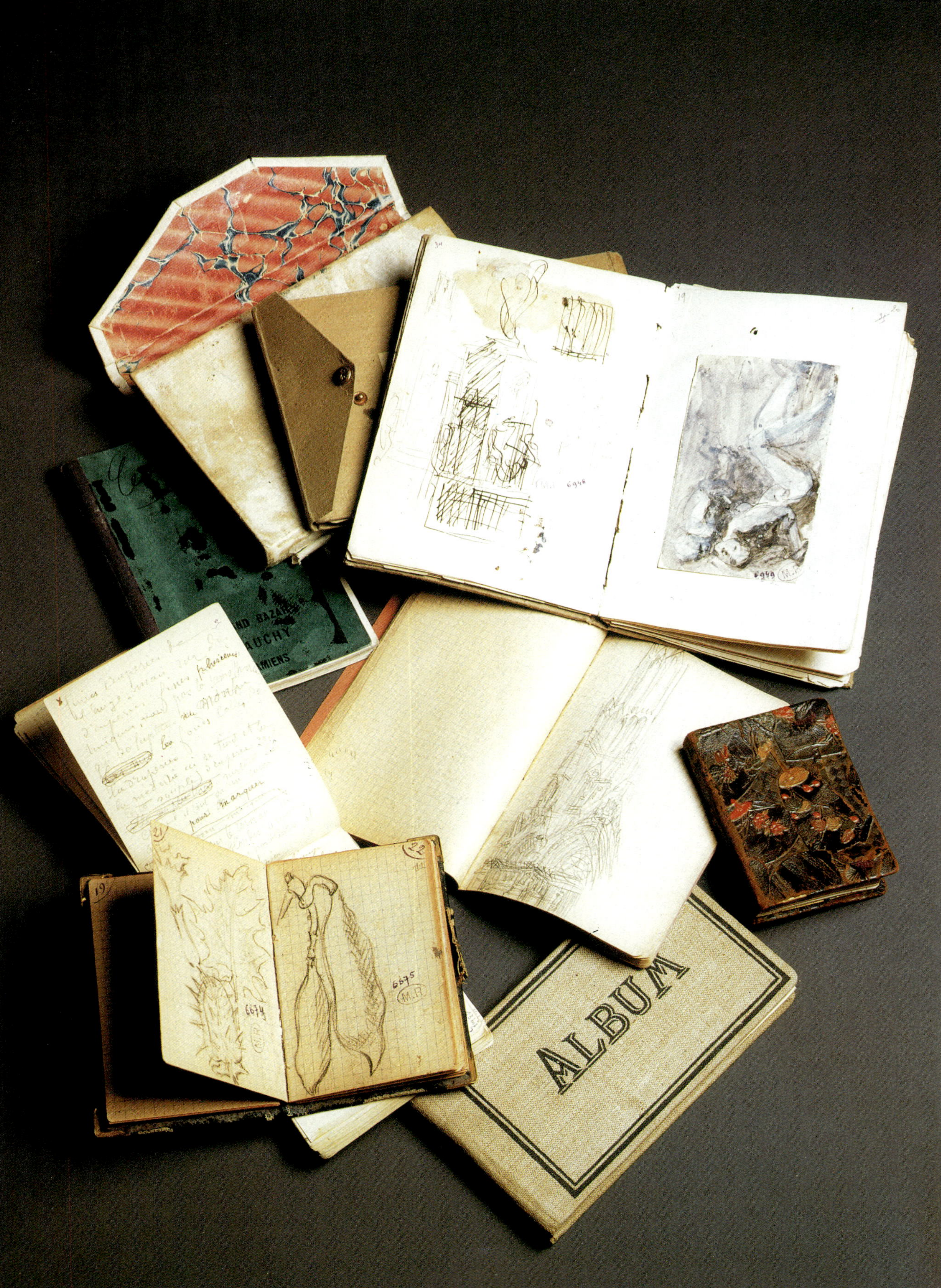
ALBUM

Architectural drawings

Claudie Judrin

The publication of *Les Cathédrales de France* in March 1914, just before the outbreak of World War I, was not something that happened by chance. From the close of the nineteenth century, reacting against restorations in the spirit of Viollet-le-Duc, Rodin had become the defender of French architecture, of our "old Living Stones." That is how he put it in the jottings in his notebooks and in a newspaper article in *Le Matin* of 23 December 1909 entitled "National sacrilege. We are allowing our cathedrals to die": "In snow, rain or sunshine you will find me before them, like a great vagabond wandering through France, and I am incessantly discovering them: I am always seeing them for the first time. To understand them you need only to be able to respond to the emotional language of these lines swollen by shadow and reinforced by the worn shape of the plain or decorated buttresses. To understand these lovingly modelled lines you have to be fortunate enough to be in love: for drawing comes from the mind, but modelling from the heart."

Rodin embarked on this pilgrimage to his sources on his first journey to Italy when he left Brussels at the end of 1875. He stopped at Rheims where the cathedral made a strong impression on him. During the autumn of 1877 he set out on a tour of cathedrals and from then on such journeys were one of his habits. Rose Beuret would see him leave home sometimes for several days at a time without it being known where he was going or when he would be back; when asked where he had been he would answer "I've been looking at cathedrals." The commission for *The Gates of Hell* required a deeper knowledge of the details of a monument. Between then and the time of Rodin's death nearly 2000 drawings were amassed in his notebooks: "I'm becoming an architect, I have to, for that will give me what I need for my door." When he drew a corner of the porch at Notre-Dame in Tonnerre he felt impelled to note in pencil: "my door."

The sketches are always hard to identify not because they lack precision but because they show details and not complete entities. Pillars, arches, mouldings and buttresses will remain forever anonymous, remote from their context, especially as many of the notebooks have been dismembered. Rodin had a soft spot for mouldings, which are used both by sculptors and architects, being essential for the elevation of a plinth or a door. In Rodin's eyes the shade and light, the dark and the fair, which he constantly mentions on his drawings to increase his awareness of the relief, epitomize the whole harmony of French architecture.

Rodin's sketchbooks
Rodin donation, 1916

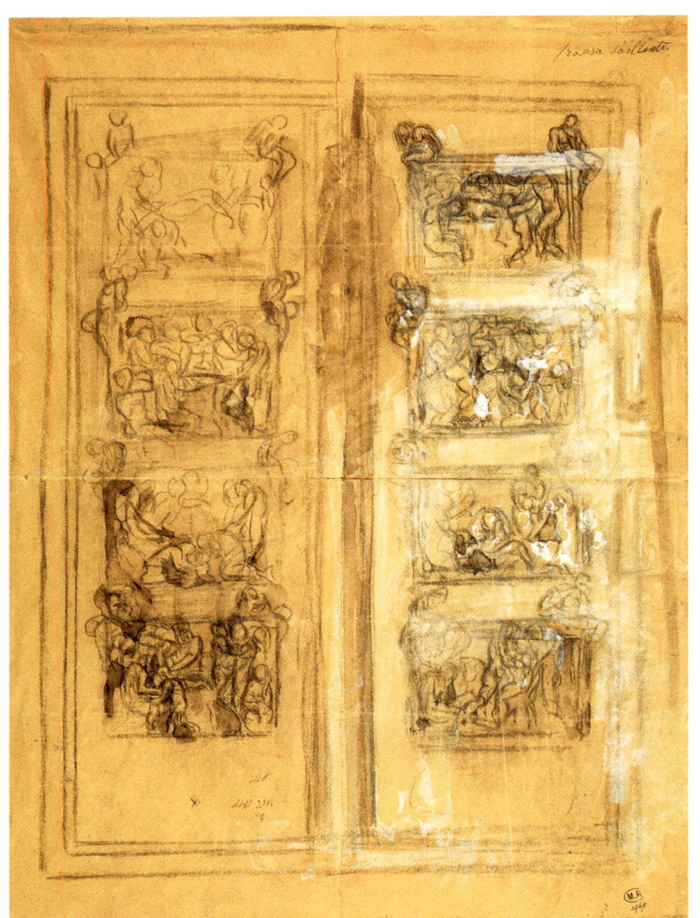

Proposal for the Gates of Hell with Eight Panels, *c.*1880
Charcoal, grey wash and gouache on paper. 55.7 x 44.7
Rodin donation, 1916
Inv. D.1969 and D.1968 verso

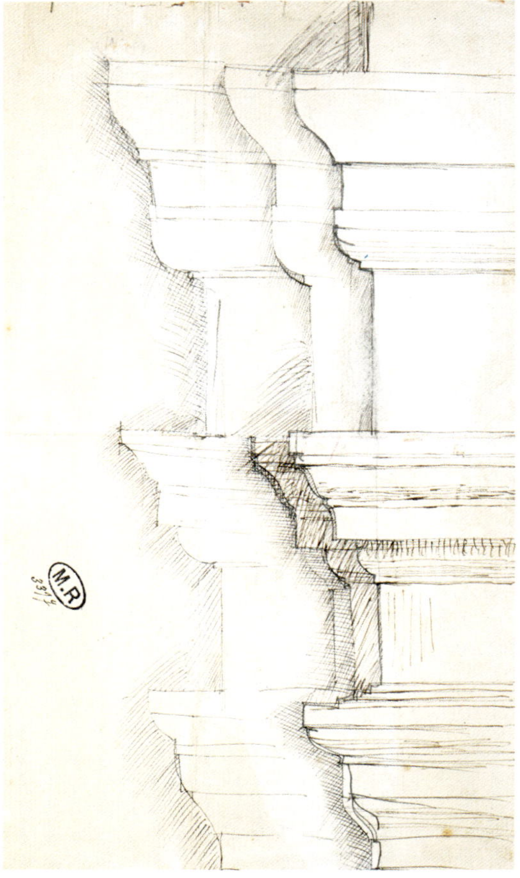

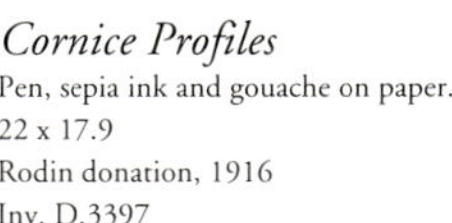

Cornice Profiles
Pen, sepia ink and gouache on paper. 22 x 17.9
Rodin donation, 1916
Inv. D.3397

Contrary to the impression created by the book on cathedrals and the commentary in it, Rodin was fonder of drawing churches which did not qualify as masterpieces. He seems to have found that they responded more to his concerns as a sculptor and architect. He travelled across France from west to east, from Quimperlé to Toulouse by way of the châteaux of the Loire, and from Dijon to Tonnerre. He was equally affected by Romanesque, Gothic or Renaissance architecture.

"My sculpture is only drawing using all the dimensions."

"My drawings are flashes of thought."

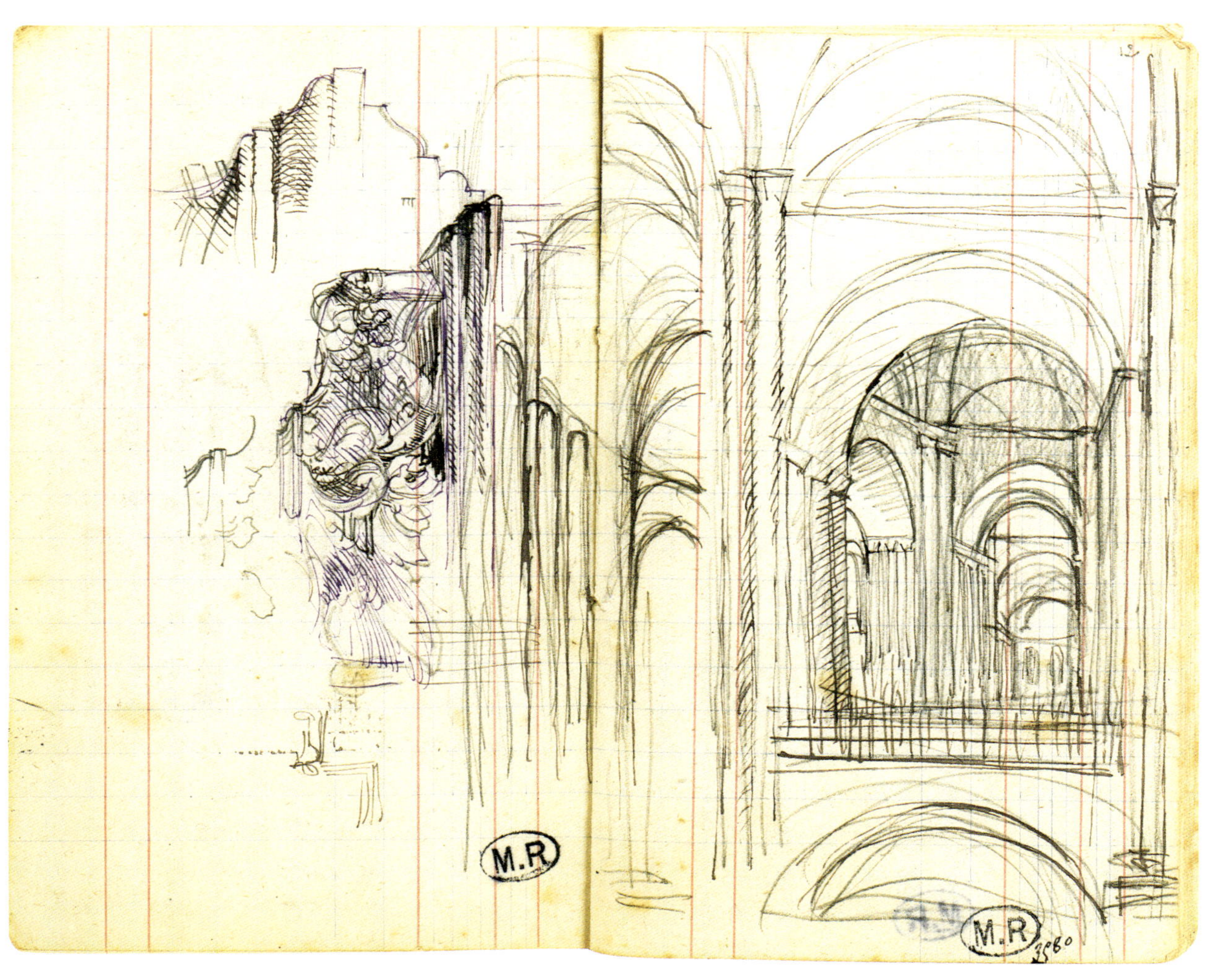

Interior of Sainte-Croix Church in Quimperlé,
1901?
Graphite and sepia ink on pages from sketchbook. 14.8 x 19
Rodin donation, 1916
Sketchbook, fo. 11 verso and 12 recto
Inv. D.3580

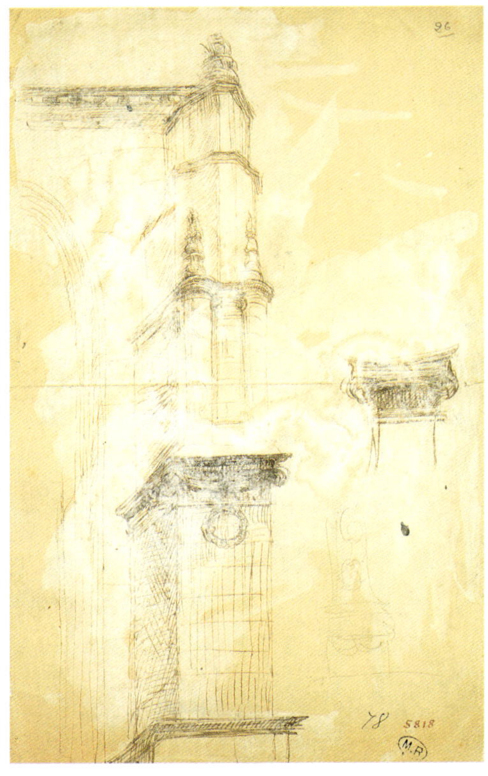

Buttress of Château d'Ussé,
*c.*1889-1890?
Graphite, pen, sepia ink and gouache on paper. 31 x 20
Rodin donation, 1916
Inv. D.5818

Dijon Palais de Justice,
*c.*1908 or 1909
Pen and sepia wash on paper.
18.7 x 14.7
Rodin donation, 1916
Inv. D.5891

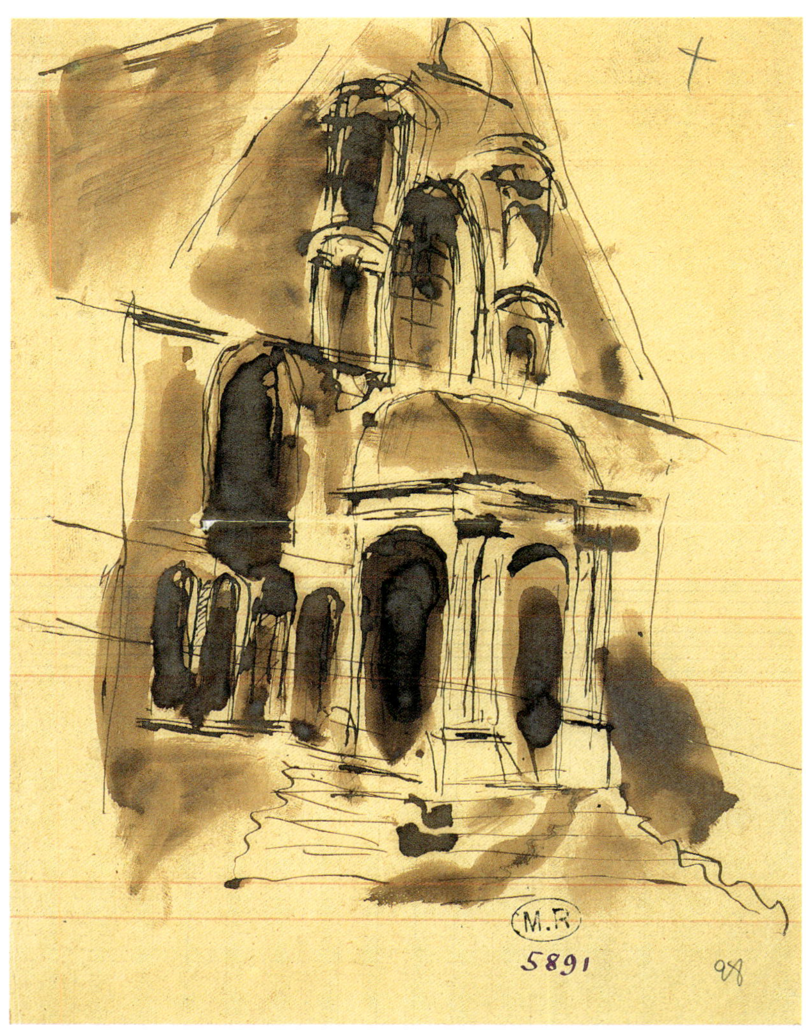

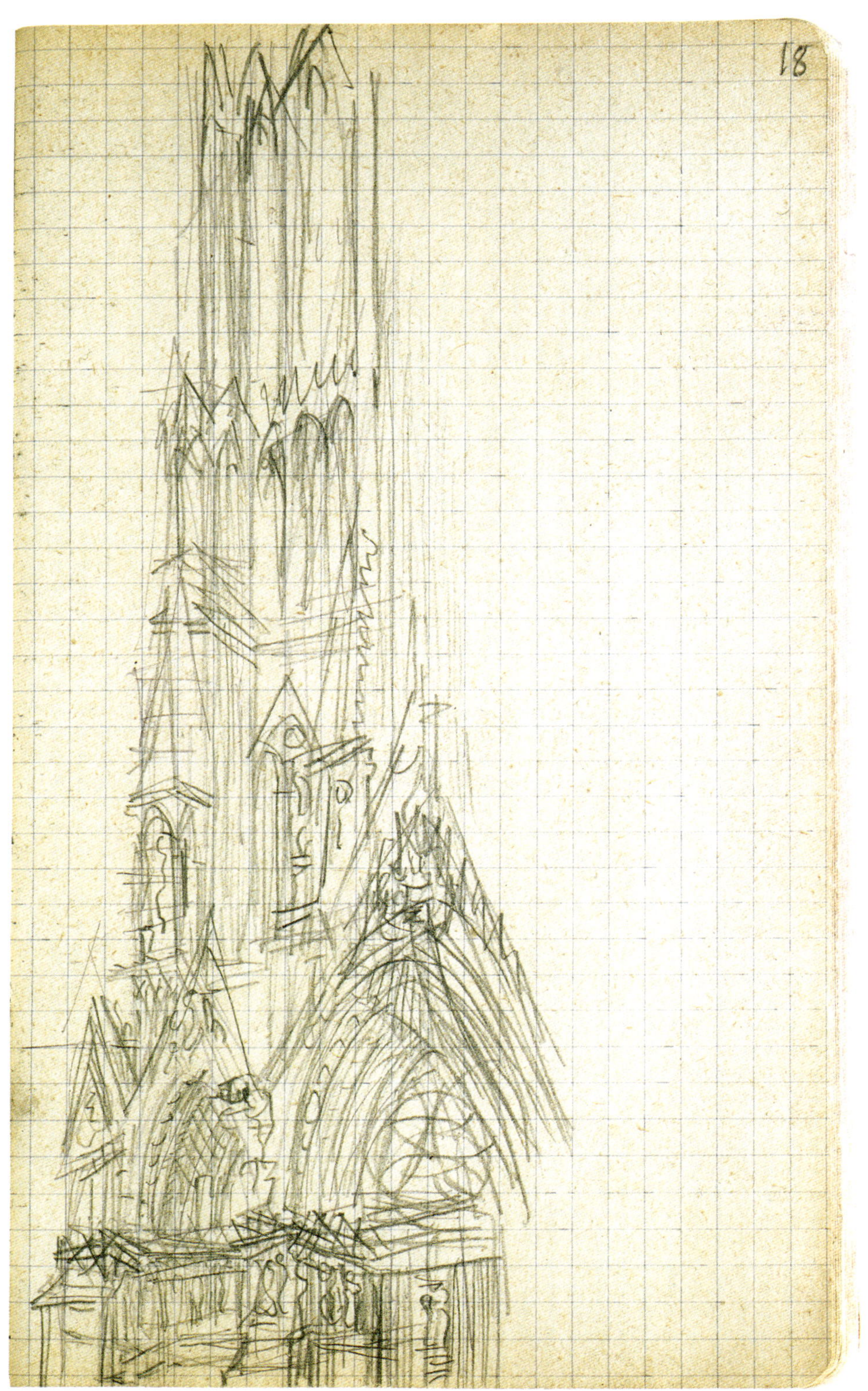

Porches and Bell Tower of Rheims Cathedral,
*c.*1905
Graphite on page from sketchbook.
15 x 9
Rodin donation, 1916
Sketchbook 55 fo. 18r.
Inv. D.7717

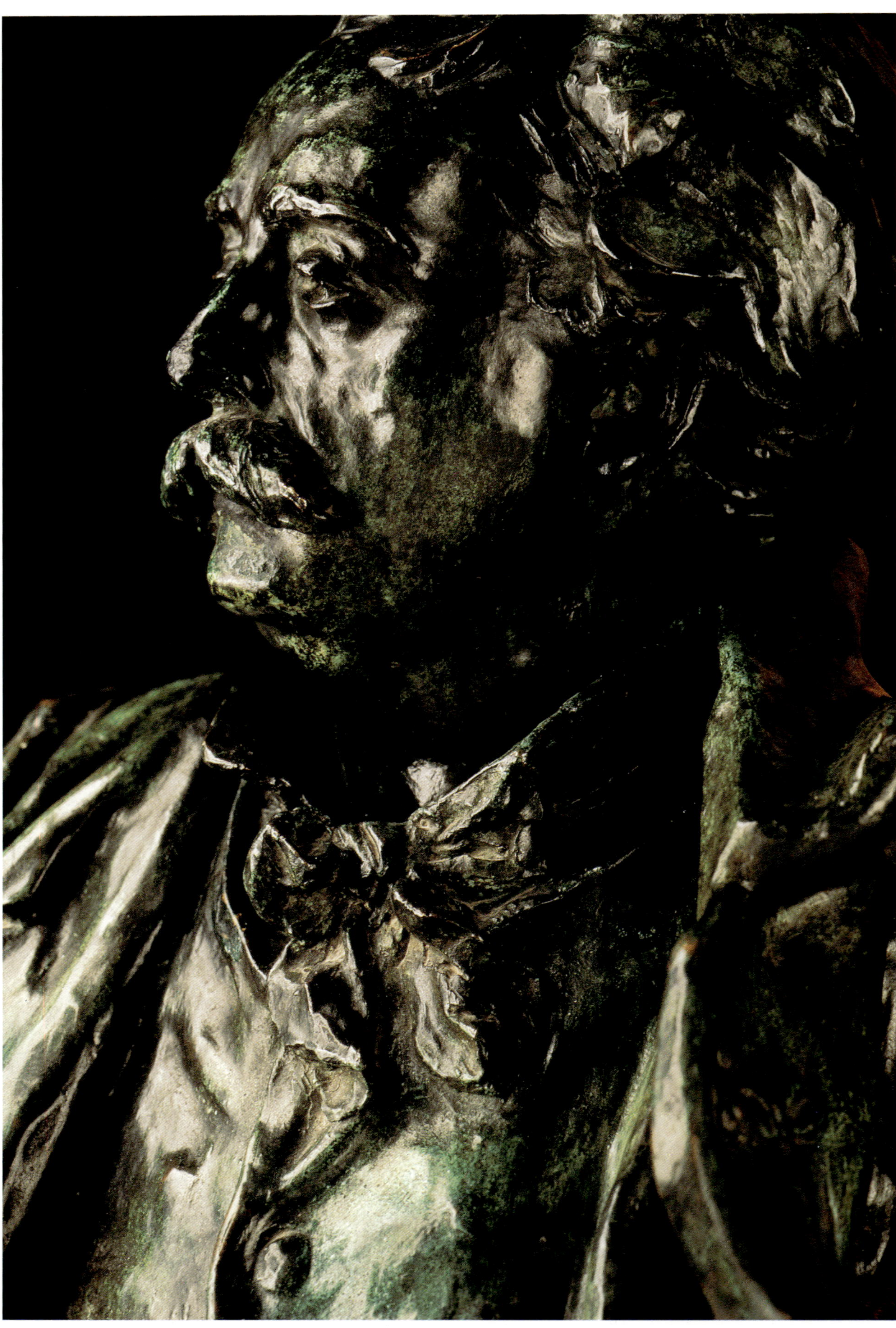

Portraits from the 1880s

Hélène Marraud

Despite his passionate enthusiasm for modelling all parts of the human figure, Rodin did not win renown as a portraitist until late in his career, but portraiture represented a substantial part of his oeuvre. "Really there is no artistic work that demands as much perspicacity as busts and portraits. It is sometimes thought that the profession of artist requires more manual skill than intelligence. One need only look at a good bust to be realise that this is a mistake. Such a work is as good as a biography" (Rodin).

Although he had carried out busts of those close to him such as his father (1860) or decorative busts under the aegis of Carrier-Belleuse at a relatively early stage in his career, it was not until the 1880s that Rodin's activity as a portraitist became known. Through his friend the journalist Bazire he met Victor Hugo and made a portrait of him before devoting himself to one of Rochefort. These busts of notabilities of the day enabled attention to be drawn to this aspect of his art. But at the time it was mainly a matter of portraits of friends, artists and close associates who posed for the sculptor free of charge. These busts were often the best, for "the fact that the artist is not being paid leaves him free to carry out the portrait completely as he likes" (Rodin). It was under these conditions that he made likeness of *Legros, Laurens, Carrier-Belleuse, Haquette, Becque, Dalou, Henley*, and *Proust*. Women, who were so dear to his heart, are less well represented: *Rose Beuret, Madame Victoria* (1884), apparently the only commission among the twenty or so busts carried out before 1900, *Madame Roll* and finally *Camille Claudel* and *Mrs Russell.*

Very few busts were made in marble, a particularly expensive material, at this period when Rodin was working mainly in clay and plaster. He gradually perfected his technique, always based on a very close study of all the profiles, and completed by working with small balls of clay which were grafted onto the face to accentuate the relief.

"People will never sufficiently credit how much tenacity is required to make a bust, and how one has to struggle to find and convey the true character, with the accentuation and highlighting of solid, supple, ample and free models," Rodin later told Dujardin-Beaumetz in his *Entretiens*. Going from the portrait to the allegorical portrait, Rodin used the features of Mrs Russell in *St George* (1888-89) and those of Camille Claudel in *The Farewell* and *France* (1905).

Albert Carrier-Belleuse
(detail), 1888
Bronze, cast by Montagutelli.
49 x 43.2 x 30.4
Rodin donation, 1916
Inv. S.983

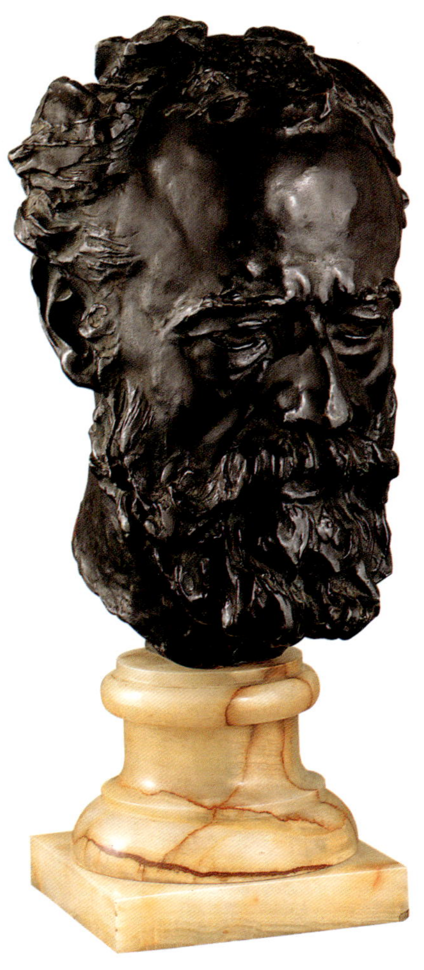

Alphonse Legros,
1882
Bronze, cast by Alexis Rudier.
32 x 20 x 23.5
Rodin donation, 1916
Inv. S.1060

"A fine bust shows the model in his moral and physical reality, tells his secret thoughts, sounds the innermost depths of his soul, his greatnesses and his weaknesses; all the masks come down" (Rodin). This is especially true of the portraits of men, which reveal an uncompromising truthfulness, not always understood by the model. Chéruy who was the sculptor's secretary tells us that in the bust of a man "Rodin saw first and foremost his character".

It is the features of Camille, as shown in the portrait executed in 1884, that crop up again in *The Farewell*, a symbolic vision showing the face and two hands seeming to send a final kiss.

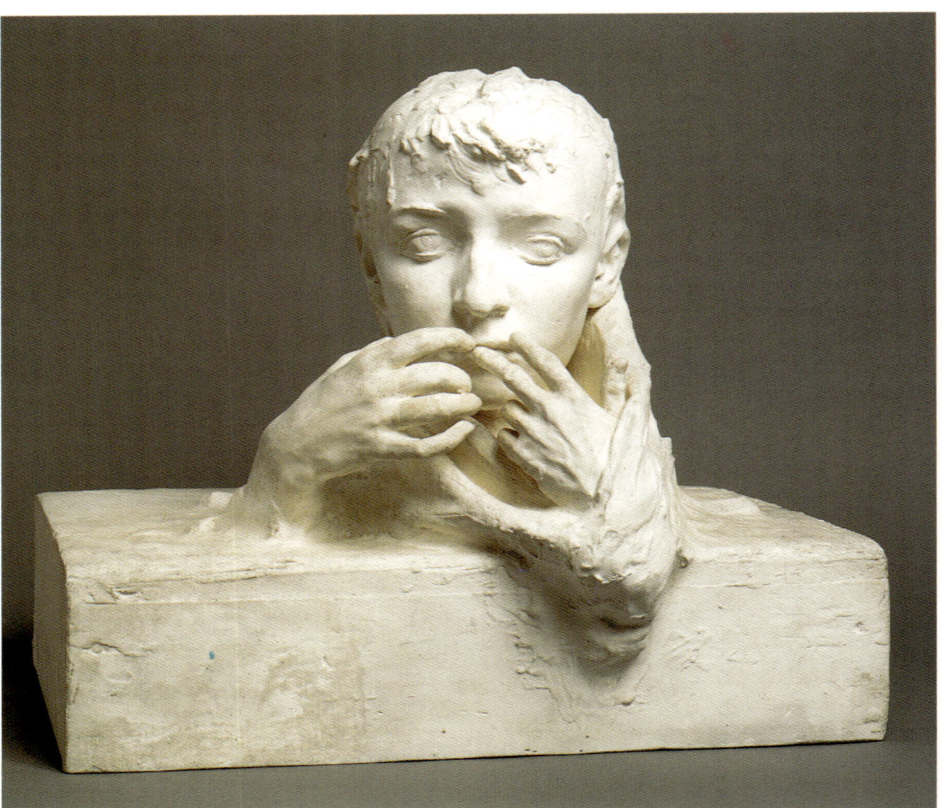

The Farewell,
1892?
Plaster. 38.8 x 45.2 x 30.6
Rodin donation, 1916
Inv. S.1795

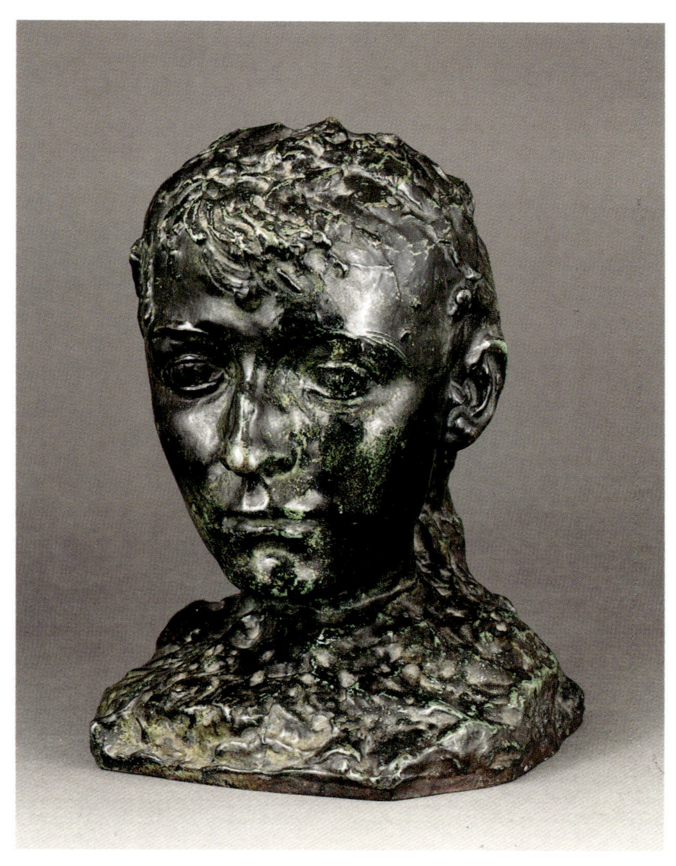

Camille Claudel,
1884
Bronze. 27.2 x 21.3 x 21.5
Rodin donation, 1916
Inv. S.1005

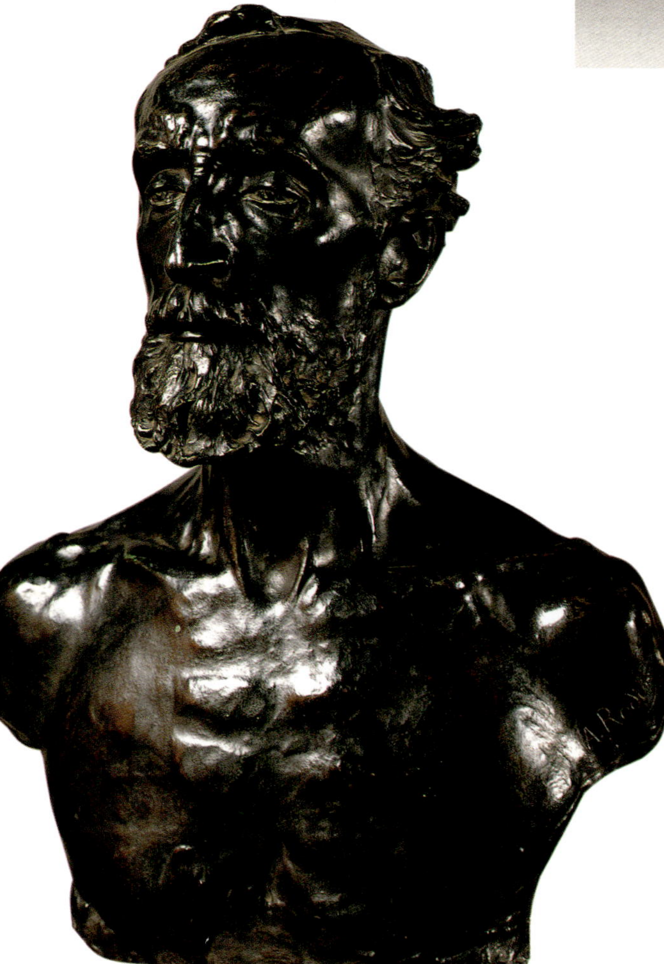

Jules Dalou,
1884
Bronze, cast by Alexis Rudier.
52.2 x 42.9 x 26.7
Rodin donation, 1916
Inv. S.982

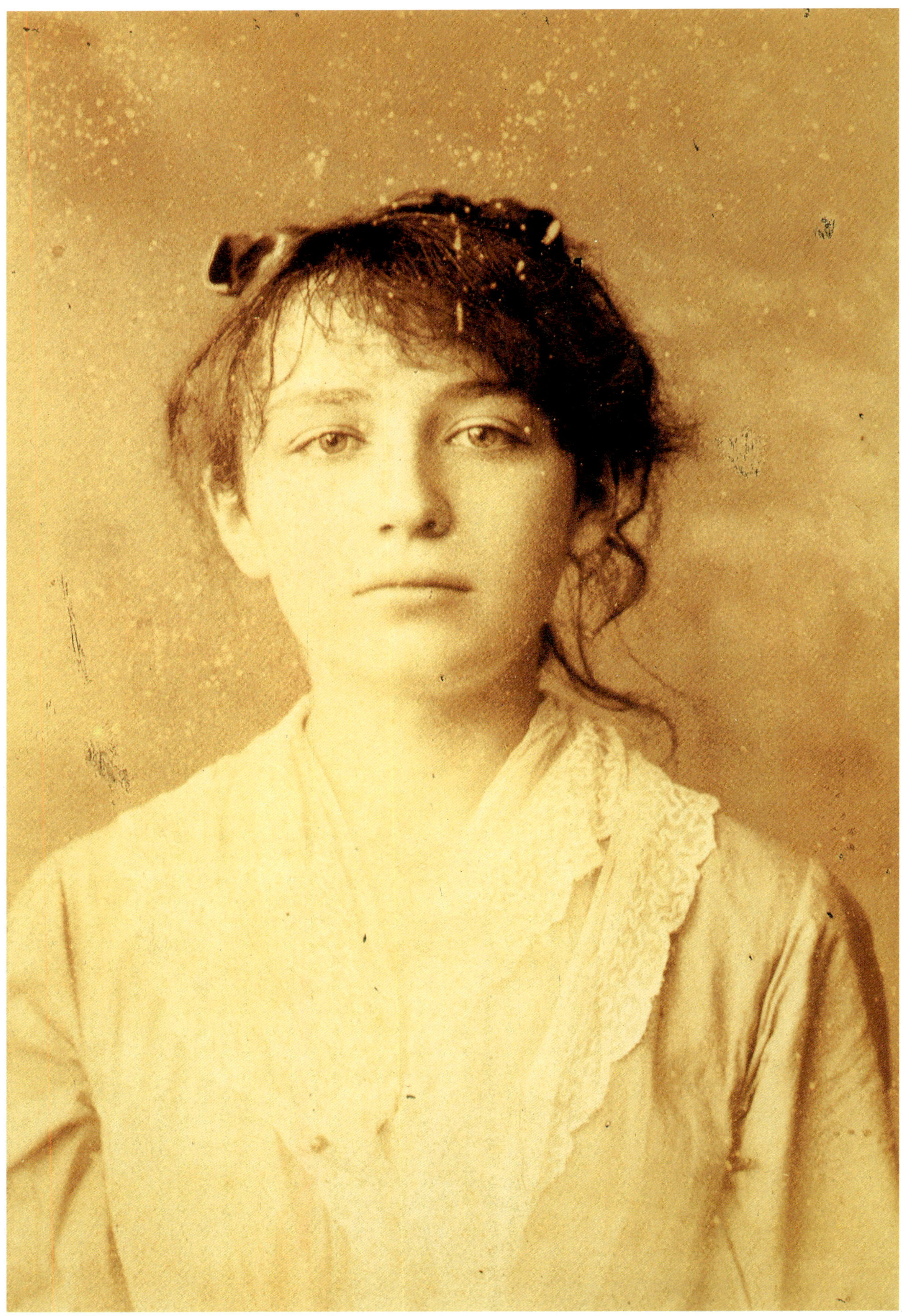

Camille Claudel

Jacques Vilain

"My very dearest down on both knees before your beautiful body which I embrace." Letter from Rodin to Camille Claudel (end of 1884 - beginning of 1885). These few ardent words evocative of the eroticism of *The Eternal Idol* perfectly convey the passion that united the two sculptors. Camille (1864-1943) was born into a modest family; her brother was the famous writer Paul Claudel (1868-1955). She decided at a very early age to become a sculptor, and in 1881 she took up residence in Paris, sure of her destiny and of her beauty: "A superb brow above magnificent eyes of that rare blue so seldom encountered outside the covers of a novel," Paul observed in 1951.

She met Rodin in 1883 and entered his studio the following year. Rodin's talented pupil very soon became his mistress; he was then in the midst of creating *The Gates of Hell* and *The Burghers of Calais*. The two artists had a mutual influence on one another; her *Jeune Fille à la Gerbe* of 1887 was a precursor of Rodin's *Galatea*, and the *Three Female Fauns* are the inspiration for the female figures in Camille Claudel's *La Vague*.

However, it was not until the early 1890s that Camille demonstrated the full measure of her art, at a time when her relationship with Rodin was beginning to deteriorate, as is demonstrated by the cruelty of the barbed drawings which Camille devoted to Rose and Rodin as a couple: the *Système Cellulaire*, *Réveil*, *Collage* ... Camille realised that she would never be Rodin's wife and would never succeed in ousting Rose Beuret; the final break between the lovers came in 1898, and the wound it caused was commensurate with the ardour of the love that the two artists had experienced for more than ten years. Camille never recovered from the separation, even if her art then started to break free of the influence of her famous master, with *La Valse* in 1892, taken up again in 1895 and produced in a large edition by Eugène Blot after 1905; *Clotho* in 1895; the various versions of the *La Petite Châtelaine*, started in 1893, or *L'Age Mûr* in 1895, taken up again in 1898 and 1907: a cruel statement of abandonment, Rodin leaving Camille, on her knees begging him to stay, to go back to Rose. The most profoundly original examples of Camille's work were produced at the turn of the century; with works such as *Les Causeuses*, 1897, and *La Vague*, 1900, she embarked on a new style derived from the *japonisme* fashionable at the time, and deeply anchored in Art Nouveau. Using onyx, a rare material, she based her compositions on an elegant play of curves; thus Camille was a sculptor in tune with the art of her day. Unfortunately the first signs of paranoia were starting to become evident.

From 1906 the madness became more pronounced and destructive. The Museum has fifteen of her sculptures and it is here that the most representative selection of Camille's art can be seen. This is as Rodin wished; we need only

César
Portrait of Camille Claudel, *c.*1884
Albumen print. 15.5 x 10.3
Gift of Stephen Back, 1992
Inv. Ph.527

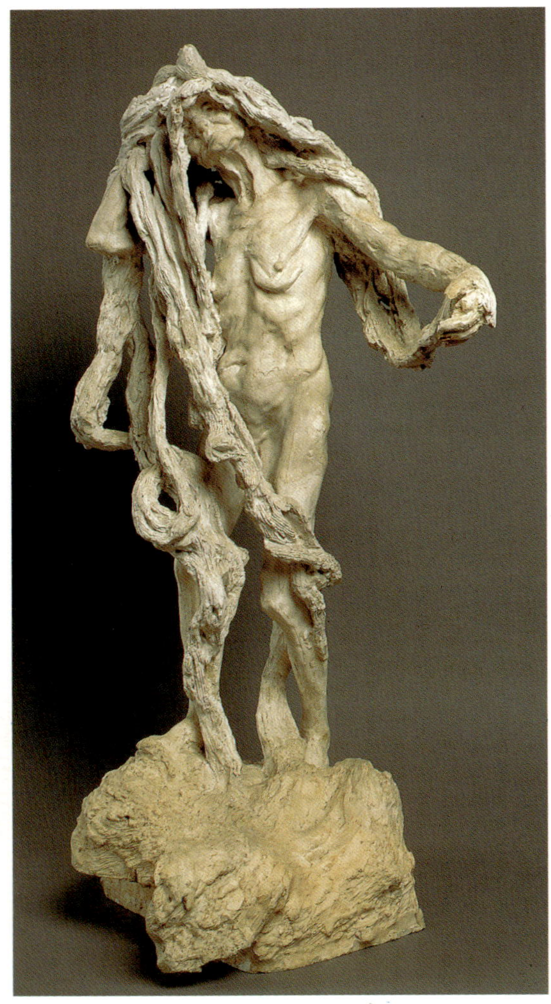

Camille Claudel
(1864-1943)
Clotho,
1893
Plaster. 89.9 x 49.3 x 43
Gift of Paul Claudel, 1952
Inv. S.1379

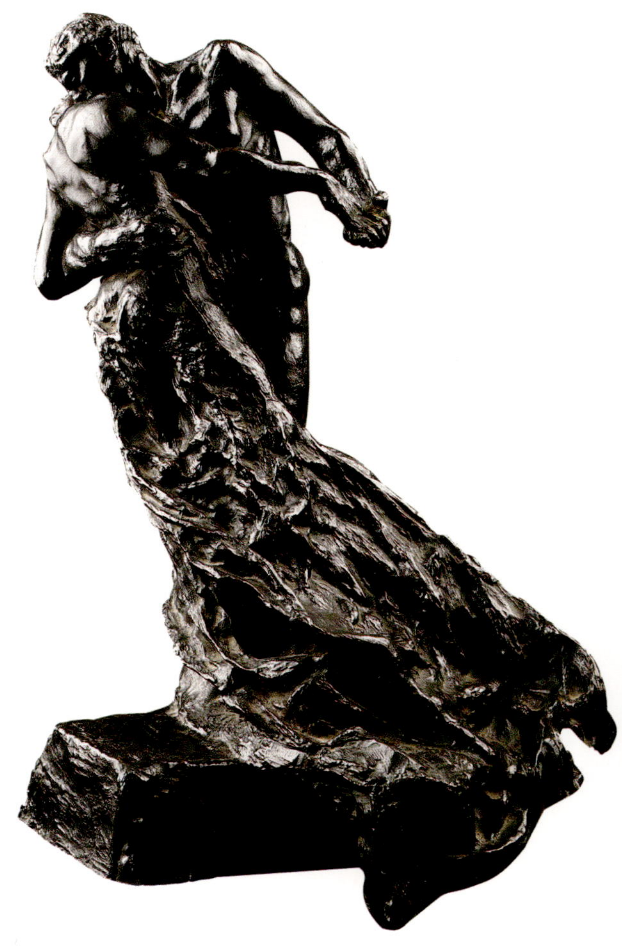

Camille Claudel
La Valse,
1895
Bronze. 43.2 x 23 x 34.3
Acquired in 1963
Inv. S.1013

quote the words he wrote to his friend Morhardt in 1914 when the museum project was taking shape: "With regard to the Hôtel Biron, nothing is settled yet. The idea of including some sculptures by Mlle Say [a phonetic pseudonym for Camille Claudel, Mademoiselle C., based on the French pronunciation of "c"] would please me very much. This house is quite small and I don't know how the rooms will be arranged. There could be a few buildings for her and for me." Following the 1951 exhibition Paul Claudel gave the museum the plaster version of *Clotho*, *L'Age Mûr* in bronze and *Vertumne et Pomone* in marble. In 1963 the museum acquired the onyx version of *Les Causeuses*, and it seemed only natural this should be joined in 1995 by *La Vague*, a masterpiece in bronze and onyx also purchased by the museum. Therefore it is in Rodin's own house that Camille's work can best be appreciated in all the power and originality of her own individual genius, stripped of the media hype which has tended only to distort it.

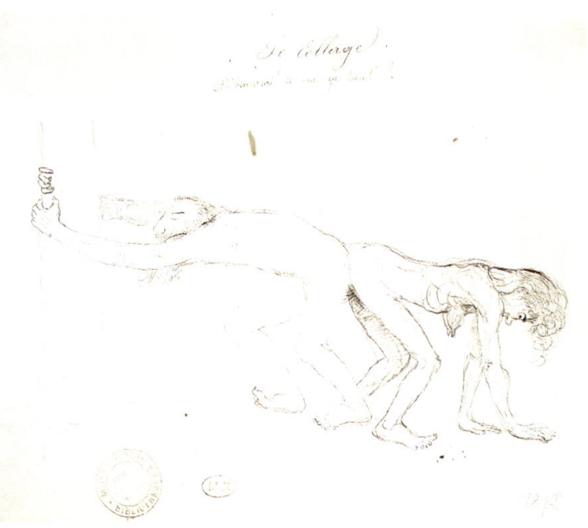

Camille Claudel
Le Collage. Ah! Ben Vrai! Ce que Ça Tient!,
*c.*1894
Pen and sepia ink on cream paper.
21 x 26.2
Rodin donation, 1916
Inv. D.7634

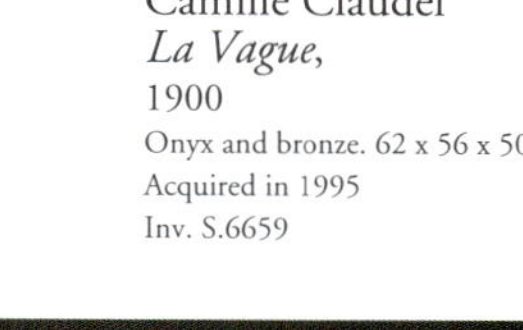

Camille Claudel
La Vague,
1900
Onyx and bronze. 62 x 56 x 50
Acquired in 1995
Inv. S.6659

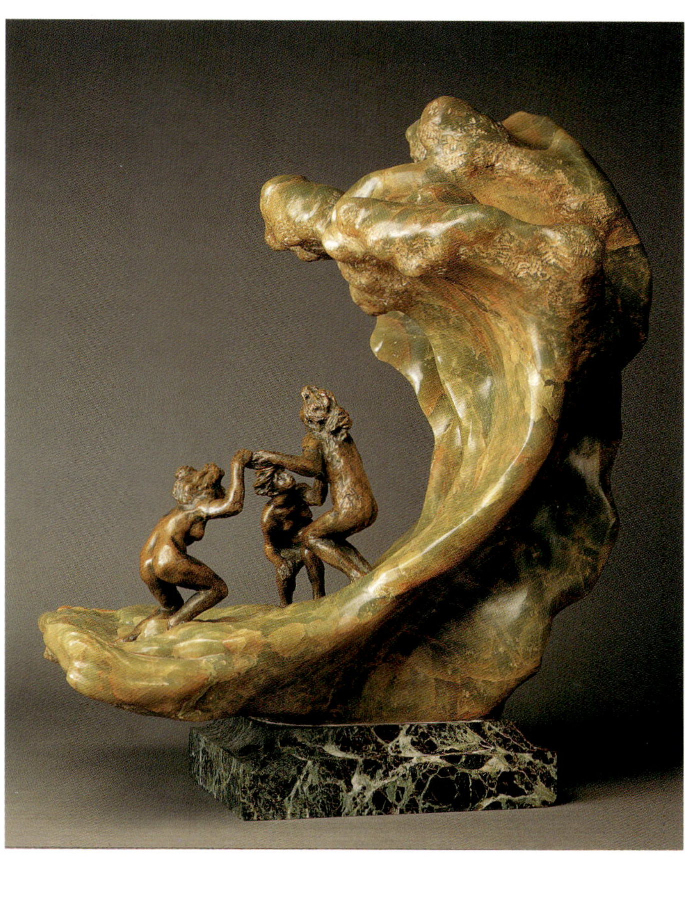

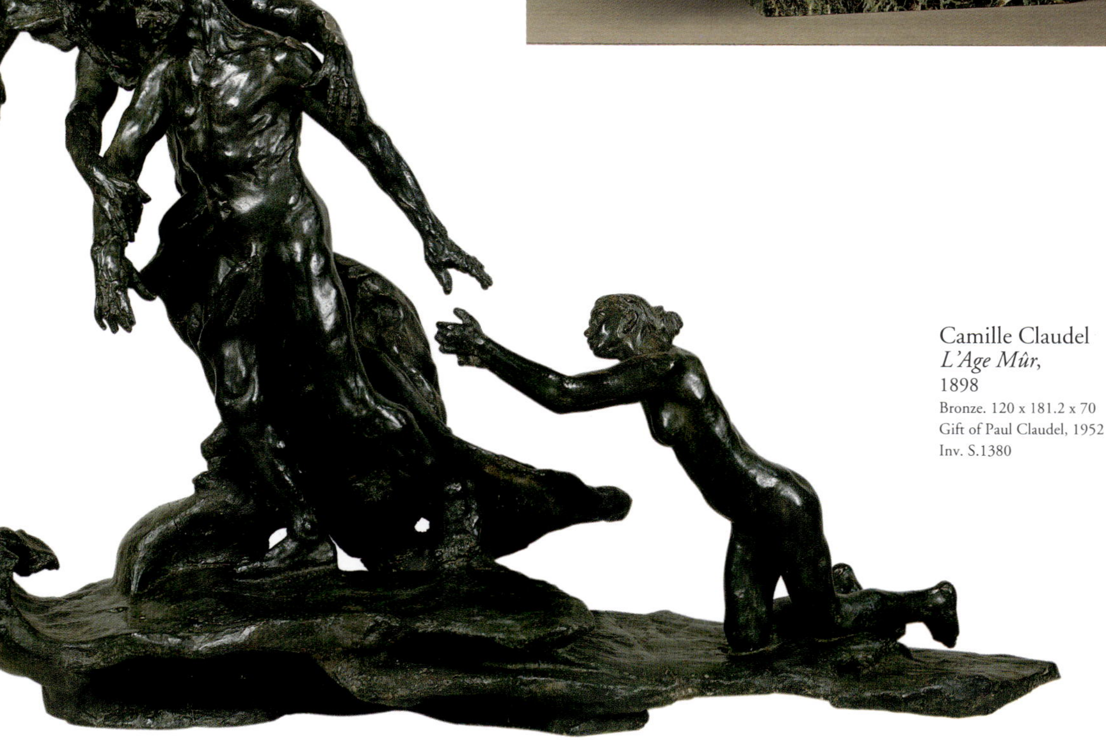

Camille Claudel
L'Age Mûr,
1898
Bronze. 120 x 181.2 x 70
Gift of Paul Claudel, 1952
Inv. S.1380

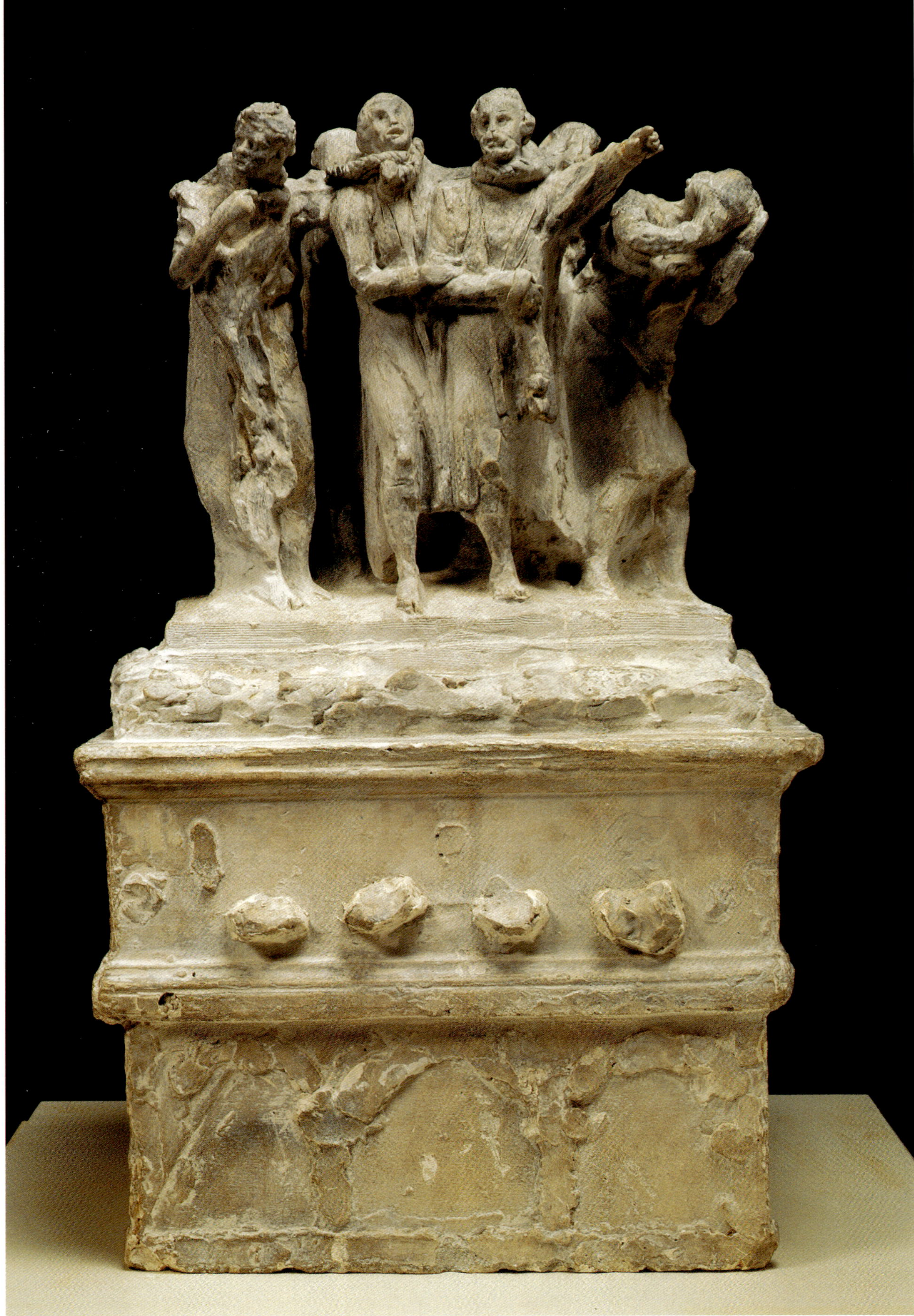

The Burghers of Calais

Hélène Marraud

In 1885, five years after *The Gates of Hell*, Rodin, though he had certain misgivings, was delighted to receive the commission for a "monument to Eustache de Saint-Pierre and his companions: I am very hard pressed at the moment trying to get my door over and done with as I must get it finished at all costs," he wrote to Omer Dewavrin, the mayor of Calais and chairman of the committee responsible for the monument, *c.*1888. "After that I will get back to the Calais figures which as you know are well advanced."

Several schemes for a monument celebrating the self-abnegation and heroism of Eustache de Saint-Pierre had already been under consideration since 1840, but none had been carried out. From 1885 when it was commissioned to 1895 when it was unveiled in Calais the story of this monument, which can be very faithfully charted thanks to the correspondence between Rodin and Omer Dewavrin, is an object lesson in more ways than one.

Rodin drew his inspiration from Froissart's *Chronicles*, recounting the episode of the surrender of Calais after it was besieged by King Edward III of England in 1347 and the heroic act of six prominent citizens prepared to sacrifice themselves to free their town. In an attempt to convey historical probability he gave his characters both a symbolic aspect (they are clothed in shirts with bare heads and feet, with a rope round their necks) and a naturalistic one, by studying models local to the region, like Rodin's friend the painter Cazin, who posed for Eustache de Saint-Pierre.

Rodin very quickly produced a *First Maquette* conceived in a heroic manner, with the six Burghers standing together on a raised plinth, differing from the proposals of the other sculptors approached which included only a single figure. The second maquette, made in July 1885, presented the figures at a third of their final size; Rodin dealt with each figure separately, naked in order to put beneath the drapery "bone structures, nervous systems, all the organs of life, flesh and blood creatures" (Geffroy, 1889) then clothed, while at the same time ensuring great cohesion within the group. "They are voluntarily bound to the same sacrifice but each of them plays the role suited to his individuality given his age and position" (Rodin). The composition is contained within a rectangle, not following the classic pyramidal plan placing a single individual in the position of honour, but evoking "the slow procession ... the walk towards death by the whole group" (Geffroy, 1889).

The "Monet-Rodin" exhibition in 1889 gave the sculptor an opportunity to show the final model of the monument successfully, but the collapse of the bank responsible for financing it delayed casting. A new campaign for the monu-

First Maquette for the Monument to the Burghers of Calais,
1884
Plaster. 61 x 38 x 32.5
Rodin donation, 1916
Inv. S.86

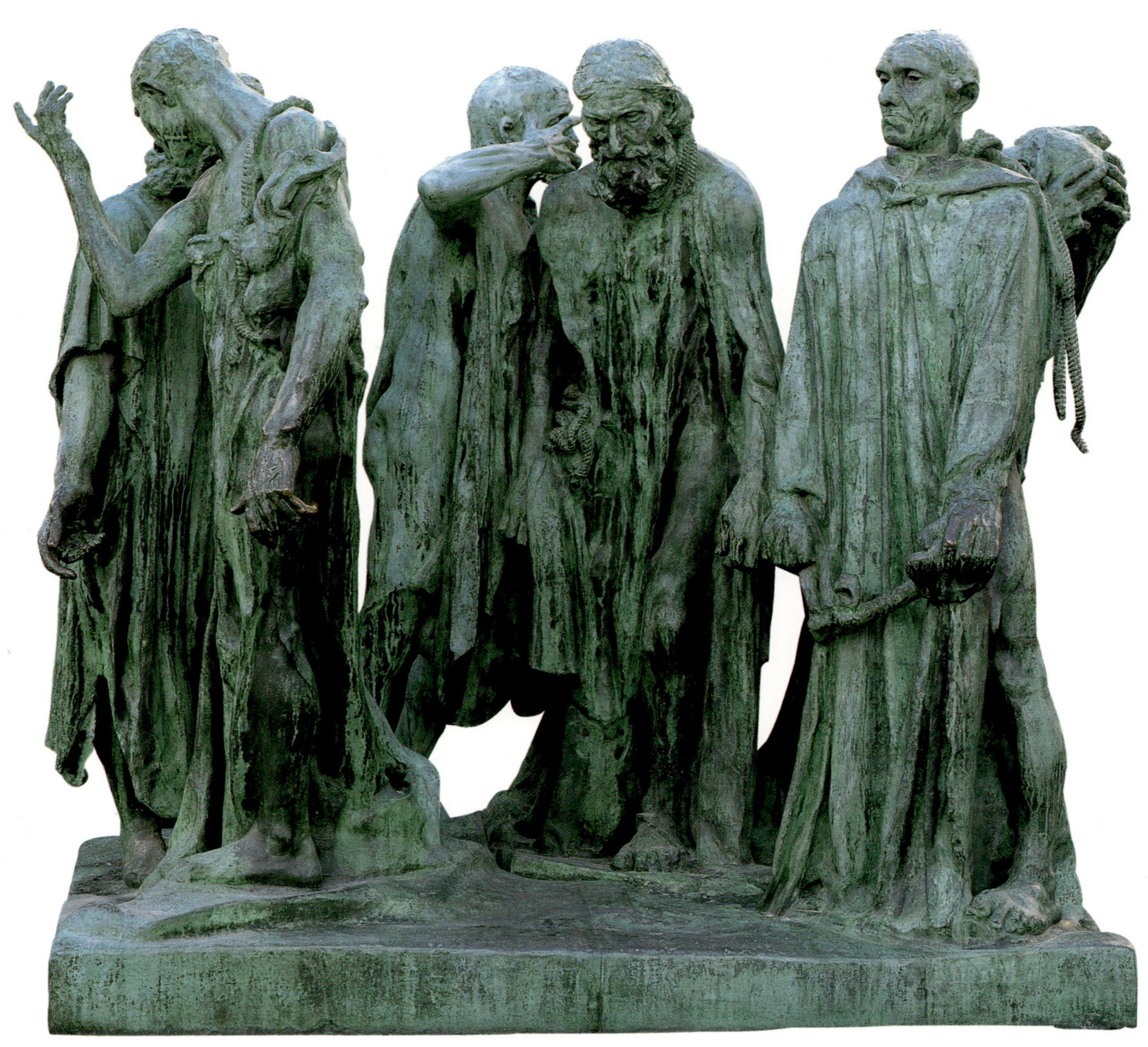

Monument to the Burghers of Calais,
1889
Commissioned in 1885 and unveiled in Calais in 1895
Bronze, cast by Alexis Rudier.
217 x 255 x 197
Cast for the Museum's collections in 1926
Inv. S.450

ment was launched in 1892 and a national subscription opened, and only on 19 November 1894 was a contract finally signed with the Leblanc-Barbedienne foundry for a sum of 12,000 francs. The monument was installed in front of a garden and unveiled in Calais on 3 June 1895 on a tall "pedestal which is as clumsy as it is superfluous," to the regret of Rodin who would have preferred it to be very low "to allow the public to penetrate to the heart of the subject, like in church entombments where the group is almost at ground level" (Rodin).

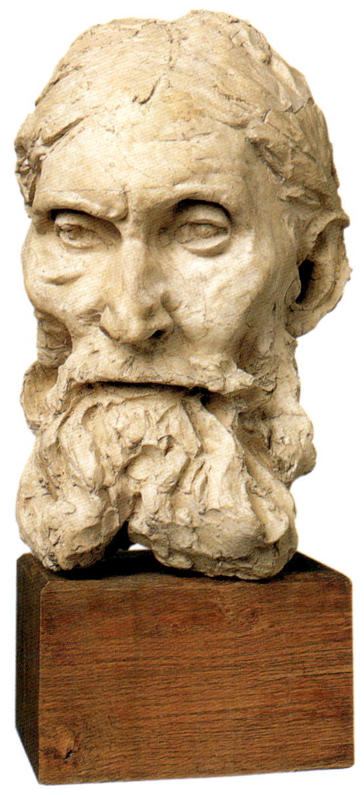

Eustache de Saint-Pierre,
1886
Patinated terra cotta.
33.7 x 21.3 x 24.8
Rodin donation, 1916
Inv. S.97

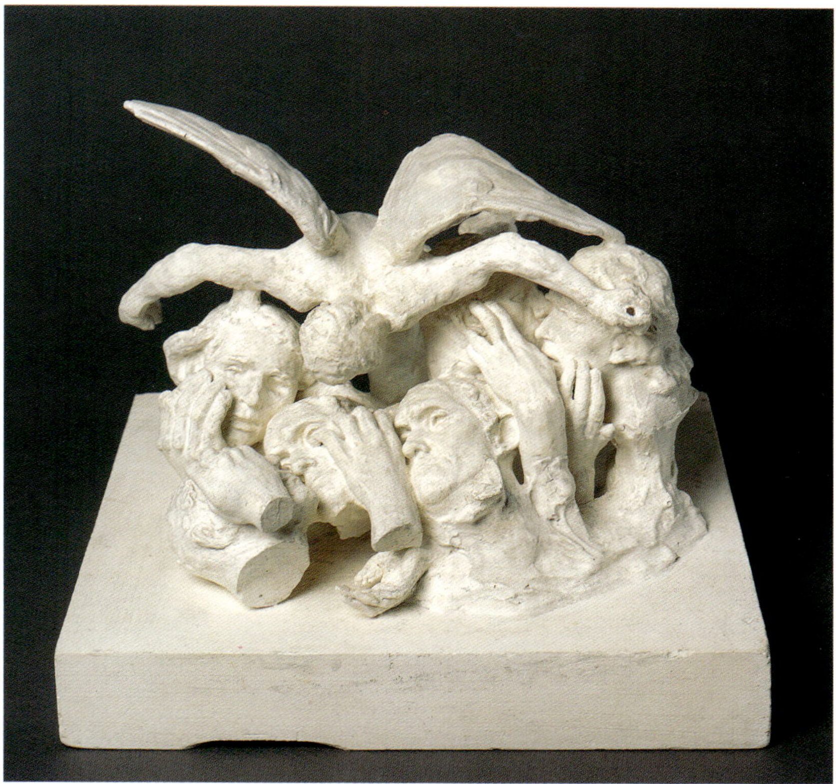

Assemblage of Heads and Hands from the Reduced Version of the Burghers of Calais, Surmounted by a Winged Figure,
*c.*1900
Plaster. 24 x 28.5 x 23.8
Rodin donation, 1916
Inv. S.849

This assemblage brings together in a single composition the reduced version of the heads of the three of the Burghers of Calais and small hands which exist independently, with a figure representing one of those damned from *The Gates of Hell* covering them with his wings.

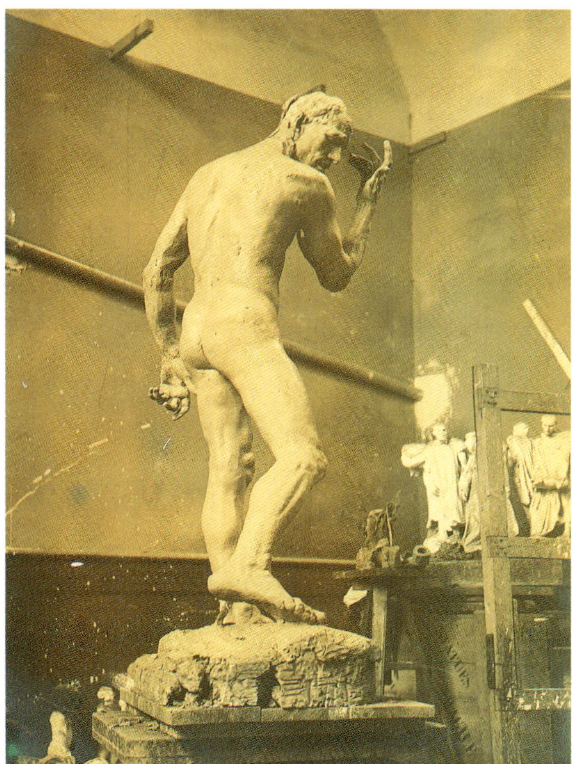

Charles Bodmer
(1809-1893)
Nude Figure of Pierre de Wissant in Unbaked Clay in the Boulevard de Vaugirard Studio,
*c.*1886
Gelatin silver print. 25 x 18.3
Rodin donation, 1916
Inv. Ph.955

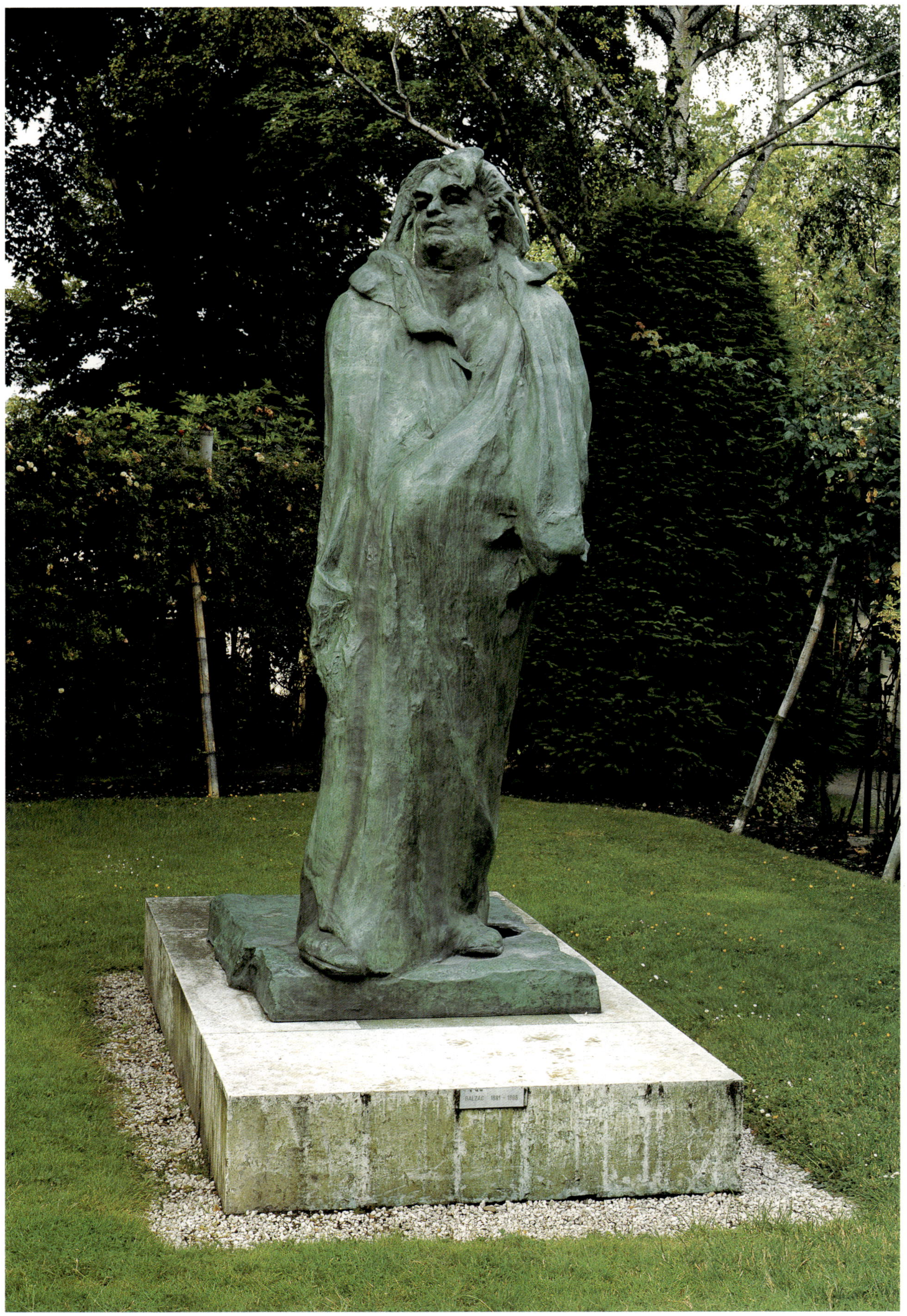
BALZAC

Public monuments

Hélène Marraud

Balzac (1799-1850)
"The most extraordinary of Rodin's adventures, the statue around which people fought as if around a flag" (Riotor) was commissioned from him in July 1891 by the Société des Gens de Lettres; Zola was president of the society and after Chapu's death he was initially responsible for having the monument made. Rodin undertook to make "a Balzac in bronze about three metres high (...) within a maximum period of eighteen months" for the sum of 30,000 francs.

Rodin, anxious to produce a historical image, truthful and not idealized, "lived entirely in this figure. He visited Balzac's native region, the countryside of Touraine (...), he read his correspondence, he studied the existing portraits of Balzac, and he went through his work again and again" (Rilke). Portraits carried out after contemporary iconographic evidence (Boulanger's portrait, Nadar's daguerreotype etc) and after models encountered in Touraine attempt to achieve a very close understanding of the writer's spirit, with the studies of heads getting gradually closer to the final version of the monument.

After *Balzac Standing in a Dominican Robe* which was favourably received by the committee in 1892 Rodin carried out many further powerful nude studies – with his legs apart, an "ace of spades" profile, as an athletic figure – and clothing studies before draping his figures *c.*1896-97. The work was eventually exhibited at the 1898 Salon where it aroused a heated polemic amplified by the publication of Zola's *J'accuse.* The Société des Gens de Lettres did not recognize Balzac in this extremely powerful figure, stripped of all anecdote, a symbol of constantly alert creativity, and turned it down. They approached Falguière who then produced a nondescript figure, seated on a bench, which was unveiled in the avenue de Friedland in 1902 while Rodin's *Balzac* had to wait until 1939 to be cast and installed at the intersection of the boulevard Raspail and the boulevard Montparnasse.

Victor Hugo (1802-1885)
Rodin was introduced to Victor Hugo by Bazire, the secretary of *La Marseillaise* newspaper, then of *L'Intransigeant.* As the poet refused to pose, Rodin managed not without some difficulty to sculpt a portrait of him in 1883, a portrait that can be found in the two monument projects, both representing Victor Hugo during his exile in Guernsey in 1855.

Balzac, monument,
1898
Bronze, cast by Alexis Rudier.
270 x 120 x 128
Cast for the Museum's collections in 1936
Inv. S.1296

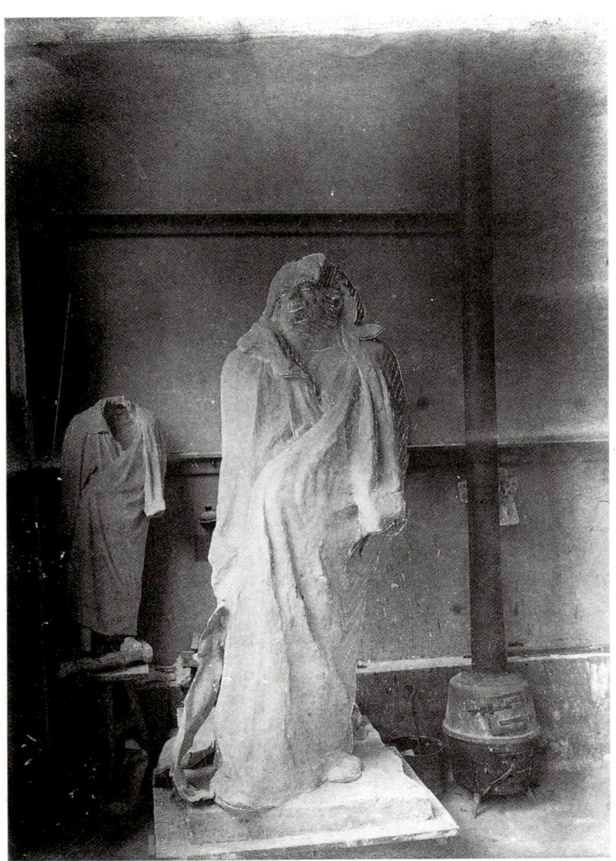

Eugène Druet
(1868-1916)
Balzac's Monument and Coat in Plaster,
*c.*1897?
Gelatin silver print. 29.7 x 19.7
Rodin donation, 1916
Inv. Ph.665

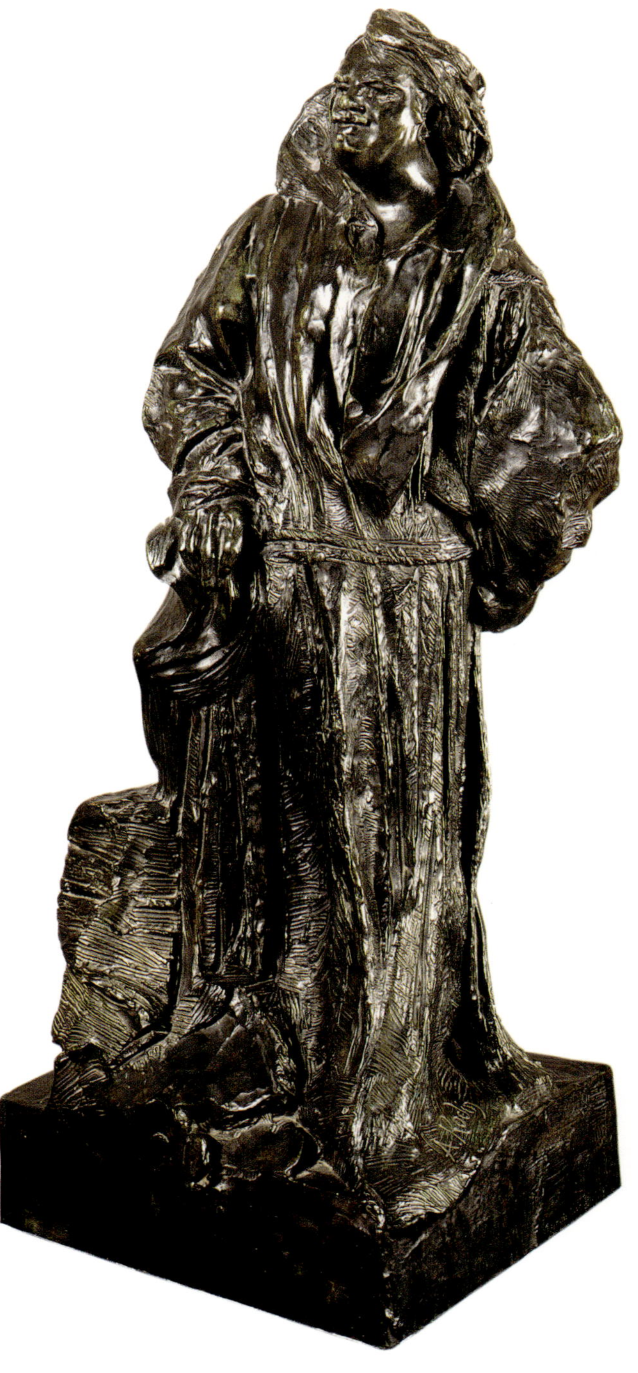

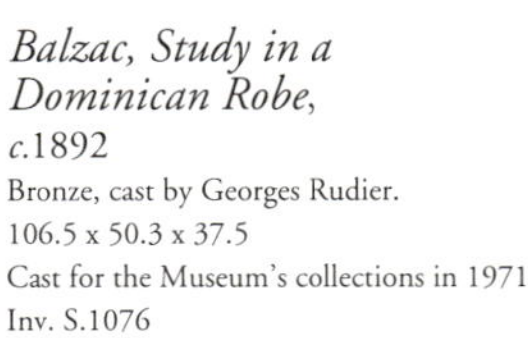

Balzac, Study in a Dominican Robe,
*c.*1892
Bronze, cast by Georges Rudier.
106.5 x 50.3 x 37.5
Cast for the Museum's collections in 1971
Inv. S.1076

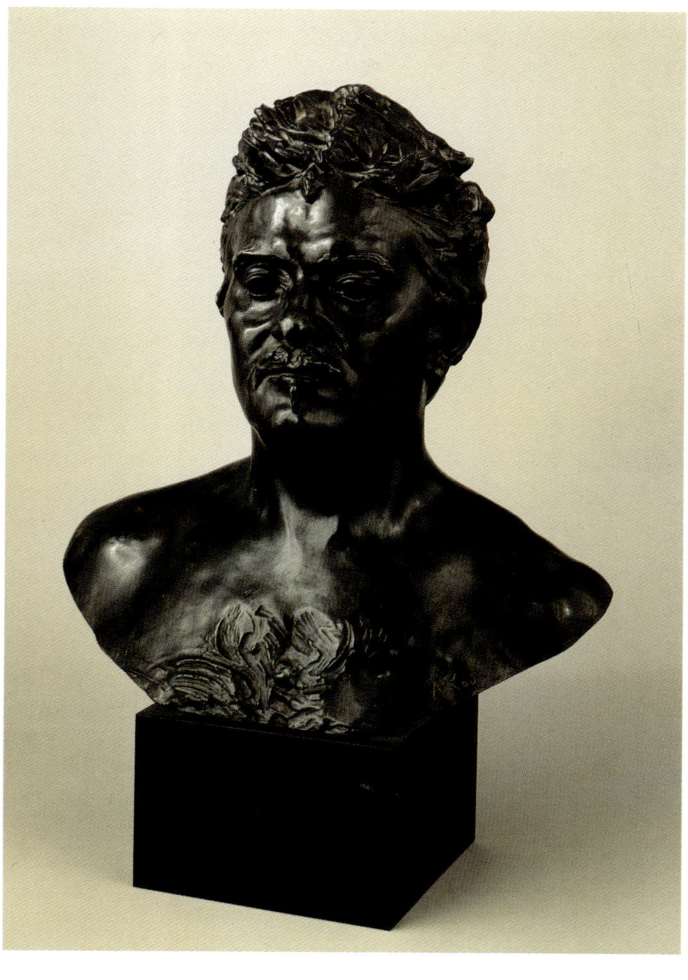

Head of Balzac after a Portrait by Devéria,
1891
Bronze, cast by Georges Rudier.
43.3 x 40.3 x 23.2
Cast for the Museum's collections in 1971
Inv. S.1082

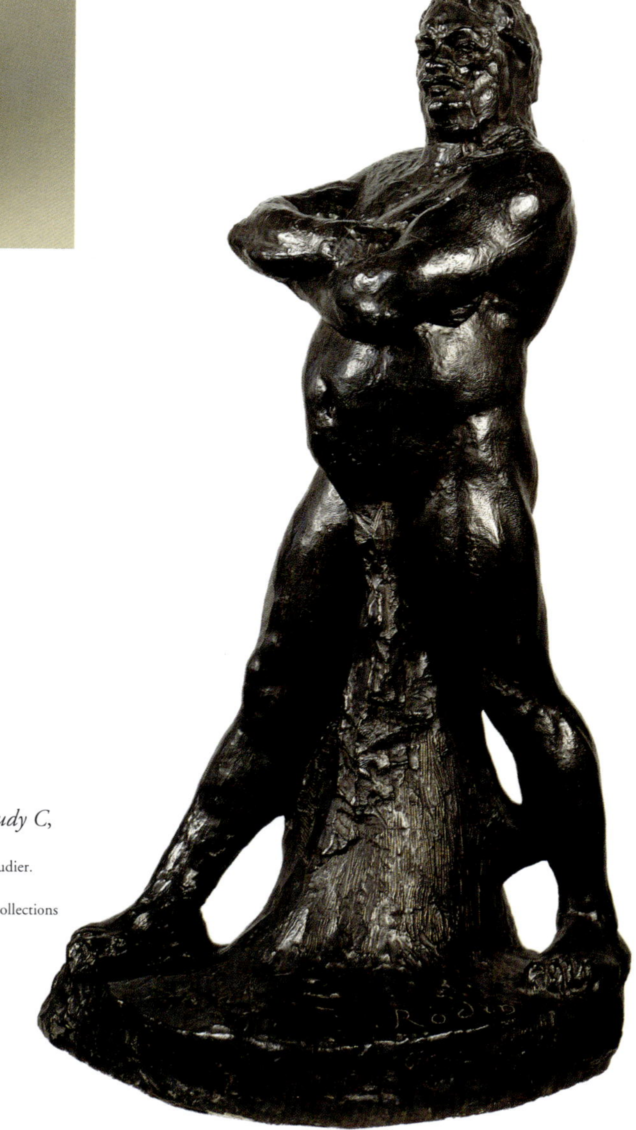

Balzac, Nude Study C,
1892-1893
Bronze, cast by Alexis Rudier.
127.3 x 50.5 x 61
Cast for the Museum's collections between 1927 and 1929
Inv. S.1074

A first commission for a *Monument to Victor Hugo* intended for the Panthéon which had been dedicated to honouring great men since 1885 was given to Rodin on 16 September 1889. The first maquette to be submitted, showing the poet sitting down already accompanied by Muses, was rejected in July 1890 as it was considered to be incoherent. But a year later the project was taken up again for the Luxembourg Gardens (it was in fact installed at the Palais Royal). Rodin then made three further maquettes before producing the final version which was exhibited in plaster at the Salon of the Société Nationale des Beaux-Arts in 1897. The monument which was still unfinished showed Victor Hugo naked, seated, with his arm outstretched as if to calm the waves, accompanied by *Meditation* without any arms, called *Inner Voice*, and the *Tragic Muse*; these independently existing figures were not included in the final Palais Royal version in marble, which has been at the Musée Rodin since 1933, but they were used separately.

However, Rodin was still giving thought to the monument intended for the Panthéon. This time he was going to make his composition harmonize with that of the monument to Mirabeau made by Injalbert which was its counterpart: a central standing figure with a mound behind it and a winged muse, the symbol of inspiration coming from above, covering it with a veil or the mound draped as with a dais, while three graceful female figures, allegories or sirens (taken from *The Gates of Hell*) enlivened the base. Separated from the composition of which it formed part the *Nude, Standing Figure of Victor Hugo* was enlarged c.1902. However, the monument was never made.

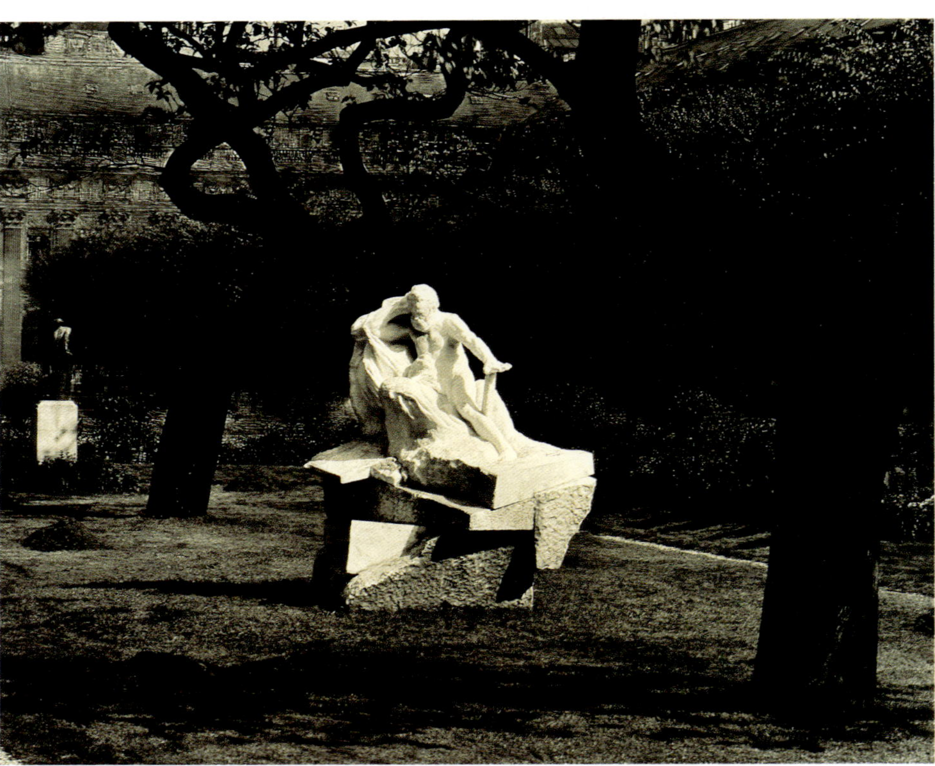

Ad. Braun & cie
Monument to Victor Hugo at the Palais-Royal,
after 1909
Carbon print. 21.5 x 27.5
Rodin donation, 1916
Inv. Ph.1194

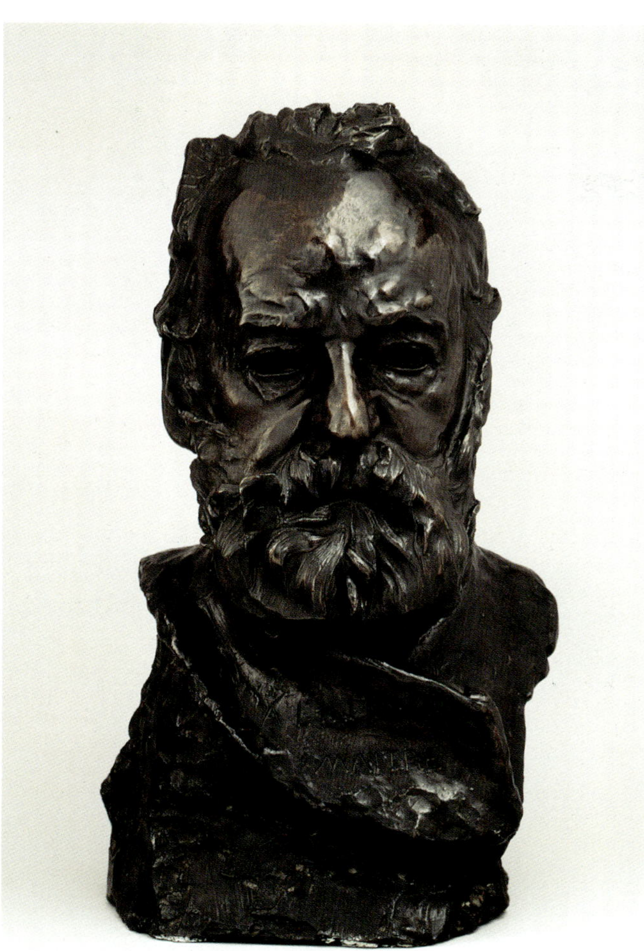

Victor Hugo,
1883
Bronze. 48.5 x 29 x 30.5
Given to Victor Hugo by Rodin
Acquired from the poet's great-granddaughter by the Museum in 1928
Inv. S.36

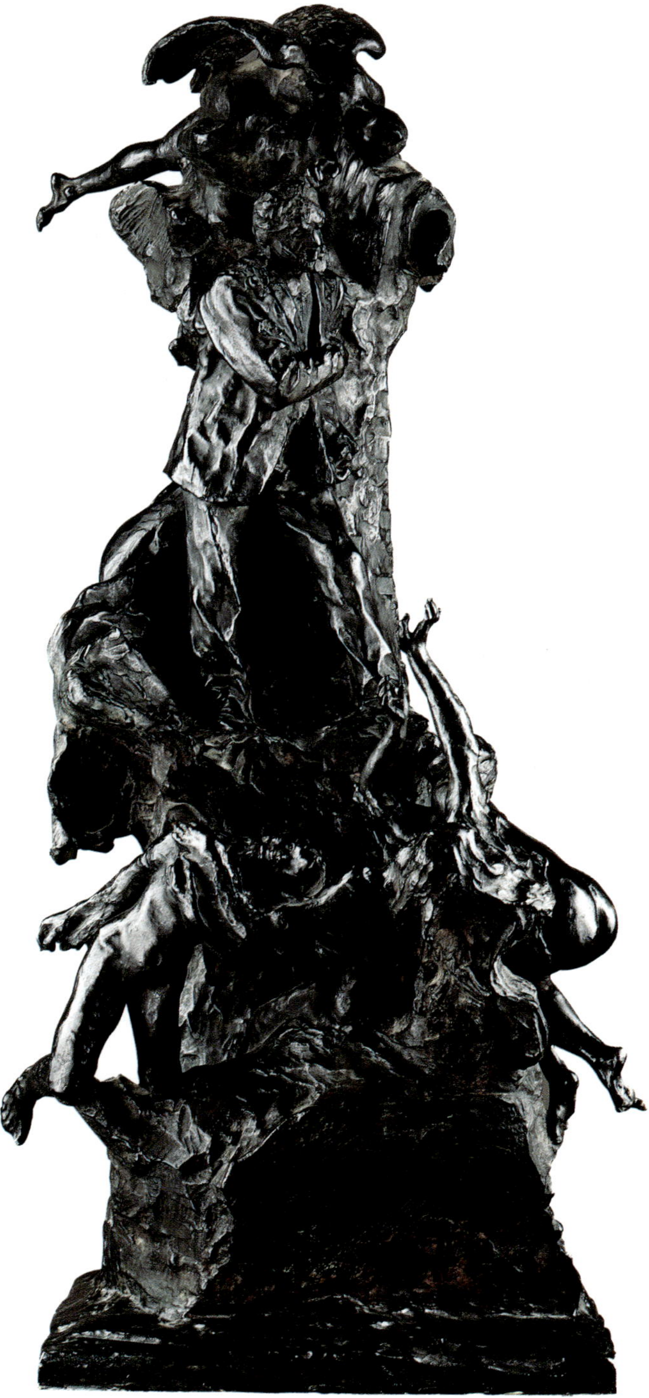

As Victor Hugo refused to pose Rodin had to adapt his method of working, making thumbnail sketches, memorizing the poet's features and then making a permanent record of them in clay. In *The Apotheosis of Victor Hugo*, the second proposal for the Panthéon, the poet appears standing, no longer seated, wearing the clothes of the period which were quickly abandoned in favour of a nude figure, an approach that was considered daring in dealing with a contemporary man of letters. The oblique plinth made up of irregular blocks on which the monument was installed in the garden of the Palais Royal in 1909 was evocative in an almost abstract way of the waves and rocks of Guernsey.

The Apotheosis of Victor Hugo,
1891-1893
Bronze, cast by Alexis Rudier.
116 x 52 x 63
Cast for the Museum's collections in 1927
Inv. S.1066

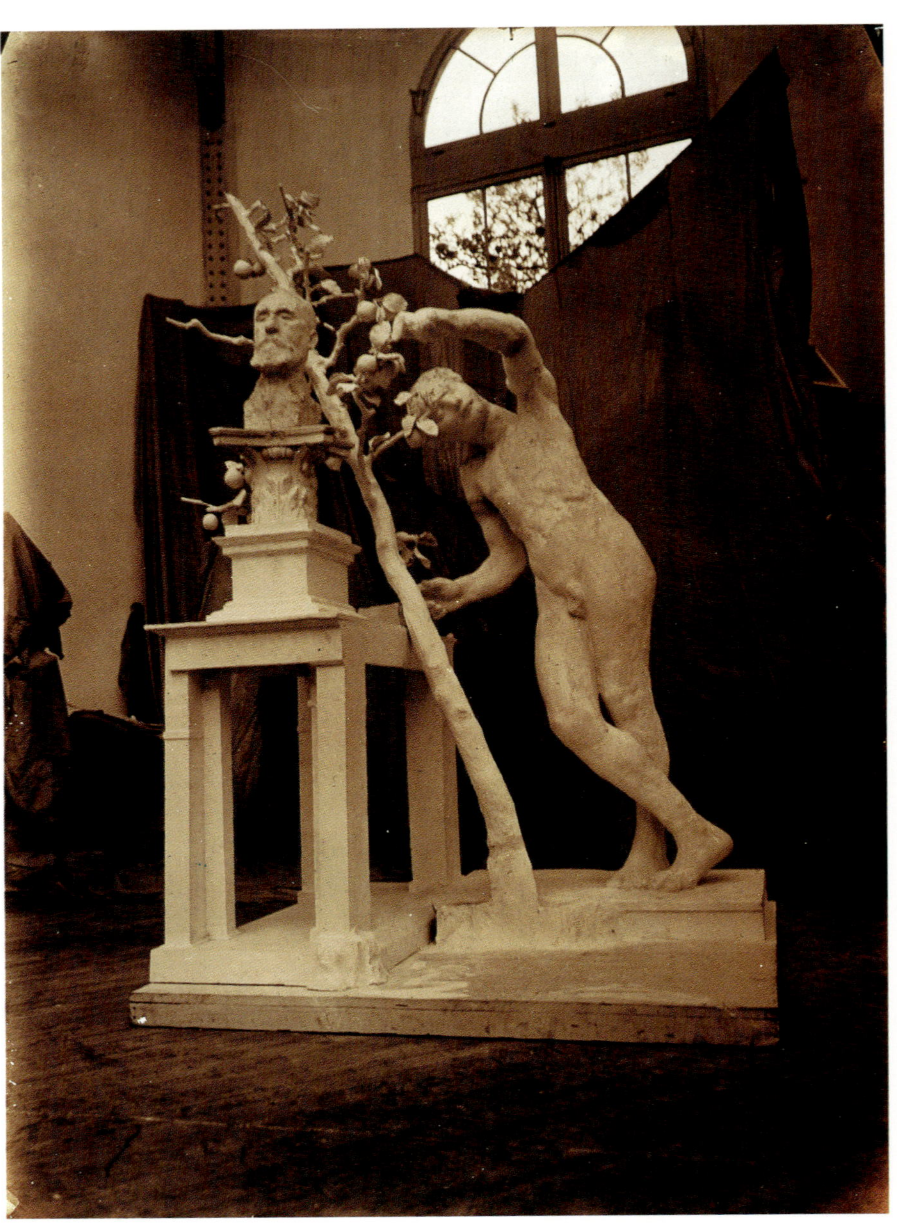

Attributed to Jean-François Limet
(1855-1941)
Monument to Puvis de Chavannes
P.O.P. print. 23.7 x 17.5
Rodin donation, 1916
Inv. Ph.384

Puvis de Chavannes (1824-1898)

"And they say that my Puvis de Chavannes is not beautiful!" Rodin was to say in his dying breath. The two men had been friends for a long time and had exhibited together on several occasions. In 1899 a year after the painter's death Rodin was asked to make a commemorative monument. He "constructed" his project by introducing the bust made in 1891 during the painter's lifetime into the centre of his composition. He then set about creating a proper allegorical setting for him: a table, a pedestal and a Corinthian capital were superimposed to carry the painter's image, with the *Spirit of Eternal Repose* picking fruit from a well stocked apple tree leaning towards the painter. The naturalism of such a presentation was a radical break with the heroic, allegorical monuments of the period. Exhibited on its own without arms at the Pavillon de l'Alma in 1900, the *Spirit* was to be produced in a marble version in 1910. The monument remained incomplete and Desbois undertook the job of carrying it out in 1924.

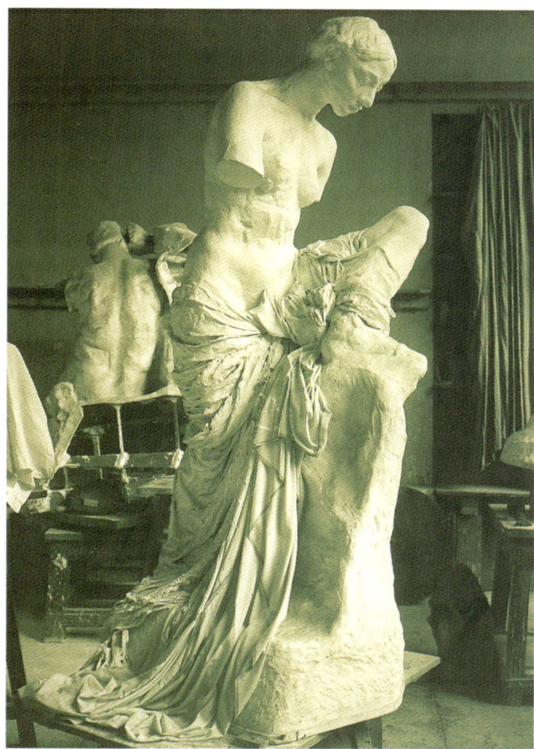

Jacques-Ernest Bulloz
(1858-1942)
Three-quarter View of Whistler's Muse, in the Dépôt des Marbres Studio,
1908
Carbon print. 36.5 x 26.5
Rodin donation, 1916
Inv. Ph.385

Puvis de Chavannes,
1911-1917
Marble executed by Aristide Rousaud.
60.7 x 60.5 x 41.8
State commission for the Panthéon in 1911
Entered the collections in 1934
Inv. S.1387

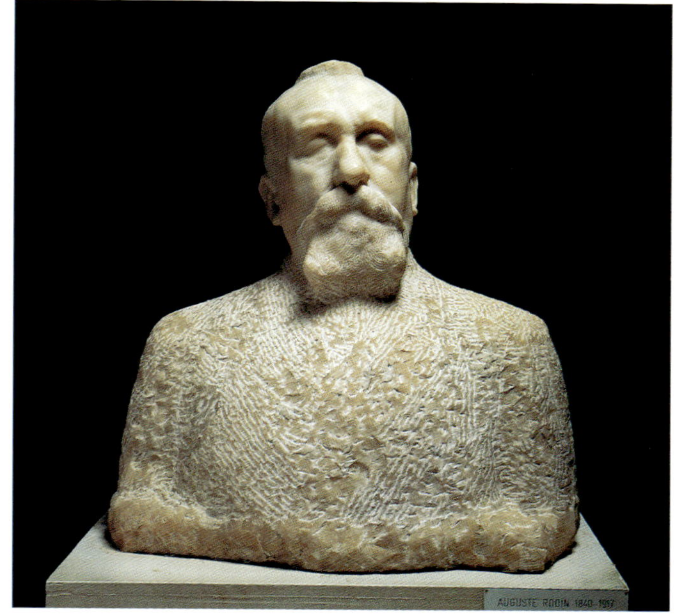

Whistler (1834-1903)
Rodin succeeded Whistler as head of the International Society of Painters, Sculptors and Gravers in London on the painter's death in 1903. Two years later a committee which had been established approached him concerning making a monument.

Rodin produced a large allegorical figure, an allegory that was very much alive: "it's flesh and blood, not a cold effigy" (Rodin). There was no direct evocation of Whistler, except later in the form of a medallion, and Rodin had moreover never produced a portrait of him. Gwen John, a young English painter, posed for the *Muse* which was shown nude and without arms at the 1908 Salon. It was intended that the monument should be completed for 1913, but it was interrupted by the war. The committee became impatient, but at the time of Rodin's death it had still not been completed. It was turned down in 1919 on the grounds that it was "not representative."

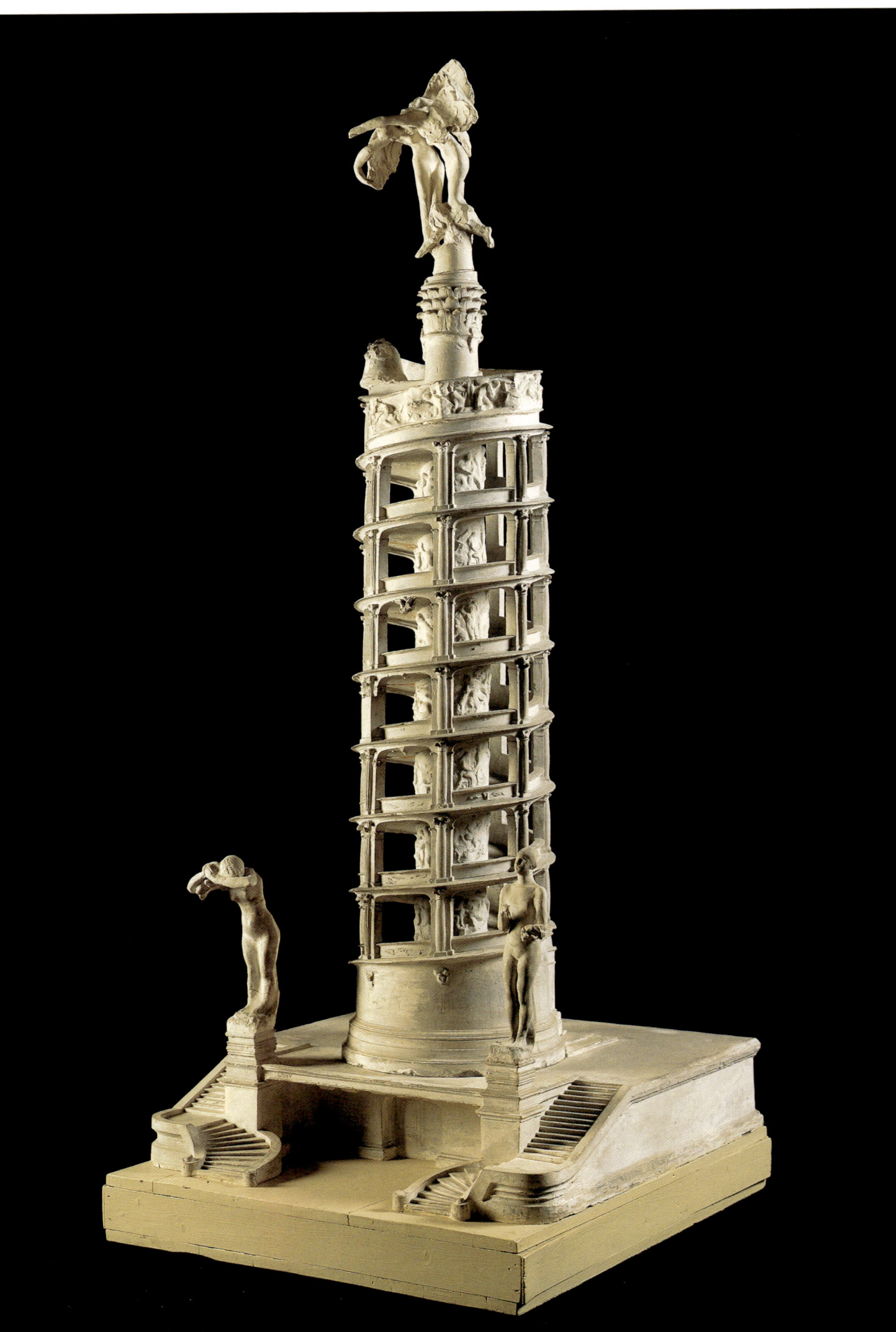

La Tour du Travail

Antoinette Le Normand-Romain

The maquette of *La Tour du Travail* has only recently been put on display again at the Musée Rodin, an ambitious project intended to celebrate "creative energy ... on equal terms with the type of energy that leaves only smoking wreckage and the painful memory of bloodstained triumphs in its wake." The initiative came from Armand Dayot, a Beaux-Arts inspector and art critic; in March 1898 he submitted the idea of a monument to labour to Jules Desbois, envisaging that it would be made in time for the Exposition Universelle in 1900. Desbois reacted enthusiastically, suggesting immediately that other sculptors should be involved in the project: Dalou (1838-1902) who had been thinking about this subject since 1889 (sketches and maquettes at the Petit Palais museum in Paris) refused to take part, but Rodin, Falguière, Baffier, A. Charpentier, Injalbert, Mercié and the Belgian sculptor Constantin Meunier (1831-1905) who also created a monument to labour of his own (unveiled in Brussels in 1931) agreed in principle, and Rodin was put in overall charge of the scheme. He could not help but be attracted by the idea of having a collective work on the stocks, similar to the cathedrals he so much admired.

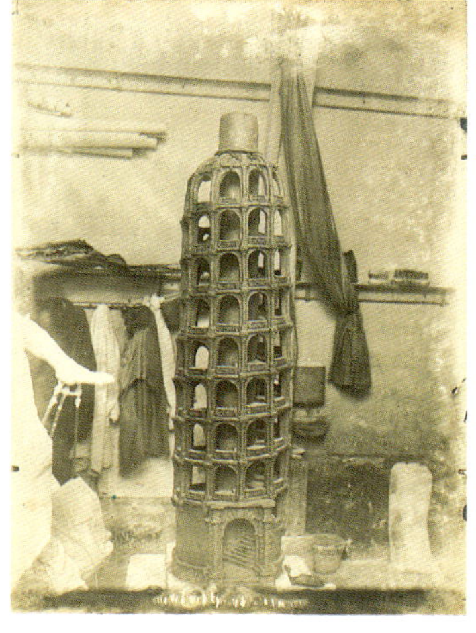

Eugène Druet
(1868-1916)
La Tour du Travail in the studio,
*c.*1898?
Gelatin silver print. 40 x 29.5
Rodin donation, 1916
Inv. Ph.403

He put forward a maquette by the end of the year: a tower reminiscent of both the Leaning Tower of Pisa and the staircase at the château of Blois, with a spiral staircase inside allowing viewers to study the reliefs covering the sides of a central column. Dominated by the *Benedictions* group, the tower rose from a plinth containing a sort of crypt. "Access underneath the tower is through a door guarded by the figures of Day and Night, symbolising the everlasting nature of labour; a huge chamber is reserved for work involving the extraction of primary materials from the bowels of the earth. In wide, almost brutally fashioned bas-reliefs in the half-light obtaining there the life of miners and divers and dark, arduous toil beneath the earth and the sea are depicted. Then we start to climb ... The farther up we go, the less rough the types of work become, the mind playing a larger role...

"The summit is where pure thought resides, the noblest profession, represented by the artist, the poet and the philosopher. Then crowning the monument against the sky, at the uppermost point of the column which now rises clear of the tower and reaches toward the blue of the heavens, are two spirits dispensing Love and Joy over Labour, for despite all the pain and hatred Labour is in fact made up of love and joy" (Coquiot, 1913).

The maquette was exhibited in 1900, but no financial backing had been found. Nor did the international committee set up in 1908 to relaunch the project get it off the ground. "Moreover, how are the tendencies, aspirations and tastes of so many conflicting personalities which if they are not opposing are at least different to be reconciled?... Cathedrals are no longer being built today." Despite the favourable reception it received *La Tour du Travail* was therefore abandoned.

La Tour du Travail,
1898-1899
Plaster. 151 x 64.5 x 67.5
Rodin donation, 1916
Inv. S.169

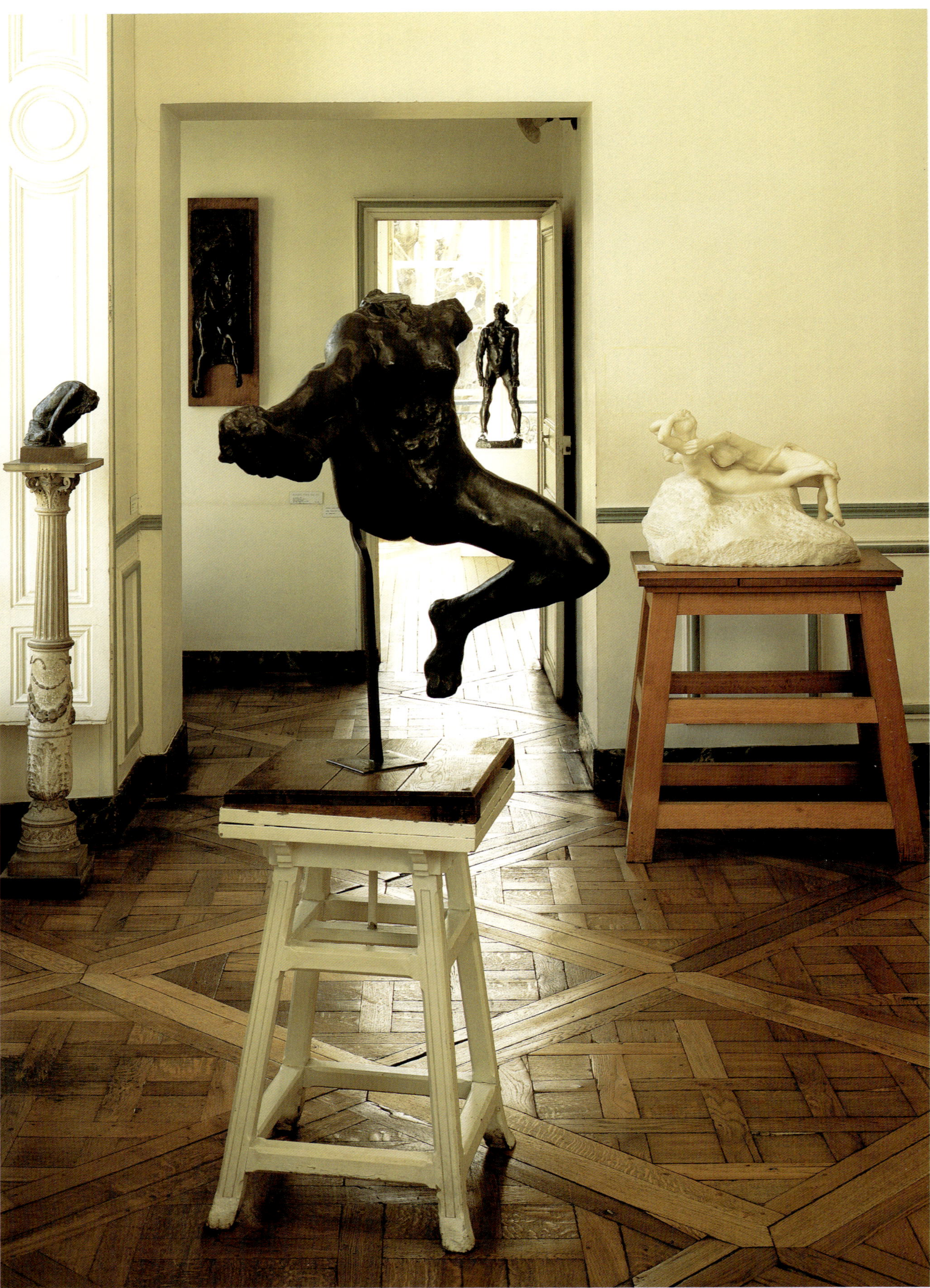

Female figures

Antoinette Le Normand-Romain

Rodin adored women because he adored nature, and made the female figure his main study. He observed women without indulgence, leaving his models free to come and go in the studio as they pleased, noting the attitudes that interested him first on paper, but also in clay. As he himself put it, "Beauty is everywhere. It is not beauty that our eyes lack, it is our eyes that are deficient in perceiving it. Beauty is character and expression. And there is nothing in Nature that has more character than the human body. Through its force and grace it evokes the widest variety of images. At times it is like a flower: the way the torso bends is like the stem ... At times it is like a supple creeper ... At other times still it is an urn... The human body is first and foremost the mirror of the soul and its greatest beauty comes from that ..." (Gsell, 1911).

For him the only ugliness came from artificiality or lying. A body that was misshapen by age, on the other hand, retained all its interest, and when he found Marie Caira as an old woman he asked her to pose for him too. She appears first at the bottom of one of the jambs on *The Gates of Hell*, then he executed the statuette simply called *Old Woman* after her - it was later named *Celle qui Fut la Belle Heaulmière* by his writer friends, while it has the name *Sources Taries* in a group where it is used twice over. As a "hunter of truth and watcher of life" Rodin was attentive in the extreme to the bodies of his models, and was surprised at having to start all over again each day on the pelvis of his *Eve*, until he discovered that the young model was pregnant. He then set aside the large model which he did not exhibit until much later to make a *Small Eve* or *Young Eve* with a smoother, more sensuous body. But one feels that for him the greatest pleasure was to show the female body in the splendour of its own special qualities, as he did in the *Eternal Idol*, and these are in fact all the more evident when the work is fragmentary: the arch of the *Torso of Adèle* highlights the voluptuousness of its forms, an element that recurs albeit more discreetly in *Eternal Spring*, though this time completed by a head and legs. In this field Rodin touched the farthest extreme with his large *Iris* which was bold in a manner unheard of at the time, and even today shocks some visitors to the Museum. As he grew older he became more responsive to a youthful, sometimes slightly awkward grace (*Devant la Mer*), reflecting the sculptor's love of life which remained just as strong to his final day.

Iris,
*c.*1890-1891
Bronze. 82.7 x 69 x 63
Rodin donation, 1916
Inv. S.1068

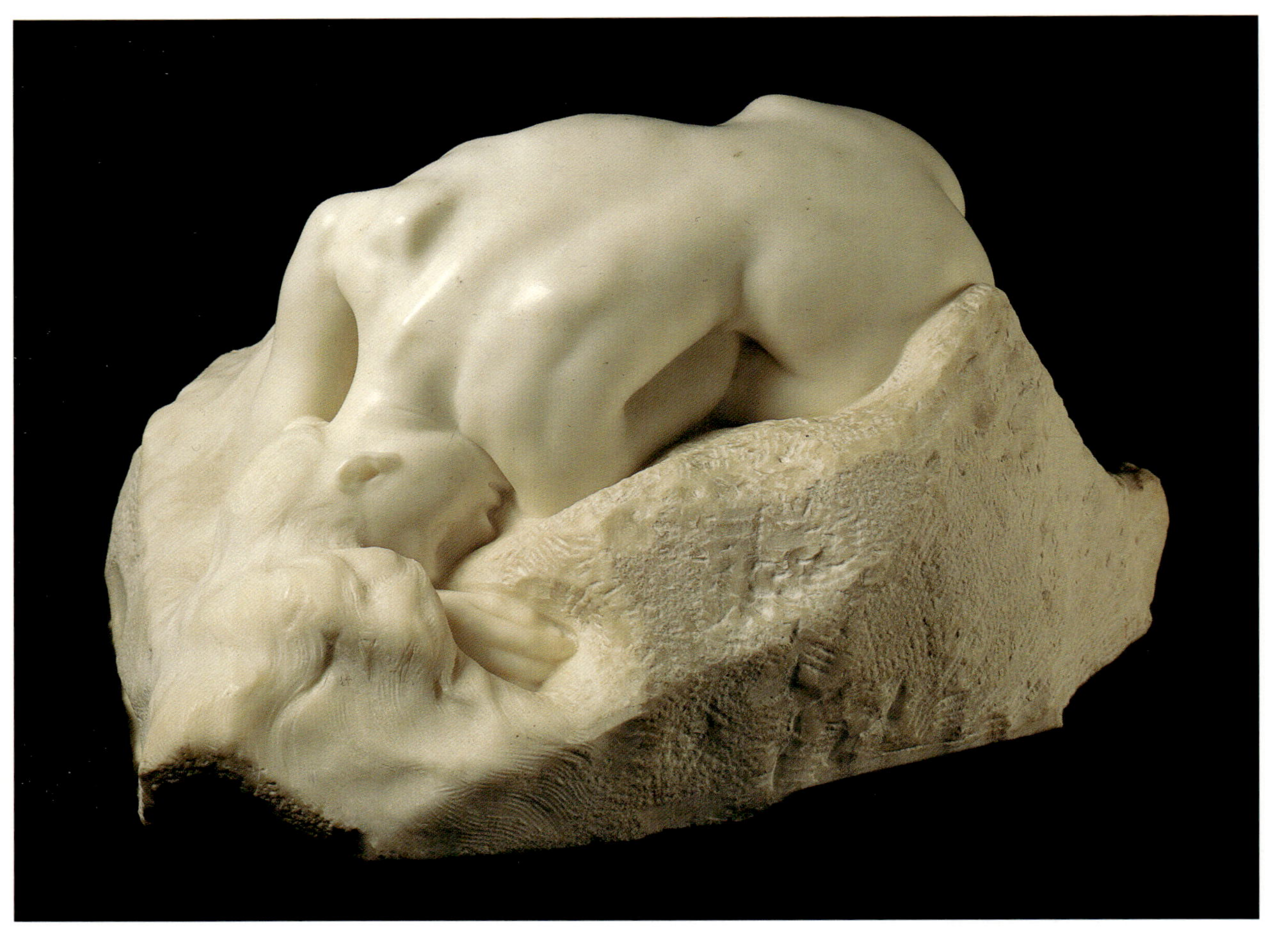

Danaïd,
*c.*1889
Marble executed by Jean Escoula.
36 x 71 x 53
Exhibited at 1890 Salon de la Société Nationale des Beaux-Arts. Acquired by the State in 1890, delivered in 1892
Musée du Luxembourg
Deposited by the Musée du Luxembourg, 1919
Inv. S.1155

"Simply walking round this marble creates a marvellous impression," wrote Rilke; "the long, very long way round the curve of that back, generously unfolding towards the face lost in the stone like a great sob, towards the hand which like a last flower once more speaks gently of the life at the heart of the eternal ice of the block." *The Danaïd*, the image of despair and a exceptionally finely executed work, aroused general admiration and replicas of it were made even before it was handed over to the State which had bought it at the 1890 Salon for the Luxembourg museum.

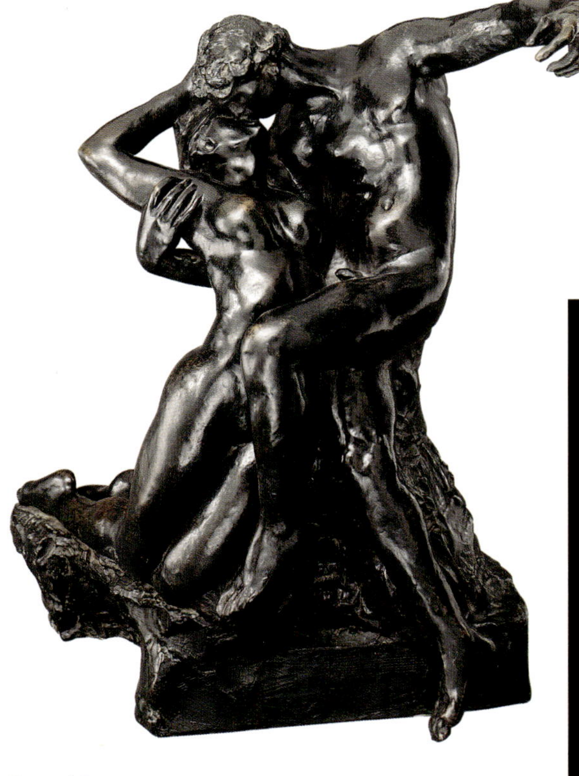

Eternal Spring,
1884
Bronze, cast by Alexis Rudier.
64.5 x 58 x 44.5
Rodin donation, 1916
Inv. S.989

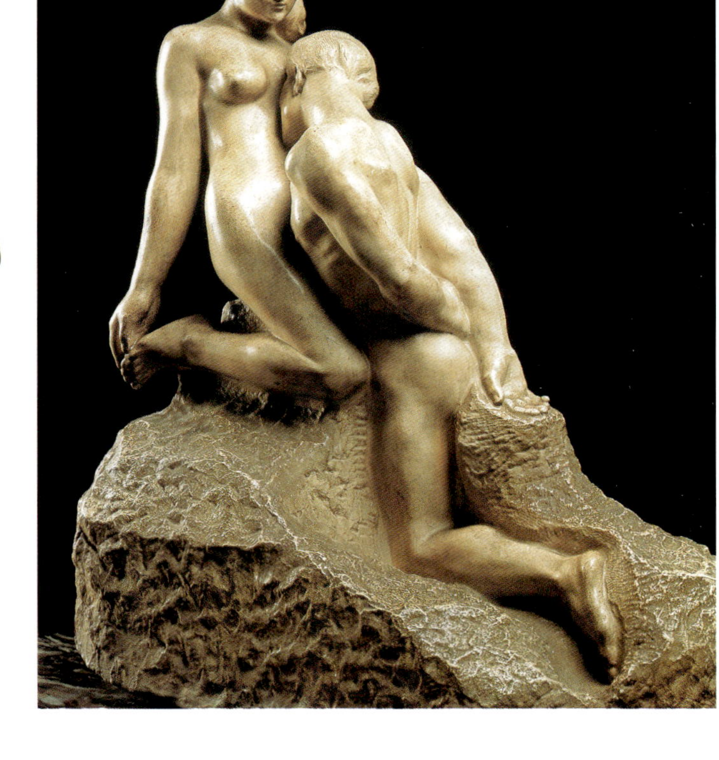

The Eternal Idol,
1889
Plaster. 73.2 x 59.2 x 41.1
Rodin donation, 1916
Inv. S.1044

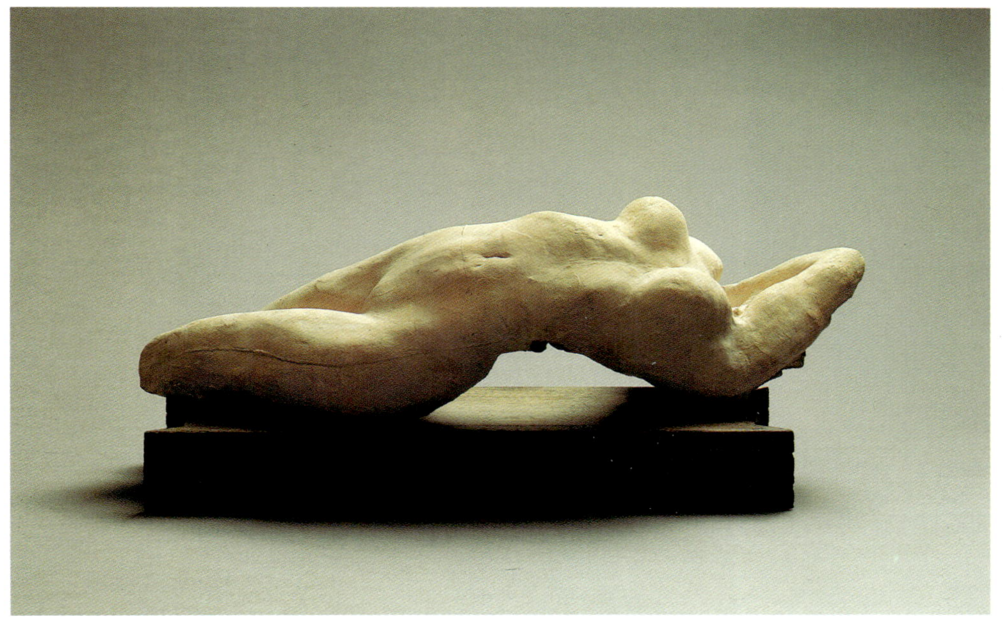

Torso of Adèle,
c.1882-1885
Terra cotta. 11 x 37.5 x 16.4
Rodin donation, 1916
Inv. S.1177

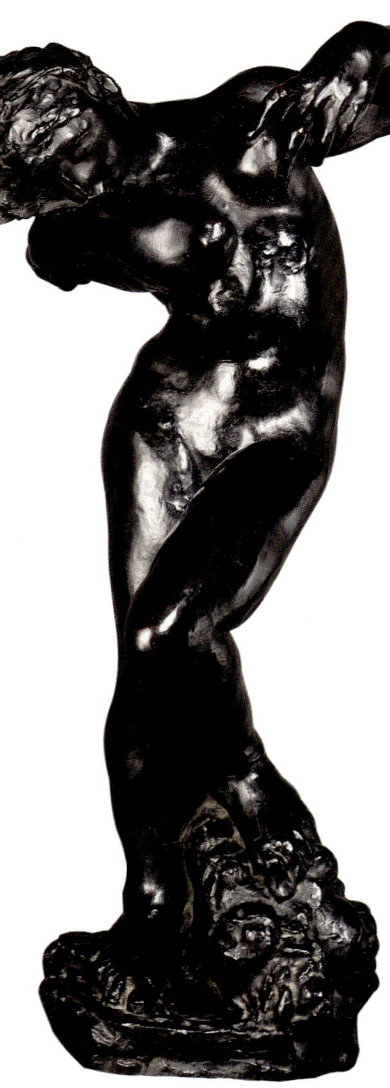

Meditation,
*c.*1885-1887
Bronze, cast by Alexis Rudier.
74.5 x 38 x 35
Gift of Léon Bérard, 1928
Inv. S.40

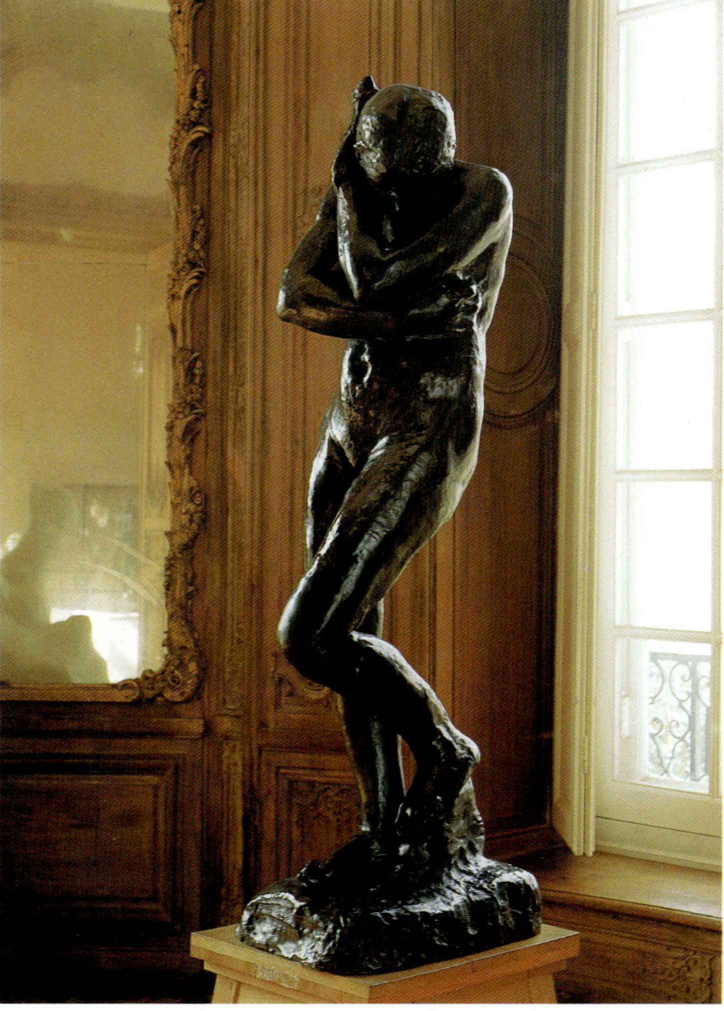

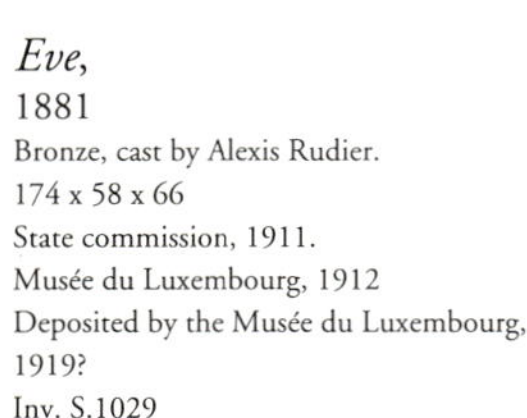

Eve,
1881
Bronze, cast by Alexis Rudier.
174 x 58 x 66
State commission, 1911.
Musée du Luxembourg, 1912
Deposited by the Musée du Luxembourg, 1919?
Inv. S.1029

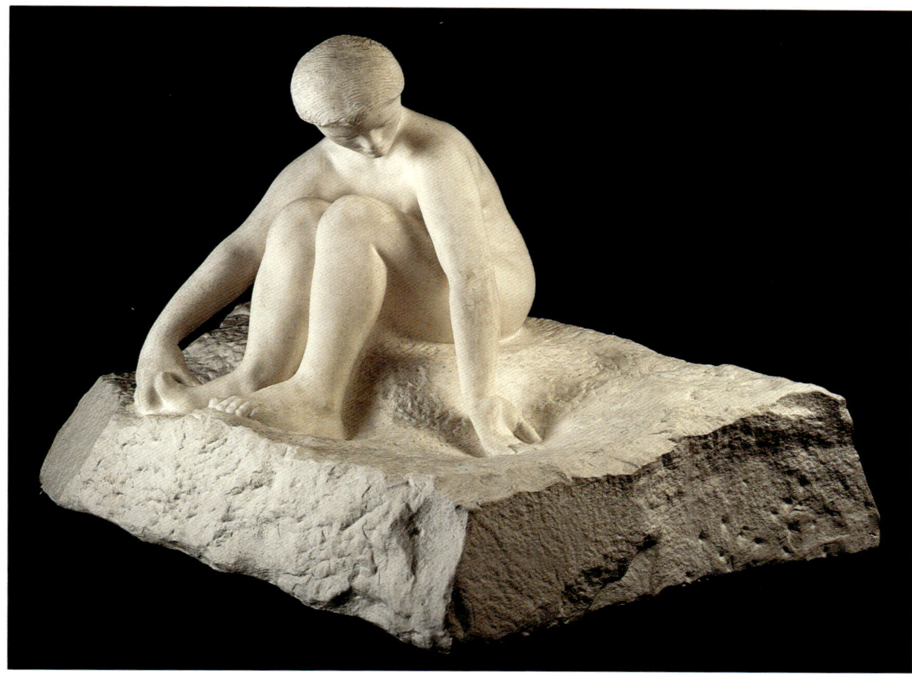

Devant la Mer,
*c.*1906
Plaster. 57.8 x 85.8 x 59.8
Rodin donation, 1916
Inv. S.1094

Rodin discovered Marie Caira through Jules Desbois who made the figure entitled *La Misère* (exhibited in 1893) after her. Camille Claudel used the same model for her *Clotho* (1893): showing these two works beside *Celle qui Fut la Belle Heaulmière* at the Musée Rodin emphasizes the interplay of influences between one artist and the other, and shows the bond that existed between them. Rodin himself used the motif of this old woman several times around the period 1887-1890.

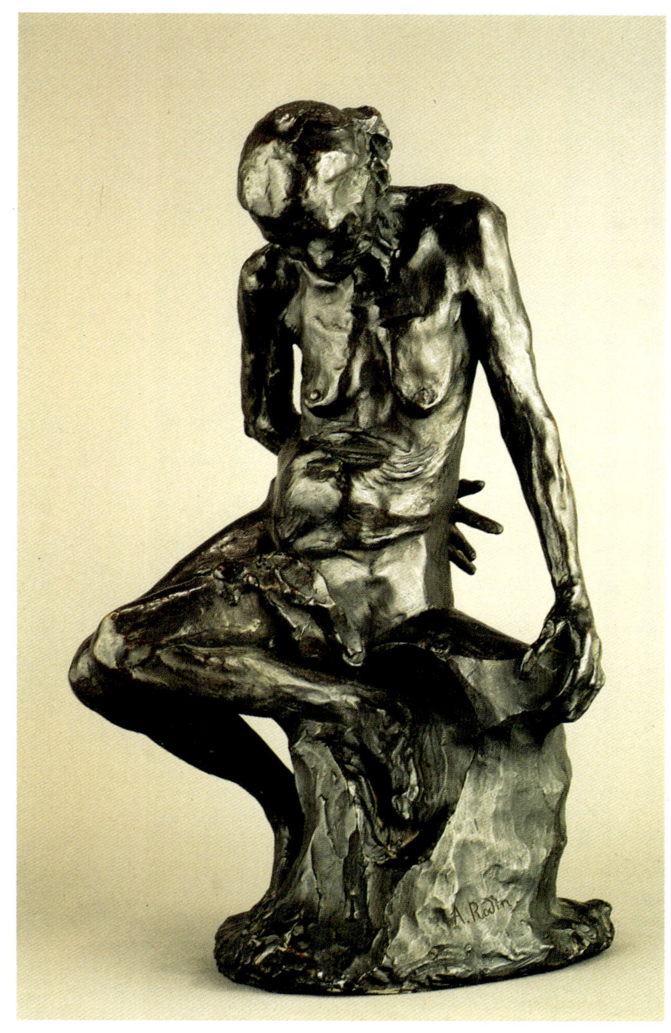

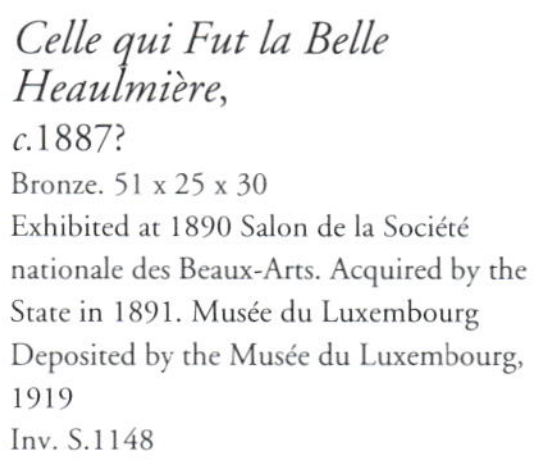

Celle qui Fut la Belle Heaulmière,
*c.*1887?
Bronze. 51 x 25 x 30
Exhibited at 1890 Salon de la Société nationale des Beaux-Arts. Acquired by the State in 1891. Musée du Luxembourg
Deposited by the Musée du Luxembourg, 1919
Inv. S.1148

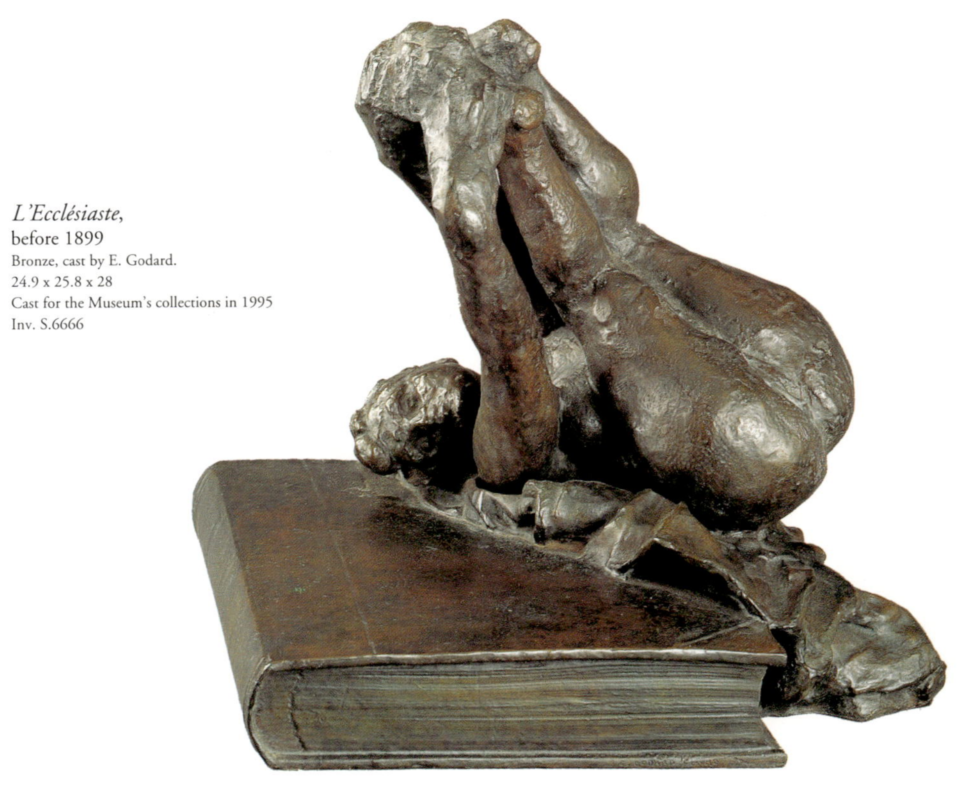

L'Ecclésiaste,
before 1899
Bronze, cast by E. Godard.
24.9 x 25.8 x 28
Cast for the Museum's collections in 1995
Inv. S.6666

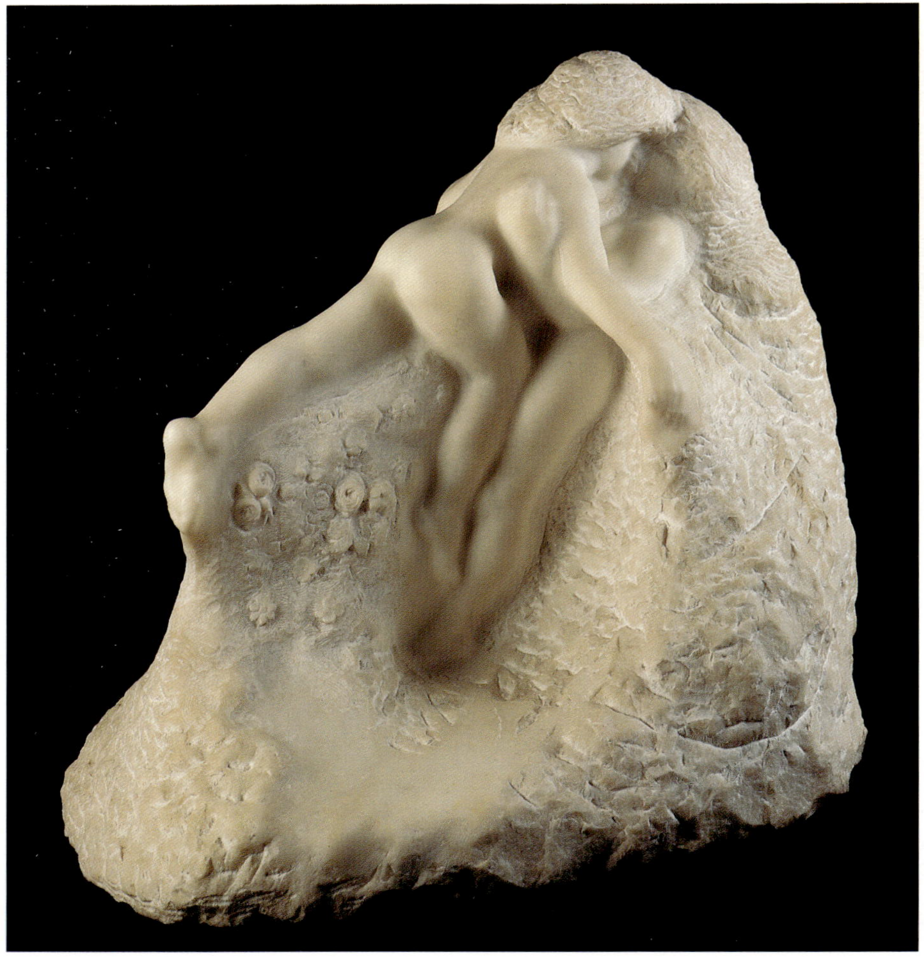

Nymphs at play,
after 1900?
Marble. 53.1 x 59 x 44.6
Rodin donation, 1916
Inv. S.1117

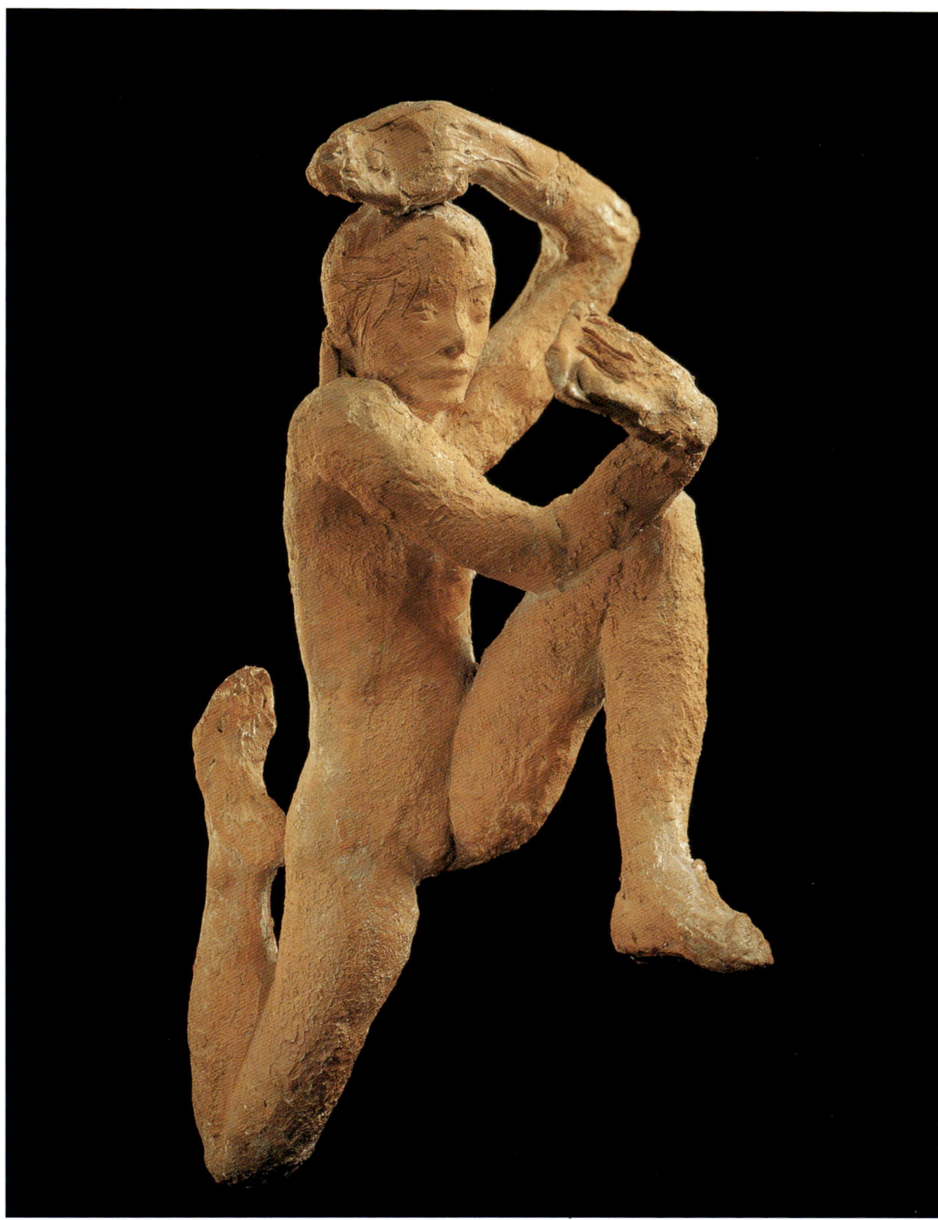

Dance Movement I,
*c.*1910?
Terra cotta. 26 x 17 x 9.8
Acquired in 1995
Inv. S.6662

Rodin was interested in the most modern forms of dance, as practised by Loïe Fuller, Isadora Duncan, Nijinsky or the French cancan dancers. His *Dance Movements* inspired by these artists are a group of clay and plaster sketches in which the laws of anatomy are flouted in an attempt to express movement, pushed to the extreme limit. These small, very free works - it is extremely uncertain when they were executed (*c.*1910?) - were never exhibited in Rodin's lifetime.

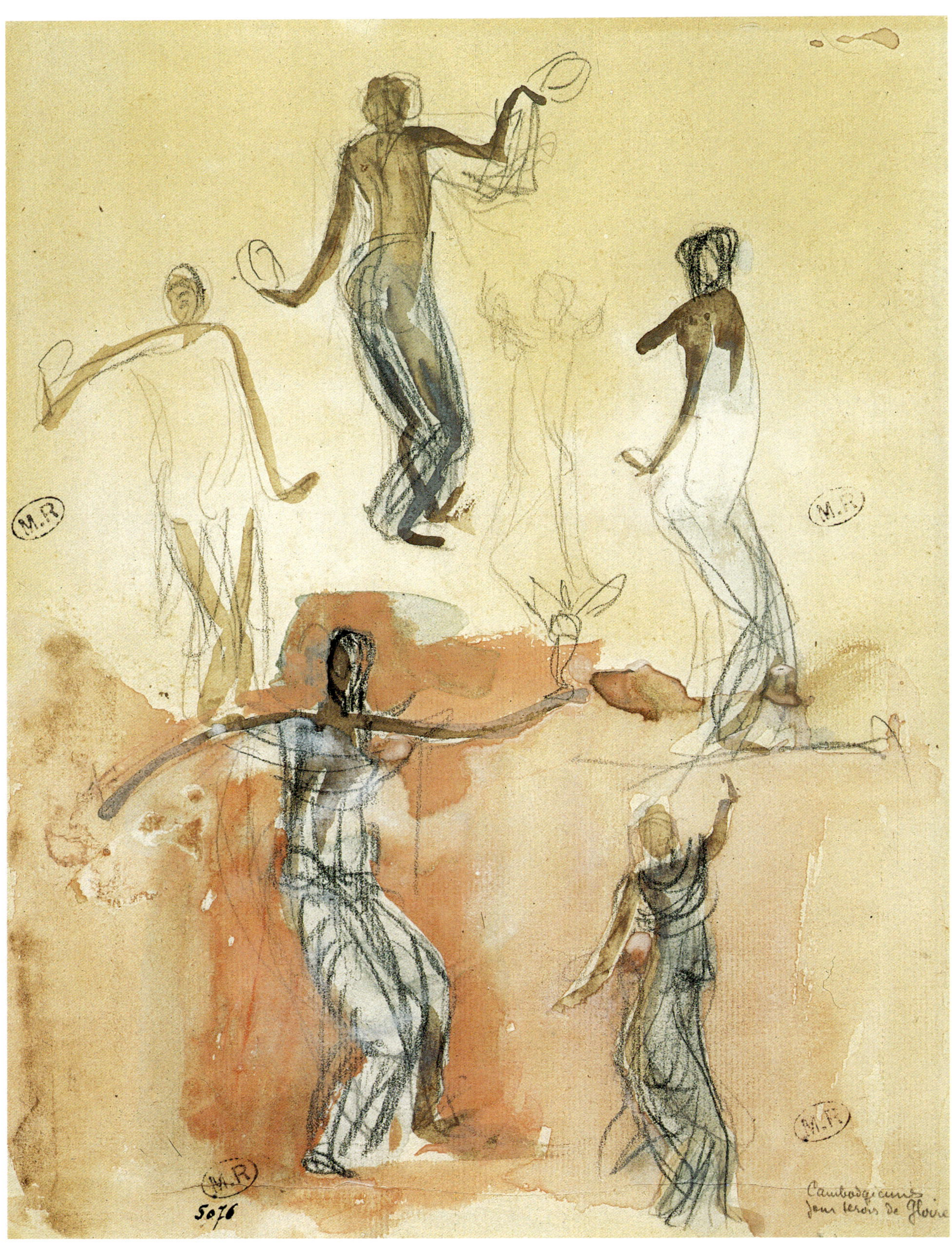
M.R
M.R
M.R
M.R
5076
Cambodgiennes

Drawings and women

Claudie Judrin

Through modesty or lack of resources Rodin did not start drawing after a model until *c.*1890. Before that his bodies do not seem to have an existence as such and we do not know if they belong to a man or a woman. Dante's damned souls are silhouettes rather than bodies. They are the product of Rodin's imagination and he then felt the need to observe.

There was no going back. The colours which had been dark became light; the format which had been modest became large; the forms which had been indeterminate became assertive; the inspiration which had been dramatic became serene. The model does not pose, rather she moves about quite freely. Rodin did not demand a certain attitude, he sketched it as it occurred with a very sure hand, without looking at his sheet of paper. He loved movement and garments which undressed the woman wearing them. The face counted for little except in the case of portraits as exceptional as that of the woman journalist Séverine - drawn in charcoal, an unusual technique for Rodin.

The nudes are anonymous but he gave them symbolic names for at that period everything was observation and everything was a symbol, using themes that were preferably cosmic, mythological, religious or literary like Salammbô or St Anthony, as a tribute to Flaubert.

Following in the train of success came the scandal of body language expressed by dance which preoccupied Rodin in his old age. "The dancing body can express more with its movements than the word. And dance which in our world has always been an erotic attribute is nowadays at last tending to become worthy of the other arts which it sums up."

Rodin approached dancing through drawing and was dazzled by it through dancing from the Far East. During the Colonial Exhibition held in Marseilles in 1906 he was fascinated by King Sisowath of Cambodia's ballet company. "I watched them in a state of ecstasy. What a void they left behind! When they left I was in darkness and cold. I followed them to Marseilles, and would have followed them even to Cairo." He felt that their movements were ancient, definitive and sacred whereas the movements in classical ballet at the nineteenth-century Opera in Paris struck him as being set and conventional.

Six Studies of Cambodian Dancers,
July 1906
Graphite, water colour and gouache on paper. 27.1 x 21.1
Rodin donation, 1916
Inv. D.5076

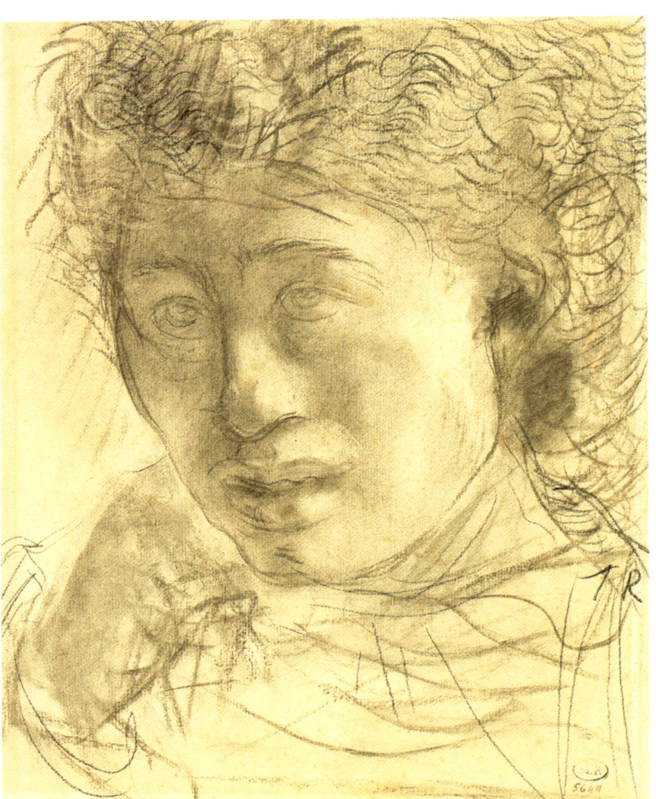

Portrait of Séverine,
*c.*1893
Charcoal on paper. 32 x 24.7
Acquired in 1924
Rodin donation, 1916
Inv. D.5644

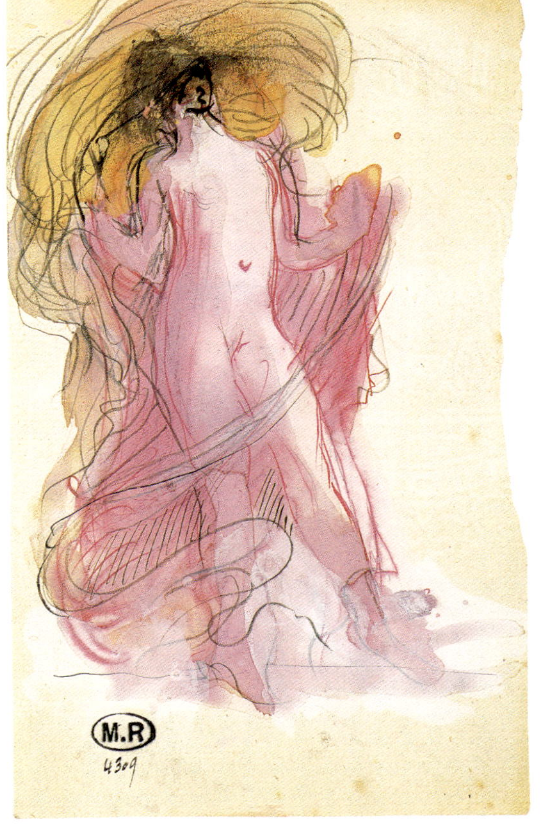

"My natural media are clay and the pencil."

"I have drawn all my life, I started my whole life by drawing; I have never stopped drawing."

Female Nude in the Movement of her Veils,
*c.*1890?
Graphite, pen, inks, water colour and gouache on paper. 17.5 x 11
Rodin donation, 1916
Inv. D.4309

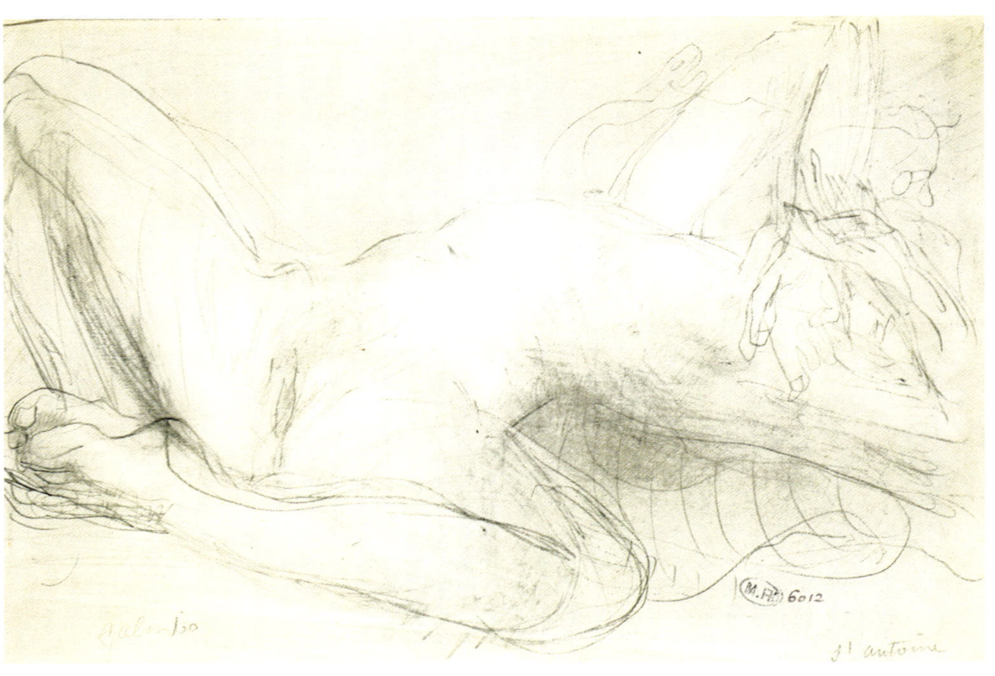

Salammbô
Graphite on paper. 20.4 x 31
Rodin donation, 1916
Inv. D.6012

The Tempest or *The Wave*
Graphite and water colour on paper
32.6 x 23.6
Rodin donation, 1916
Inv. D.4186

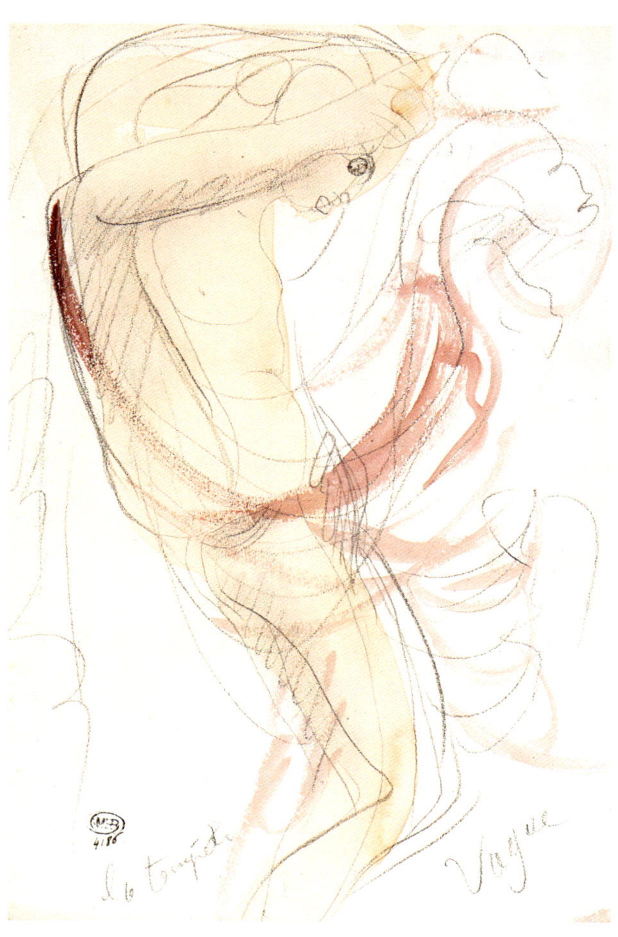

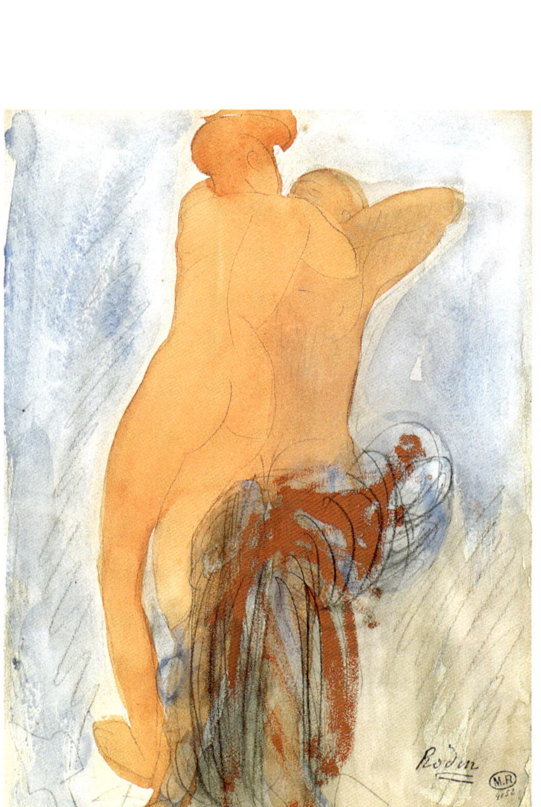

Sapphic Couple Embracing
Graphite, water colour and gouache on paper. 32.6 x 25.1
Rodin donation, 1916
Inv. D.4052

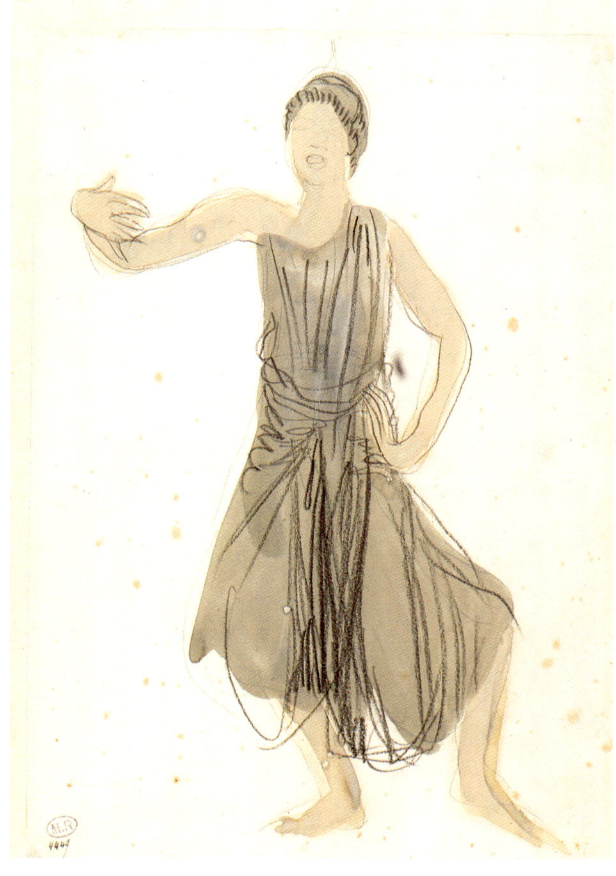

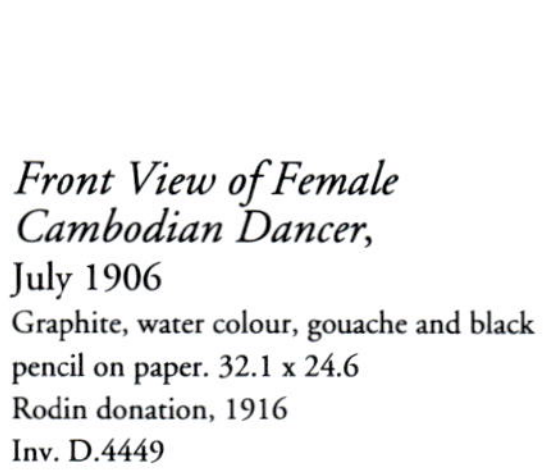

Front View of Female Cambodian Dancer,
July 1906
Graphite, water colour, gouache and black pencil on paper. 32.1 x 24.6
Rodin donation, 1916
Inv. D.4449

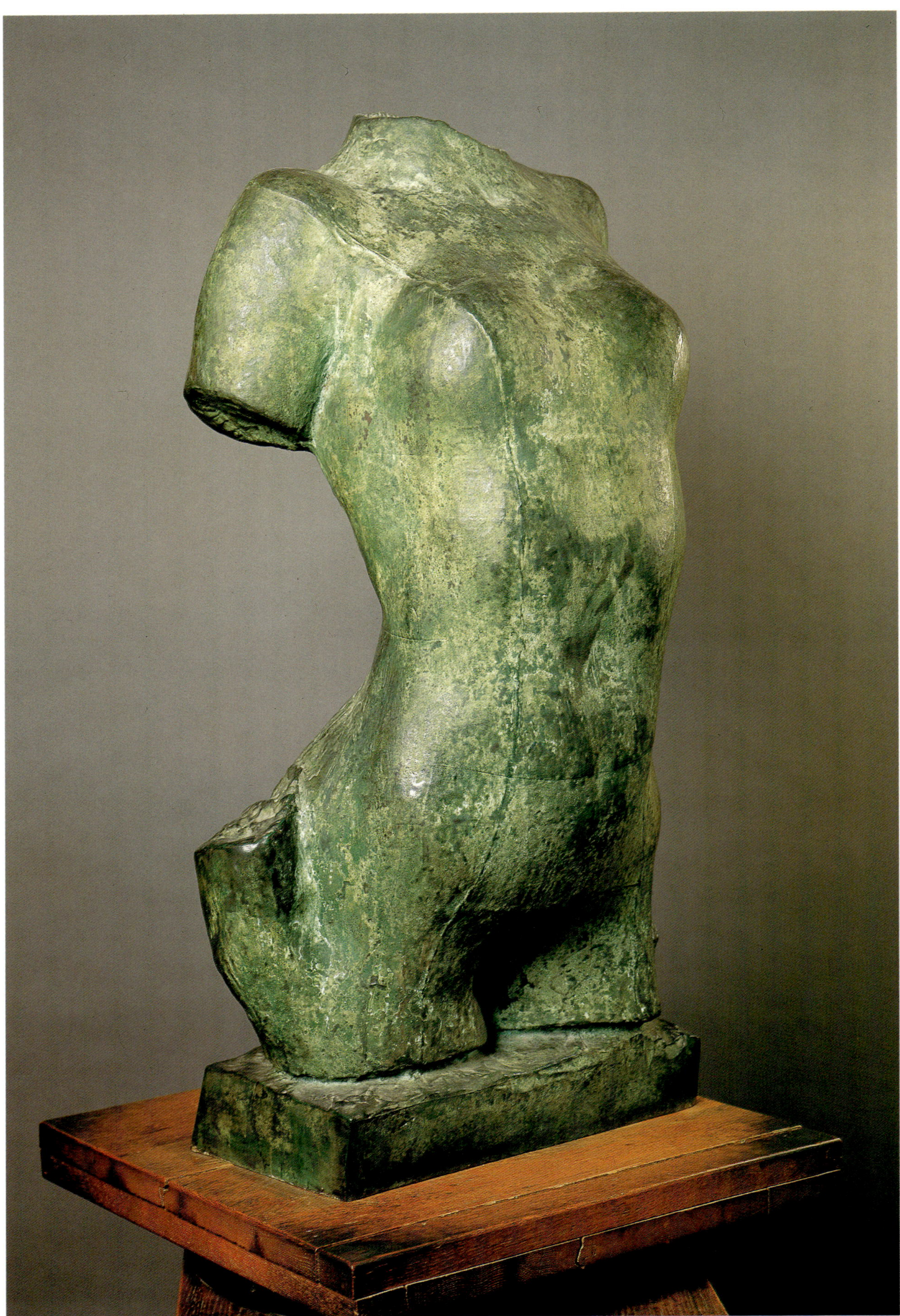

Fragments, assemblages and enlargements

Antoinette Le Normand-Romain

In 1877 Rodin removed the lance from *The Age of Bronze*, and in 1880 the cross from *St John the Baptist*. His approach was always to suppress what seemed to him to be superfluous or what gave the work too obvious a meaning. Thus in 1897 he exhibited his large *Inner Voice* with the arms cut off and the right knee broken off, maintaining that in his eyes it was nonetheless completely finished. It is true, as Rilke wrote, that "never had a human body so concentrated on what was most intimate to it, thus bowed down by its own spirit... Rodin's statues without arms lack nothing essential to them. In front of them we feel we are in front of a completed whole which admits no complement."

This state represented the culmination of a long story: created for *The Gates of Hell*, and left incomplete then because it was to be placed in the lintel, the figure was given feet, a left arm and a new face, probably in the late 1880s. In 1894 Rodin decided to make it into part of the *Monument to Victor Hugo*, removing all the elements which he found inappropriate. After 1900 he completed the figure which had been now given the name *Inner Voice* in tribute to Victor Hugo's collection of poems, *La Voix Intérieure*, or *Meditation*, but before that it had been enlarged in its fragmentary form. It is in this form which the artist preferred that it was exhibited.

This was the first time that Rodin so clearly accorded the status of a finished work to a figure that looked incomplete. He reconfirmed his intentions soon afterwards with *The Walking Man*, often regarded as the symbol of pure creativity finally relieved of the weight of the subject. The very image of movement for all that it is in fact an intellectual reconstruction of it, the small *Walking Man* had passed almost unnoticed in 1900, and it was not until 1911 that a group of art lovers had a first bronze cast (Musée d'Orsay) of the large version exhibited in 1907 to make a gift of it to the French State. Meanwhile at the Salon there had been the large *Three Shades* with no arms (1902), the *Muse* from the *Monument to Whistler* (1908) and finally in 1910 *The Prayer* and the *Torso of a Young Woman, Arched*, the latter equalling the masterpieces of Antiquity in its plastic perfection. After 1900 Rodin looked at antique works with a new eye, and the fragmentary state in which the majority of Greco-Roman sculptures have

Torso of Young Woman, Arched,
1910
Bronze, cast by Alexis Rudier.
86 x 48.1 x 32.2
Acquired by the State in 1911
Musée du Luxembourg
Deposited by the Musée du Luxembourg, 1919
Inv. S.1064

come down to us must inevitably have had some influence on his own ideas. He had noticed that it in no way diminished their beauty or their expressive power: "Here is a hand ... broken off at the wrist, it no longer has any fingers, just a palm, and it is so true that to look at it, to see it alive, I do not need the fingers. Mutilated as it is, it is still sufficient in itself because it is true," he commented admiringly. Or again: "Life is in the relief, the soul of a sculpture is in the piece; the whole sculpture is there."

But the public found this hard to understand, and were critical of these "formless experiments" which they felt reflected an intolerably casual attitude towards viewers. In 1910 they took perverse pleasure in praising Bourdelle's big *Héraklès Archer* to the skies, the splendid athlete's body seeming to epitomize sculptural perfection.

After his first visit to Meudon in 1902 Rilke wrote: "One feels that conceiving of the body as a whole is more the scholar's approach, while the artist's is to create from these elements new relationships, new entities, greater, more legitimate, more eternal..." *The Walking Man* is a superb example of an assemblage, but Rodin had actually been using the process since the 1880s, with *I am Beautiful* providing a very early example. It enabled him very rapidly to create new groups in which he could let his imagination have free rein, drawing on the huge repertory of forms at his disposal. This is nowhere more obvious than in the assemblages of fragments of bodies and vases coming from Rodin's collection: these works - a woman seated in the hollow created by a snake coiled round upon itself, the *Little Female Faun* leaning over the edge of a cup and almost tipping it over, *Ugolino's Son* placed symmetrically opposite *The Despairing Adolescent* to serve as a handle for the remains of an antique vase - are attractive as much for the combination of different materials and colours as for the ever alert imagination they reveal.

The same inventive spirit lay behind the transformation of some figurines; quite frequently it is possible to present side by side a sketch in earth or plaster (the plaster figures sometimes being dipped in a milk which blurs the outlines) and different groups in which the sketch is combined with other fragments. This is the case for instance where a *Male Nude* is placed beside either *Day* from *La Tour du Travail* or beside a female figure to form the group entitled *Man and his Thought*, a group which would later be translated into marble as the very visible "points" demonstrate. The final stage of this game is reached with groups made up of multiples of one figure: an example of this from very early in Rodin's work is *The Three Shades* from *The Gates of Hell* of which there is a small and a large version.

The large version postdates 1900 for Rodin in fact discovered the potential which enlargement could open up to him at a late stage. Rodin's loyal collaborator Henri Lebossé enlarged the groups fragment by fragment, taking care to respect the master's touch, then mounted the sculpture in Rodin's studio. By changing the proportions and hence the relationship between the work and its surroundings, enlargement could profoundly alter the meaning of the work.

Christ and Mary Magdalene,
*c.*1894
Maquette
Plaster. 84,5 x 74 x 44,2
Donation Rodin, 1916
Inv. S.1097

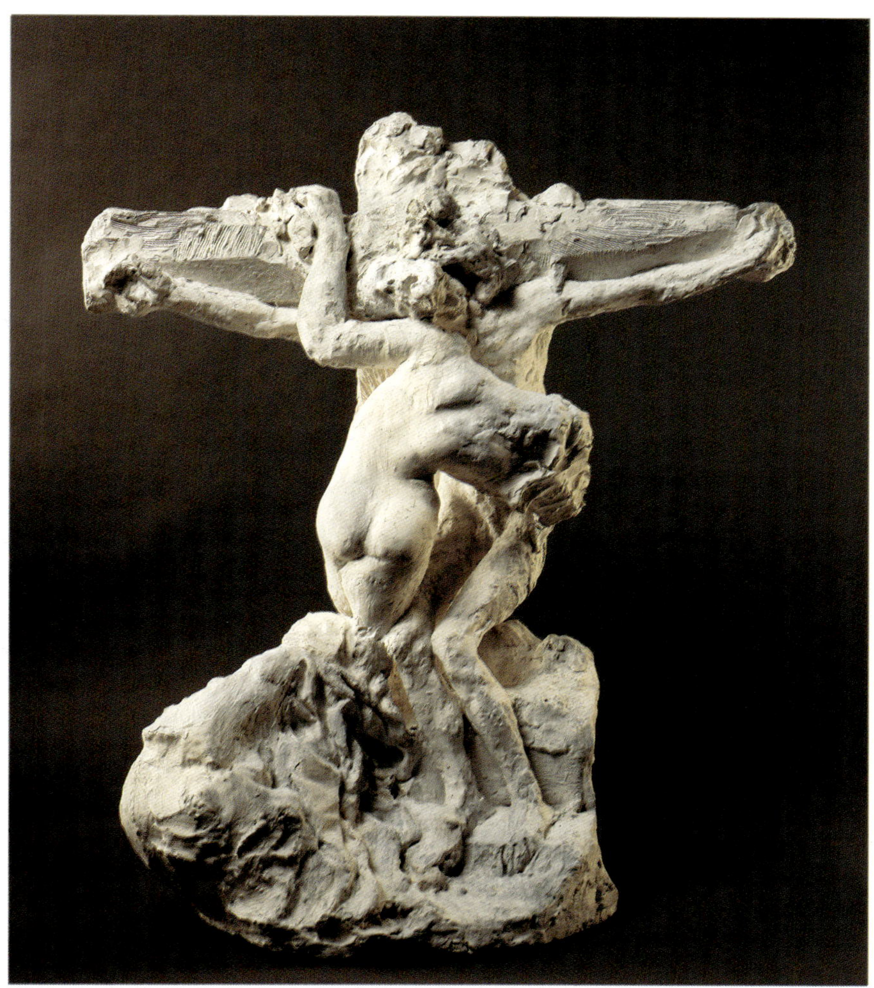

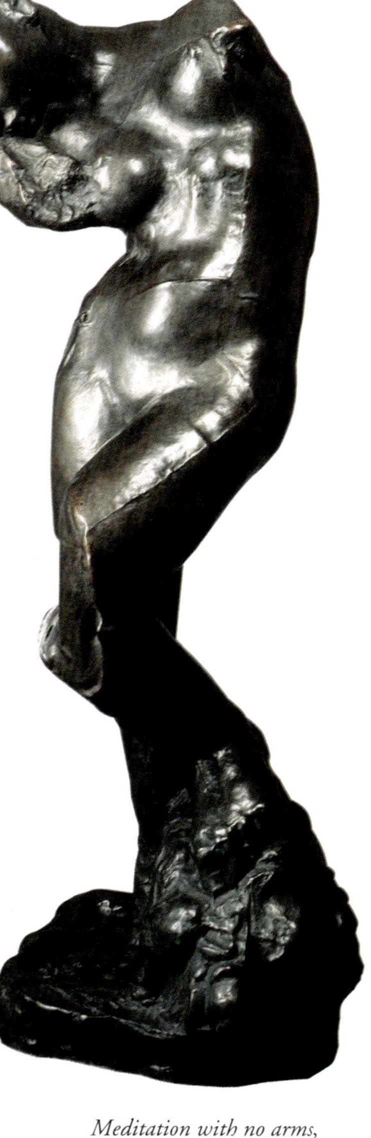

Meditation with no arms,
*c.*1896-1897
Bronze, cast by the Coubertin foundry
146 x 75,5 x 55
Cast for the museum's collections in 1981
Inv. S.792

Clinging onto the body of Christ in an attitude that is the inverse of his, *Mary Magdalen* is none other than *Meditation,* with only the body being retained, while the arms and legs have been modified. But as always when dealing with the maquette, Rodin was concerned only with specifying his idea without wasting time on pointless details: thus when we look at her from behind we discover that Mary Magdalen has three legs! From the front this "make-do-and-mend" is hidden by a drape made of a real piece of cloth dipped into plaster while it was still liquid.

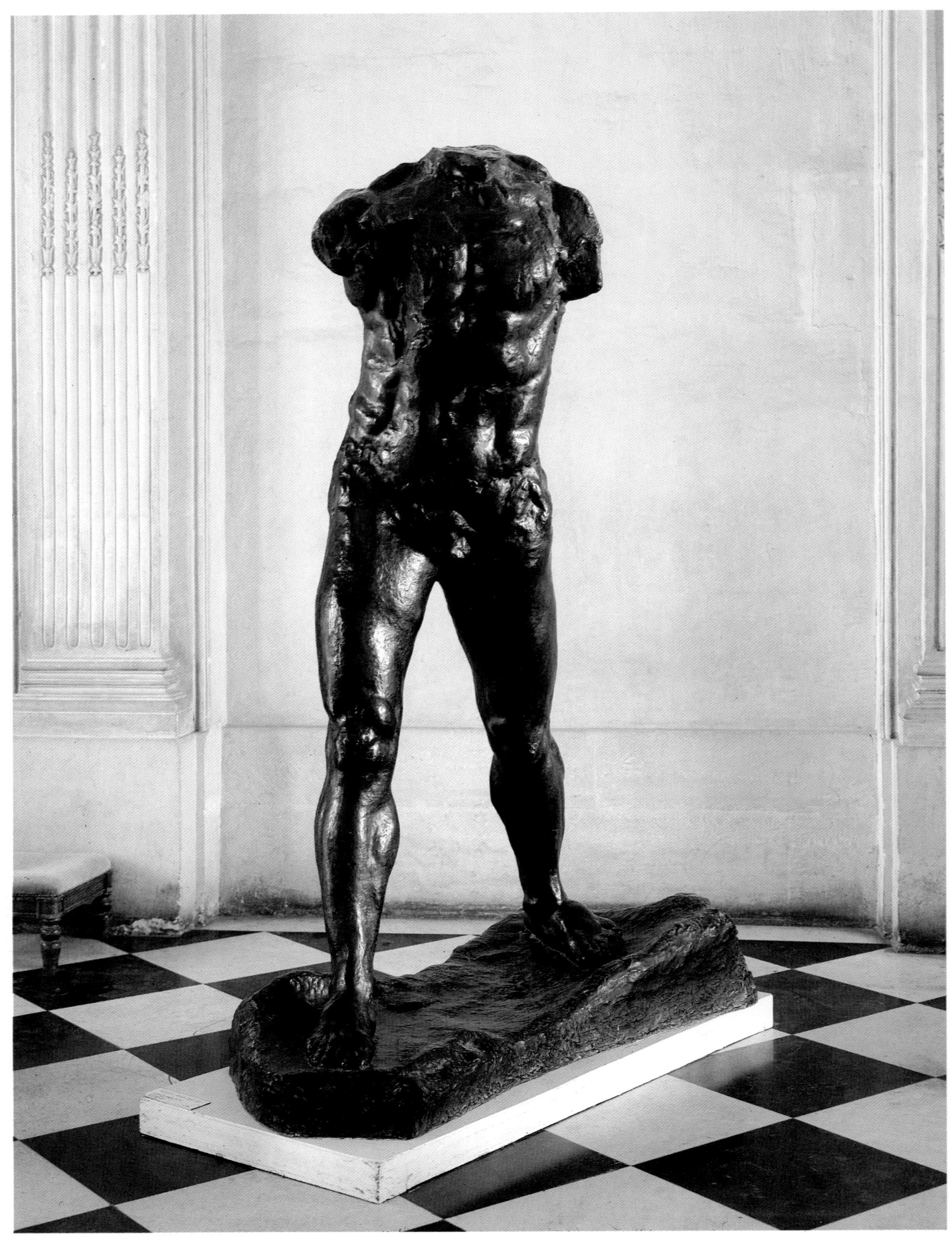

The Walking Man,
1900-1907
Enlargement.
Bronze, cast by Alexis Rudier.
213.5 x 71.7 x 156.5
Rodin donation, 1916
Inv. S.998

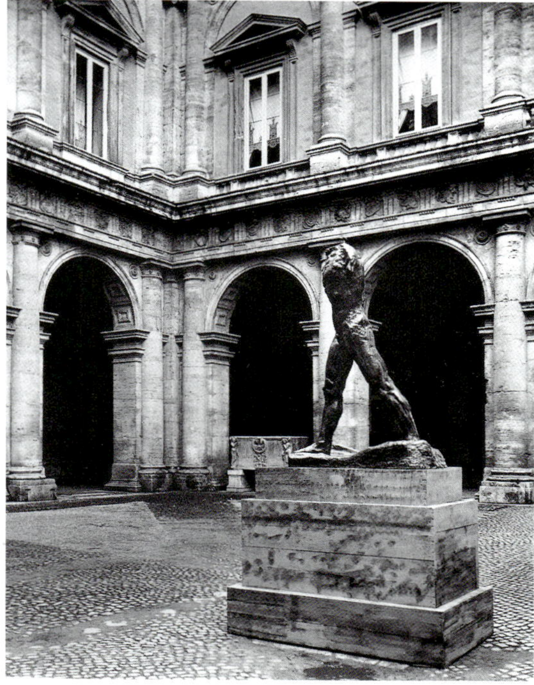

Cesare Faraglia
The Walking Man at the Palazzo Farnese in Rome,
1912
Gelatin silver print. 25,6 x 19,6
Rodin donation, 1916
Inv. Ph.1825

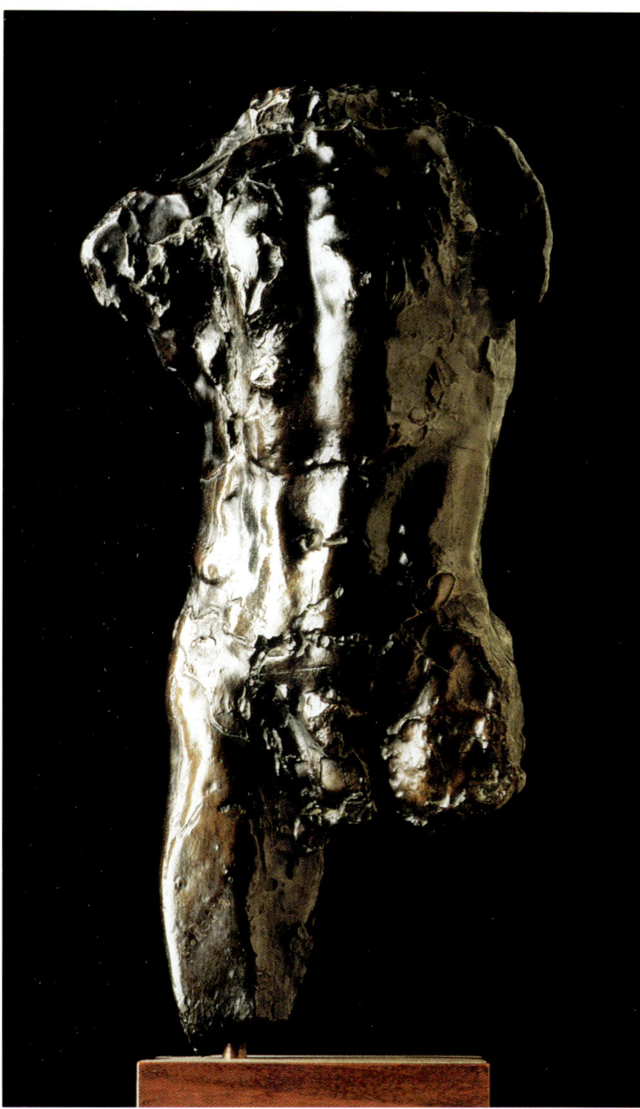

Male Torso, study for *The Walking Man,*
*c.*1878
Bronze, cast by the Coubertin fondry.
53 x 27 x 15
Cast for the Museum's collections in 1979
Inv. S.602

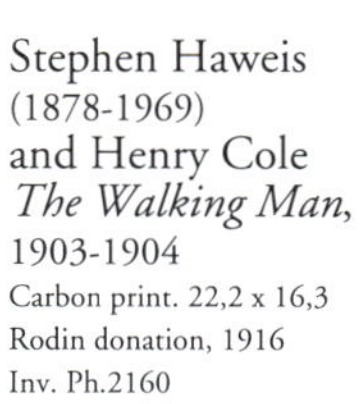

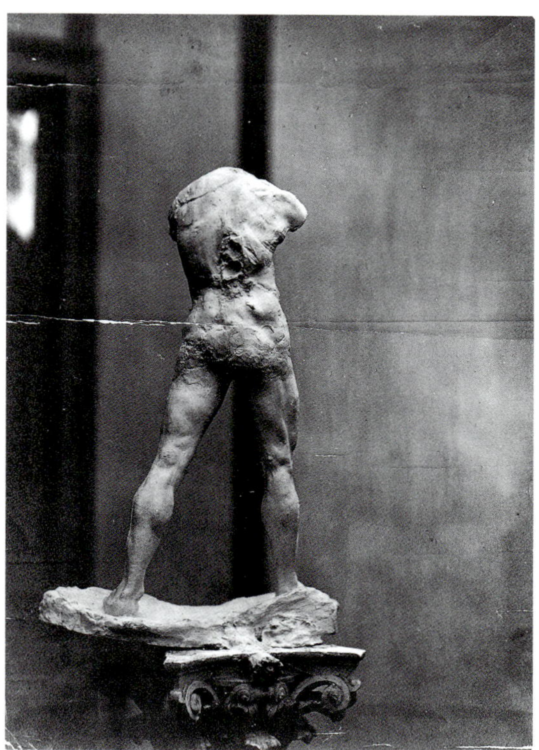

Stephen Haweis
(1878-1969)
and Henry Cole
The Walking Man,
1903-1904
Carbon print. 22,2 x 16,3
Rodin donation, 1916
Inv. Ph.2160

Male Nude,
before 1888
Terra cotta. 22 x 6.5 x 6.6
Rodin donation, 1916
Inv. S.198

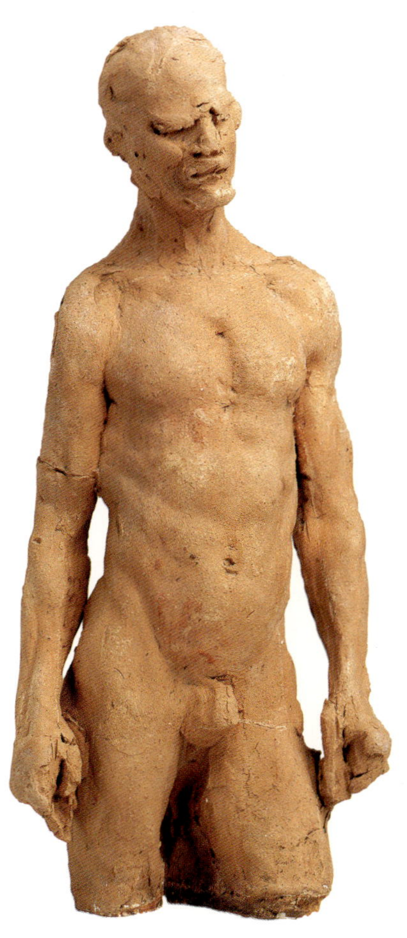

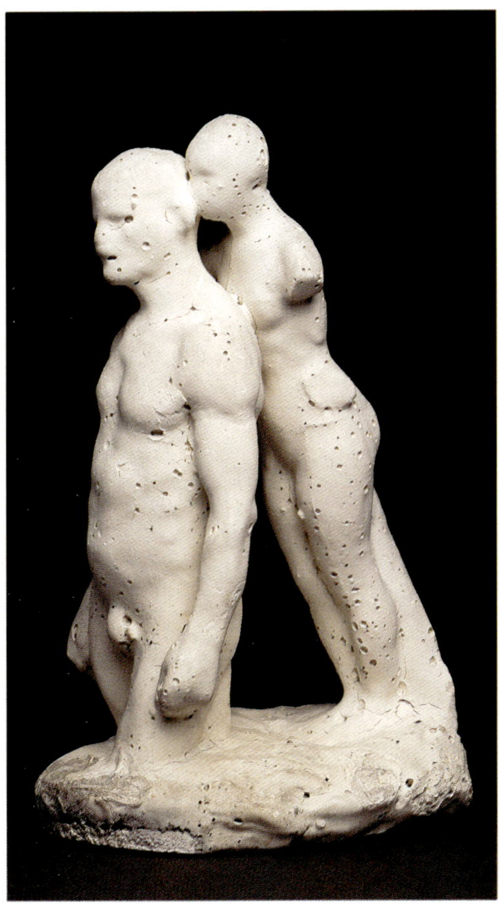

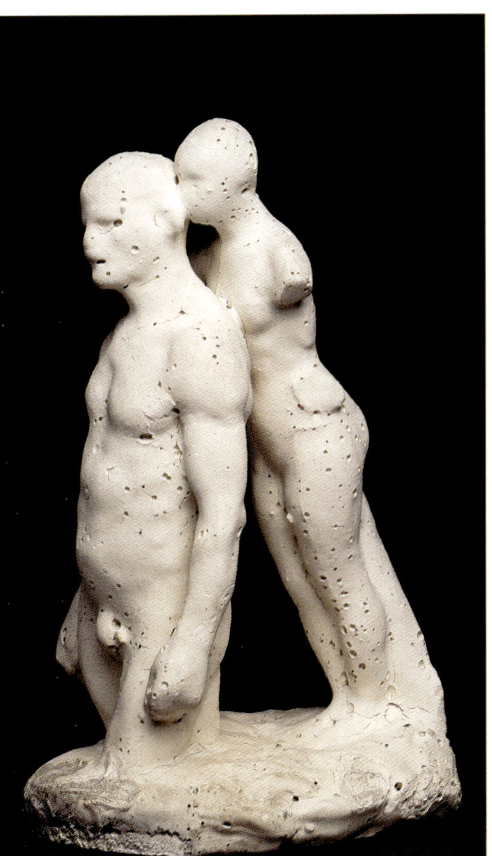

Assemblage:
Male Nude and Day
Plaster. 27.9 x 14 x 17.1
Rodin donation, 1916
Inv. S.2038

Man and his Thought,
*c.*1888
Plaster. 29.5 x 22.6 x 18
Rodin donation, 1916
Inv. S.2031

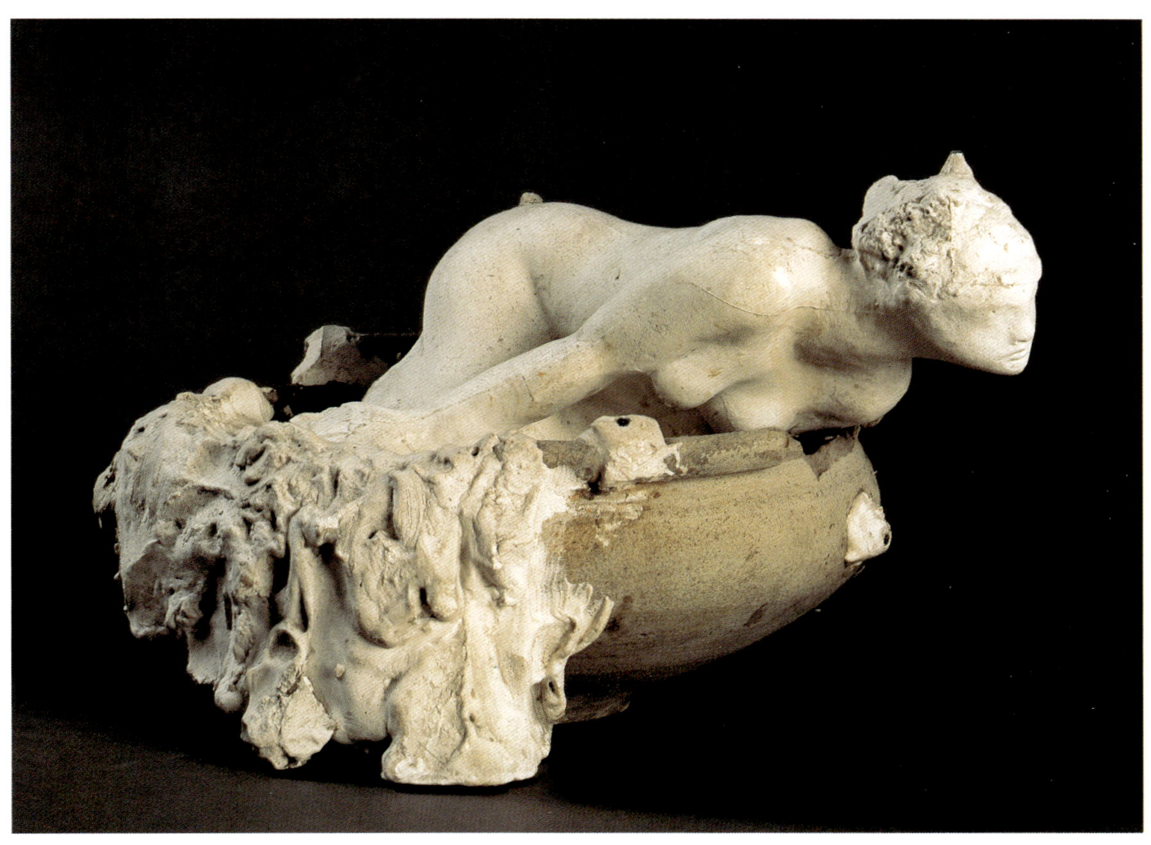

The Little Water Fairy,
before 1903
Maquette. Plaster and terracotta.
14.3 x 19.9 x 23.2
Rodin donation, 1916
Inv. S.368

Assemblage:
Vase with The Despairing Adolescent and One of Ugolino's Children
Plaster and ceramics. 45.8 x 46.6 x 27.5
Rodin donation, 1916
Inv. S.3614

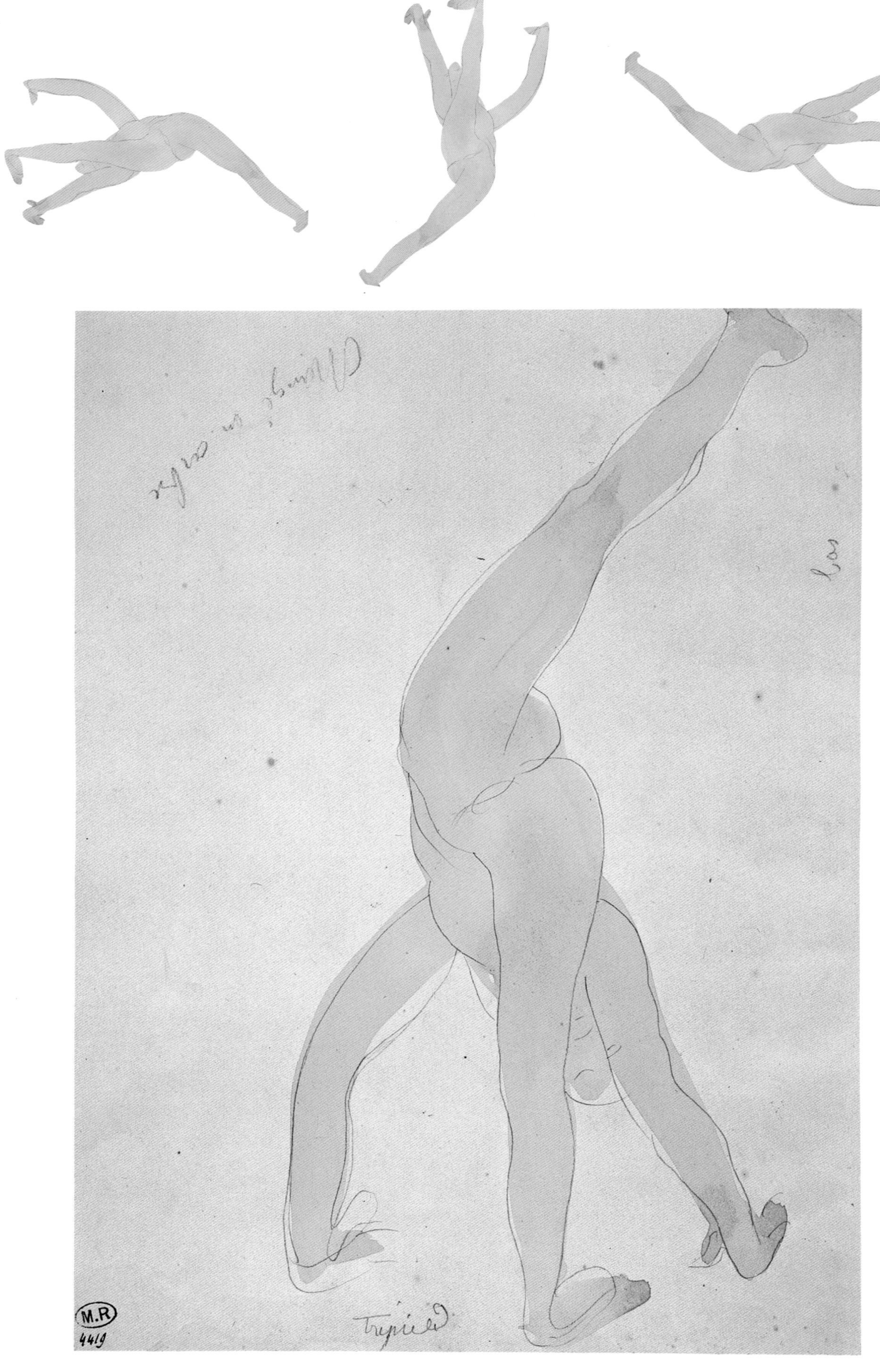

Graphic experimentation

Claudie Judrin

Rodin began to apply his curiosity to his drawing. The notebook is the prime tool of the person travelling with a pencil in his hand, his eyes on the look-out. It is often forgotten the extent to which the artist needs to record fleeting moments there and then, because with the passage of time this valuable testimony is broken up out of greed by dealers, or by museums for presentation, or finally by the creator himself, the master of his own work, deciding to cut up his own researches, as Rodin sometimes did.

His notebooks which were modest in format when he was young and penniless, in Belgium in particular, might be covered for instance with studies of works in silver and gold. There can be no doubt that Rodin amassed countless sketches when he went down to Italy from Belgium, and it is legitimate to surmise that he cut them up and put them together as the spirit moved him once back in Brussels.

When he places twelve studies of Victor Hugo's head from different angles side by side on the same sheet of paper Rodin is multiplying his observations to get a better grasp of his famous model who, at the height of his fame, was unwilling to pose. In 1883 Goncourt noted that Rodin must have made sixty lightning thumbnail sketches, almost all in a kind of shorthand, with Hugo reading, thinking or eating and often showing only his forehead.

When he reveals that his "sculpture is only drawing using all the dimensions" and that he turns his sheet of paper round several times, it is as if he were rotating his model on a turntable to view him or her from all sides. To leave no doubt in the viewer's mind he writes in various titles with the writing running in two or three different directions.

Rodin looked at the female body with a completely new eye, going so far as to include the curves of a nude in the outline of a moulding or to note a daring pose in a water colour wash in the form of an egg symbolizing creation. His boldest experiment was to cut out silhouettes which he then left unattached, not fixing them on to a support, so that he could manipulate them at will like puppets. This liking for relief led him to move from two dimensions to three. The flat subject becomes an object. Rodin sometimes gives up a cut-out he has started in such a way that we can re-form a pair of intertwining women that he had separated incompletely since the two protagonists' hands and legs pass over each other in such a way that they could not be spared from mutilation by the knife. It is a rare occurrence to be able to touch a work that is in the process of gestation.

Tripod
Graphite and water colour on paper.
32.5 x 24.5
Rodin donation, 1916
Inv. D.4419

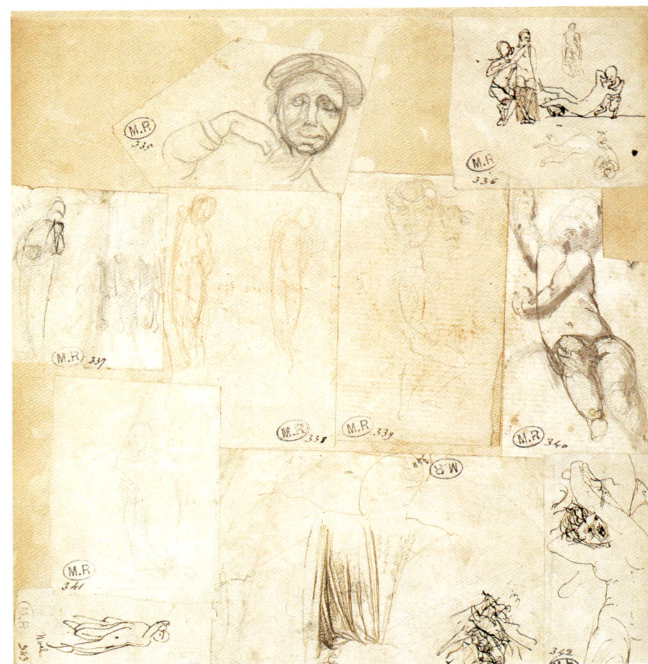

Page of sketches,
*c.*1875-1876
Graphite, pen and ink washes on paper collage. 26.3 x 26.4
Rodin donation, 1916
Inv. D.335-344

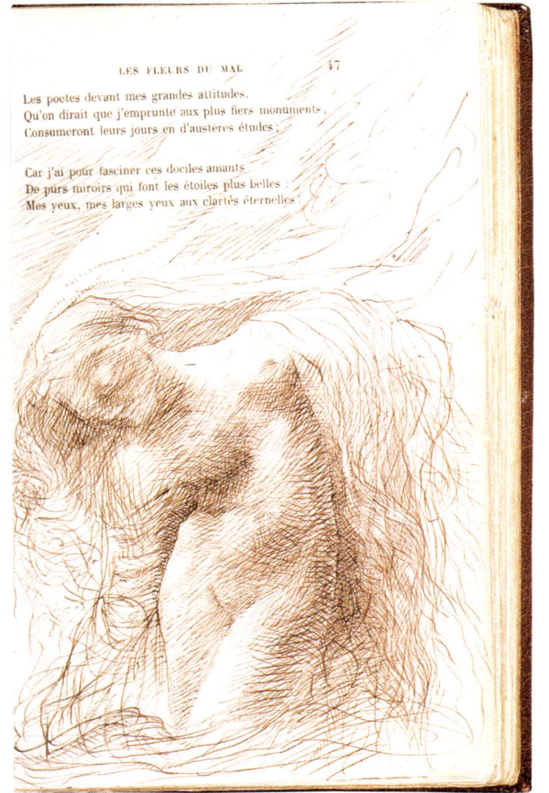

LES FLEURS DU MAL 47

Les poëtes devant mes grandes attitudes,
Qu'on dirait que j'emprunte aux plus fiers monuments,
Consumeront leurs jours en d'austères études ;

Car j'ai pour fasciner ces dociles amants
De purs miroirs qui font les étoiles plus belles :
Mes yeux, mes larges yeux aux clartés éternelles !

Beauty,
1887-1888
Graphite, pen and sepia ink on p. 47 of Charles Baudelaire, *Les Fleurs du Mal,* Paris, Poulet-Malassis and de Broise, 1857
Acquired in 1937
Inv. D.7174E

"Nothing touches me in the same way as an exhibition of my drawings. I feel that those who love me will find the sincerest expression of my effort in them."

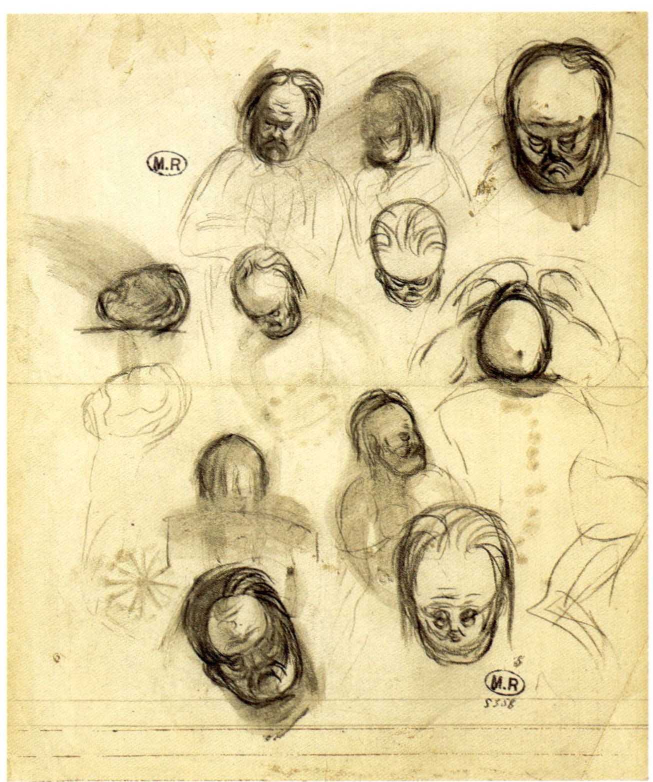

Twelve Studies of Victor Hugo's Head from Different Angles,
1883
Black crayon and grey ink wash on paper. 25.2 x 21.1
Rodin donation, 1916
Inv. D.5358

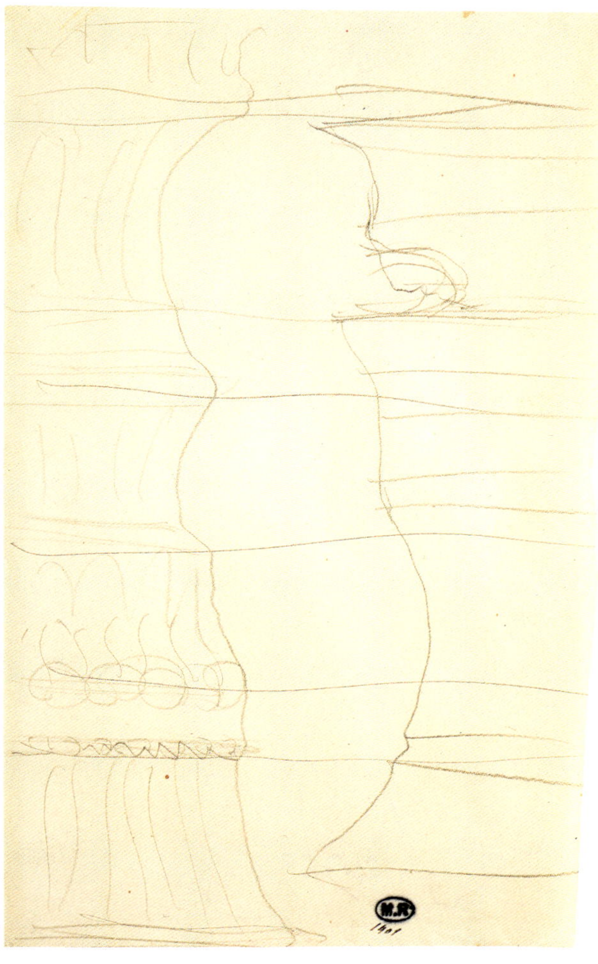

Profile of Female Nude against a Background of Mouldings
Graphite on paper. 31.2 x 20.2
Rodin donation, 1916
Inv. D.1401

"What I say about them is not said so that my drawings will be heralded to the sound of trumpets. On the contrary, they must be quietly protected so that the public does not rebel."

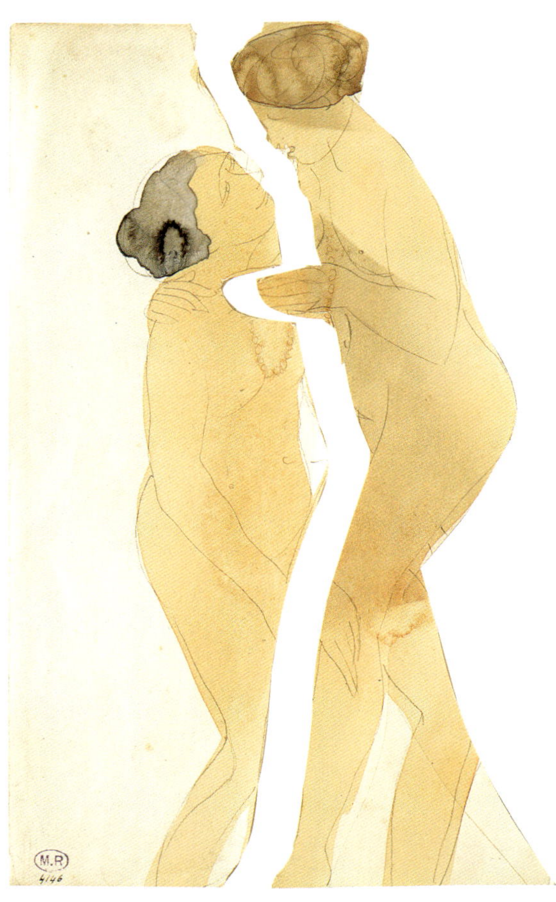

Standing Female Nude against a Nude Female in Profile with Clasped Hands
Graphite and water colour on paper cut-outs. 32.4 x 22.5
Rodin donation, 1916
Inv. D.4146-5228

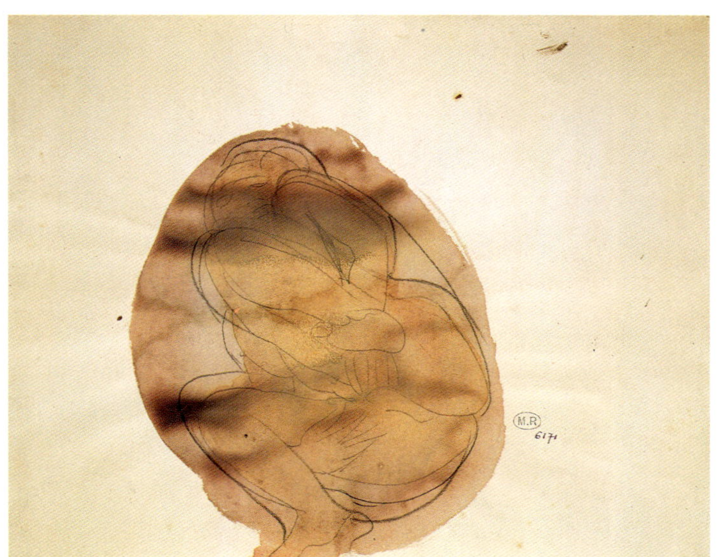

Female Nude on her Back, Holding her Thighs Raised and Apart
Graphite and water colour on paper.
25.1 x 32.8
Rodin donation, 1916
Inv. D.6171

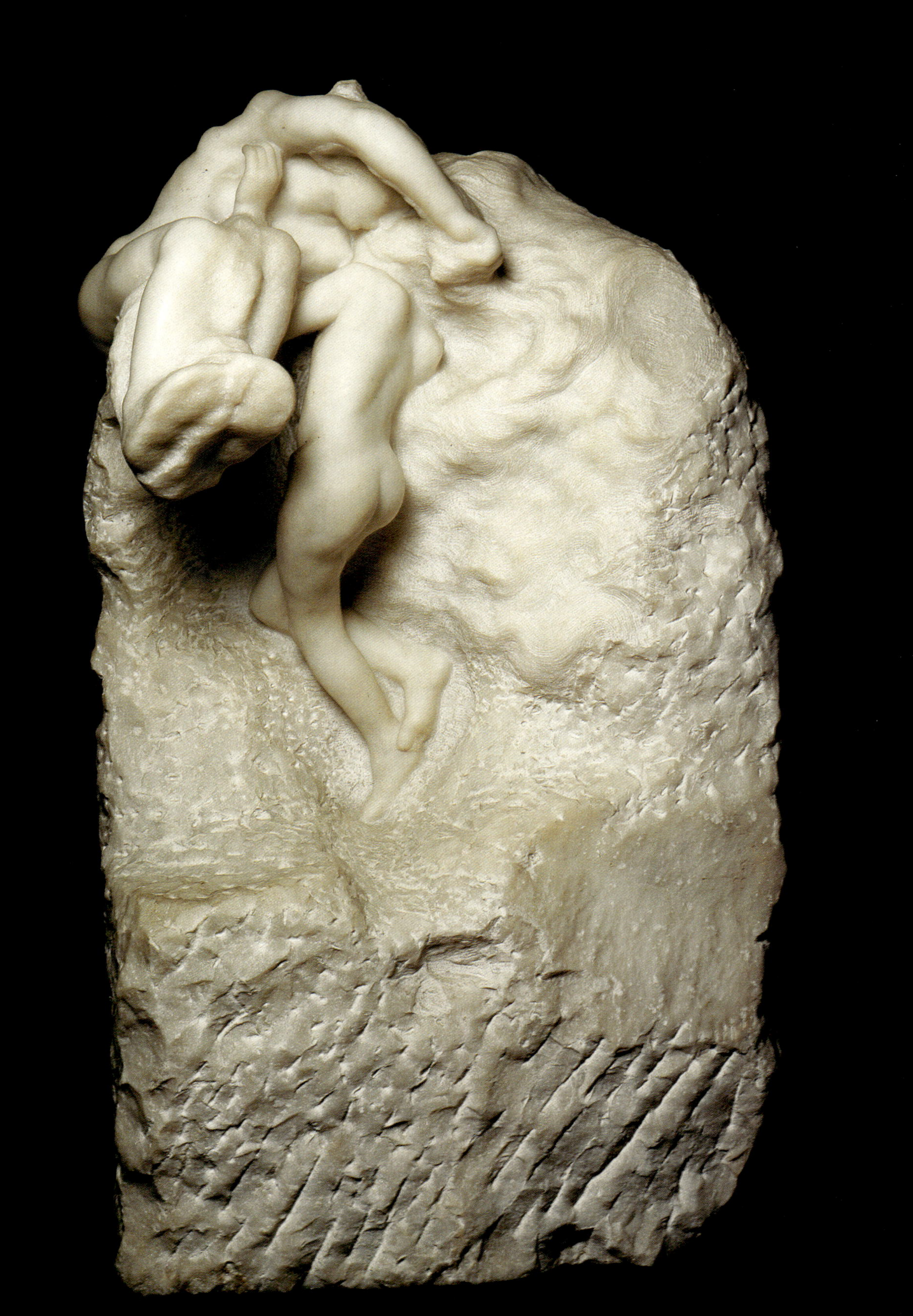

Works in marble

Antoinette Le Normand-Romain

In the nineteenth century sculptors who executed their own works in marble were few and far between. It had become customary for them to create a *model* in plaster, perfect and identical in all respects to the work they wanted to produce, then to hand it over to a *praticien* who would carve it in marble. These *praticiens* or sculptor's assistants were often excellent sculptors in their own right, like Peter, Escoula, Turcan, Pompon, Despiau, Bourdelle etc all of whom worked for Rodin.

As soon as he was able to Rodin adopted this method of working: the bust of *The Man with the Broken Nose*, exhibited as early as 1875, was already the chisel work of Léon Fourquet. As time went by, however, Rodin became ever freer in his behaviour towards his assistants, getting into the habit of handing them not a model but a sketch, a rough indication of the work to be realised, made up by assemblage from already existing works: in *The Sculptor and his Muse* the little Muse breathing inspiration into the sculptor's ear is none other than the figure entitled *The Shell and the Pearl*, raised to a vertical position. In the case of *Orpheus and the Maenads* the assemblage had been created for the tympanum of *The Gates of Hell* and was translated into marble at another time; but the vertical figure exists in isolation: it is the *Kneeling Female Faun* which reappears several times in Rodin's work. The same applies to *The Martyr* originally created for *The Gates of Hell*: fitted with wings and placed in a plunging position it becomes *The Illusion, Sister of Icarus*. This very beautiful marble was exhibited in 1896 and bought immediately by Albert Kahn.

The sale of sculptures in marble was in fact an important source of revenue for Rodin and in the final years of the nineteenth century he got into the habit of having medium-scale groups made up at his own initiative which he could show to potential buyers. By then assemblage had come to occupy an increasingly important place in his creative process; new groups created from fragments made earlier with no preconceived plan could very easily be interpreted with very different meanings inspired by the Symbolism then in vogue. Thus they seemed ideally suited to serve as the starting point for works in marble; the distance that always existed in the case of Rodin between the maquette and the finished marble gave the artist the option of altering his work as it was being executed, according to circumstances, the form and characteristics of the block of marble in particular, but no doubt also on the basis of suggestions made by the *praticiens*.

On these marbles the traces of how they were executed always remain visible: the points, the small holes made by the probe to get close to the level of the final modelling are not concealed; in places the surface is almost polished while elsewhere it seems scarcely to have been roughed out, as if the aim were to create a kind of poetic atmosphere around the work. Rodin liked this contrast which can be seen even more clearly in the marbles produced in his final years.

The Earth and the Moon, 1899
Marble executed by Raynaud?
125.5 x 78 x 58
Commissioned by the Cassirer gallery in Berlin in 1898, delivered in 1900.
Acquired in 1984
Inv. S.1439

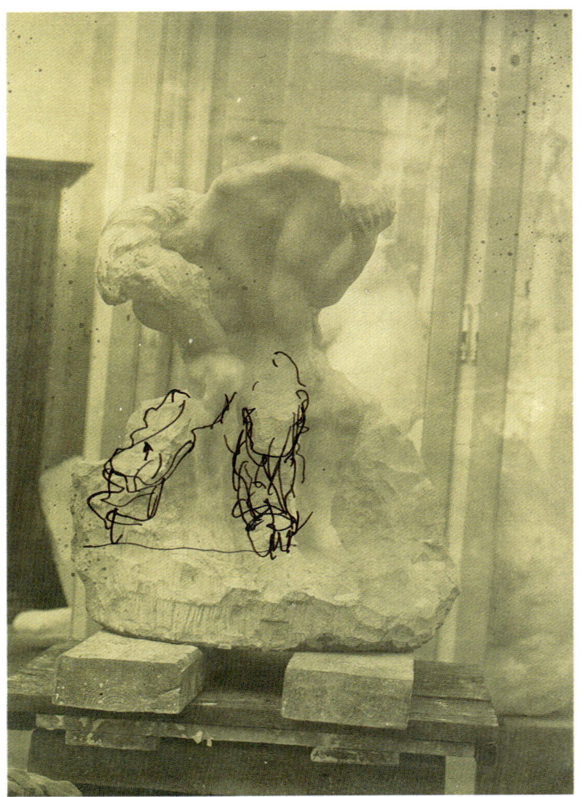

Anonymous
The Sculptor and his Muse
Gelatin silver print retouched in ink.
18 x 12.5
Rodin donation, 1916
Inv. Ph.1059

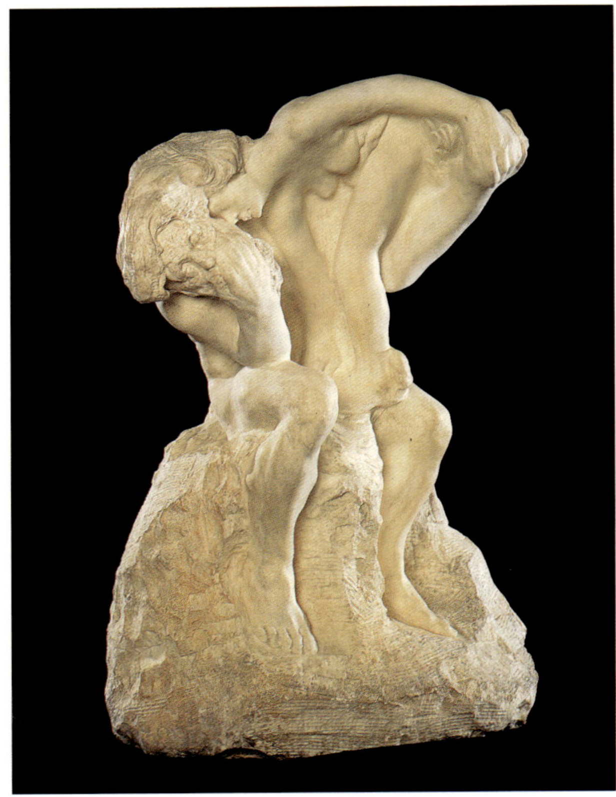

The Sculptor and his Muse
Stone executed by François Pompon
in 1894-1895.
66.3 x 58.3 x 53
Rodin donation, 1916
Inv. S.1020

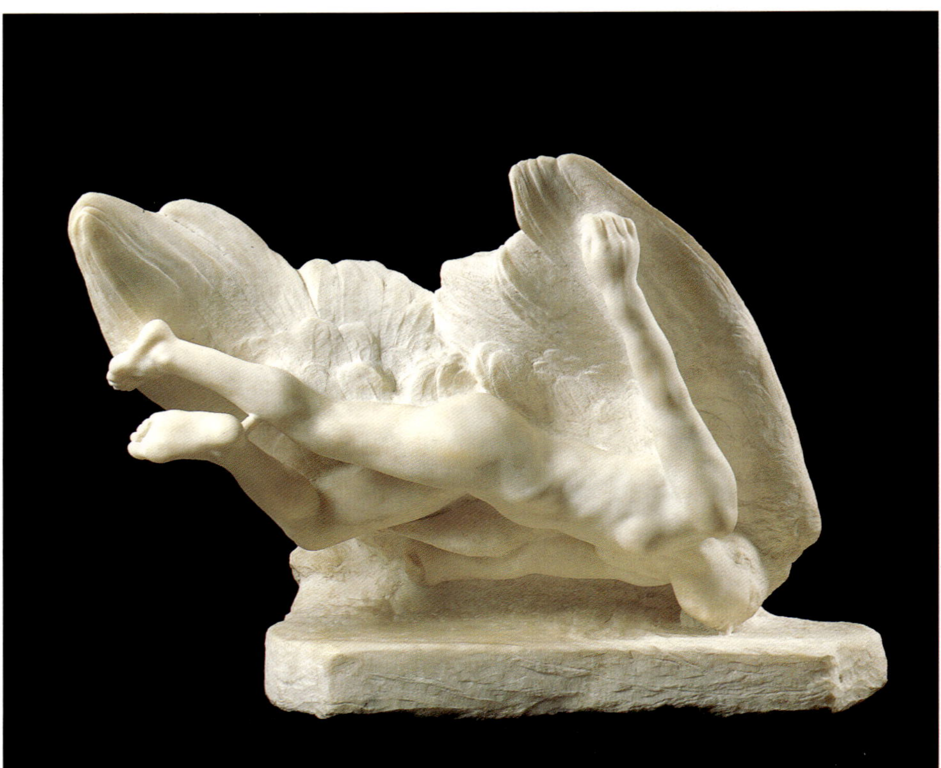

The Illusion, Sister of Icarus
Marble executed by Alexandre Pézieux
exhibited at 1896 Salon de la Société
Nationale des Beaux-Arts. 62 x 96 x 51
Previously Albert Kahn collection
Acquired in 1983
Inv. S.1385

Psyche-Spring,
1886?
Marble executed by Barthelémy?
29.6 x 48 x 40.3
Bequeathed to the town of Aix-les-Bains
by Dr Jean Faure in 1947
Exchanged for bronzes in 1948
Inv. S.1116

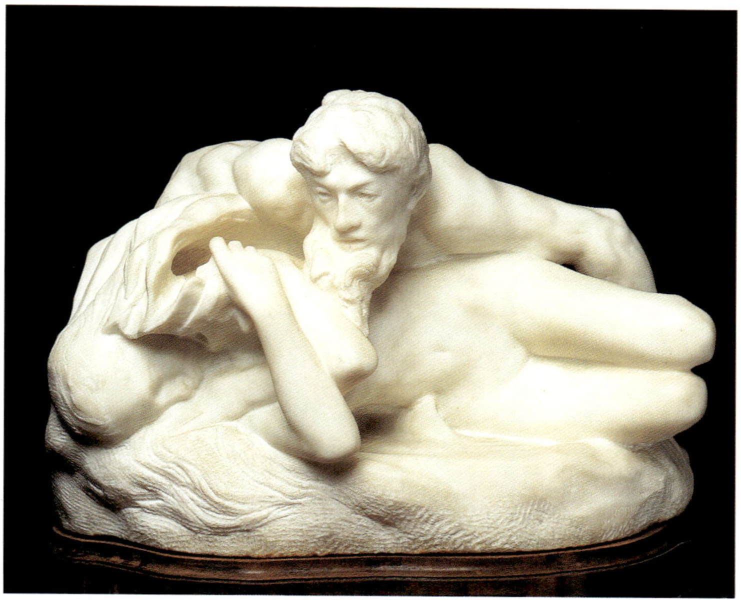

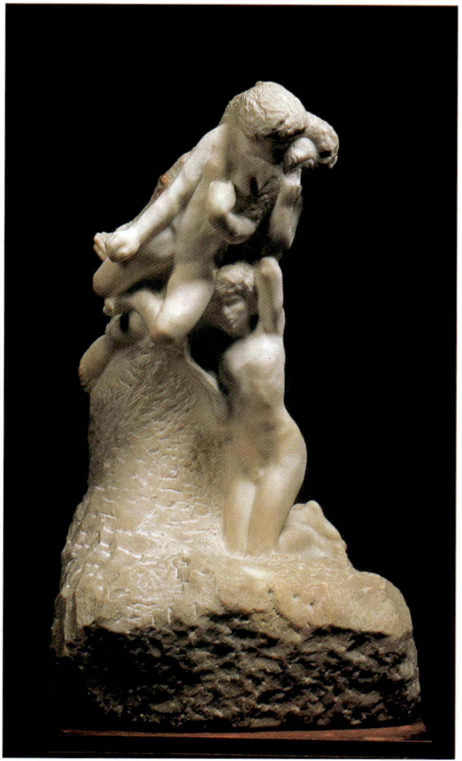

Orpheus and the Maenads,
1905
Marble executed by Ganier and
Louis Mathet. 97.5 x 60 x 63.2
Rodin donation, 1916
Inv. S. 1023

Paolo and Francesca,
*c.*1905
Marble. 81 x 108 x 65
Rodin donation, 1916
Inv. S.1423

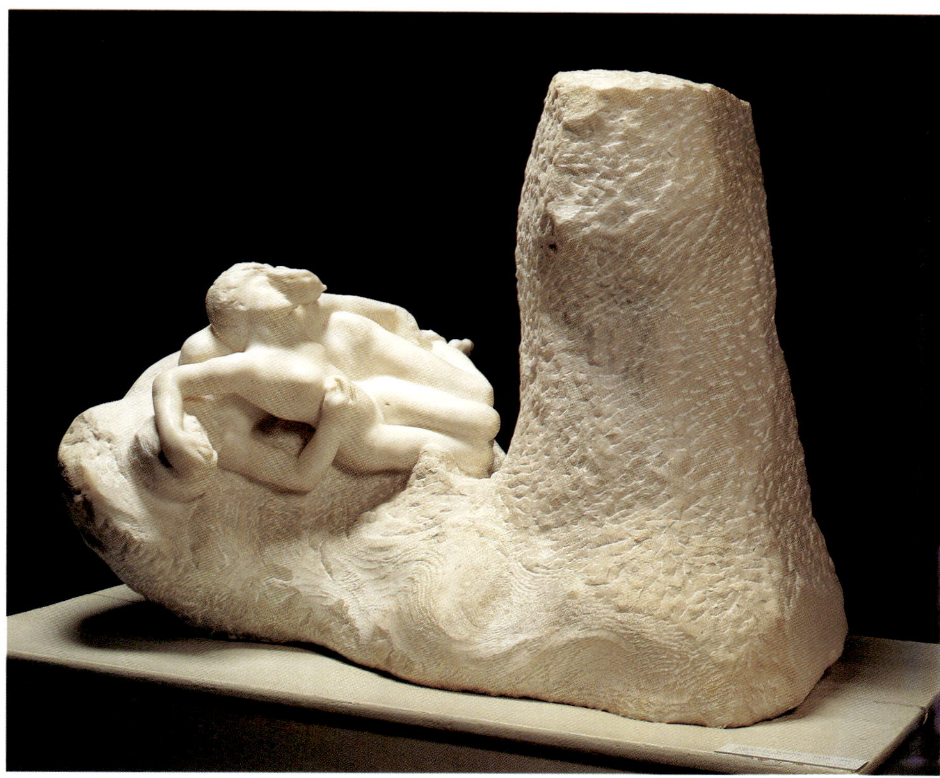

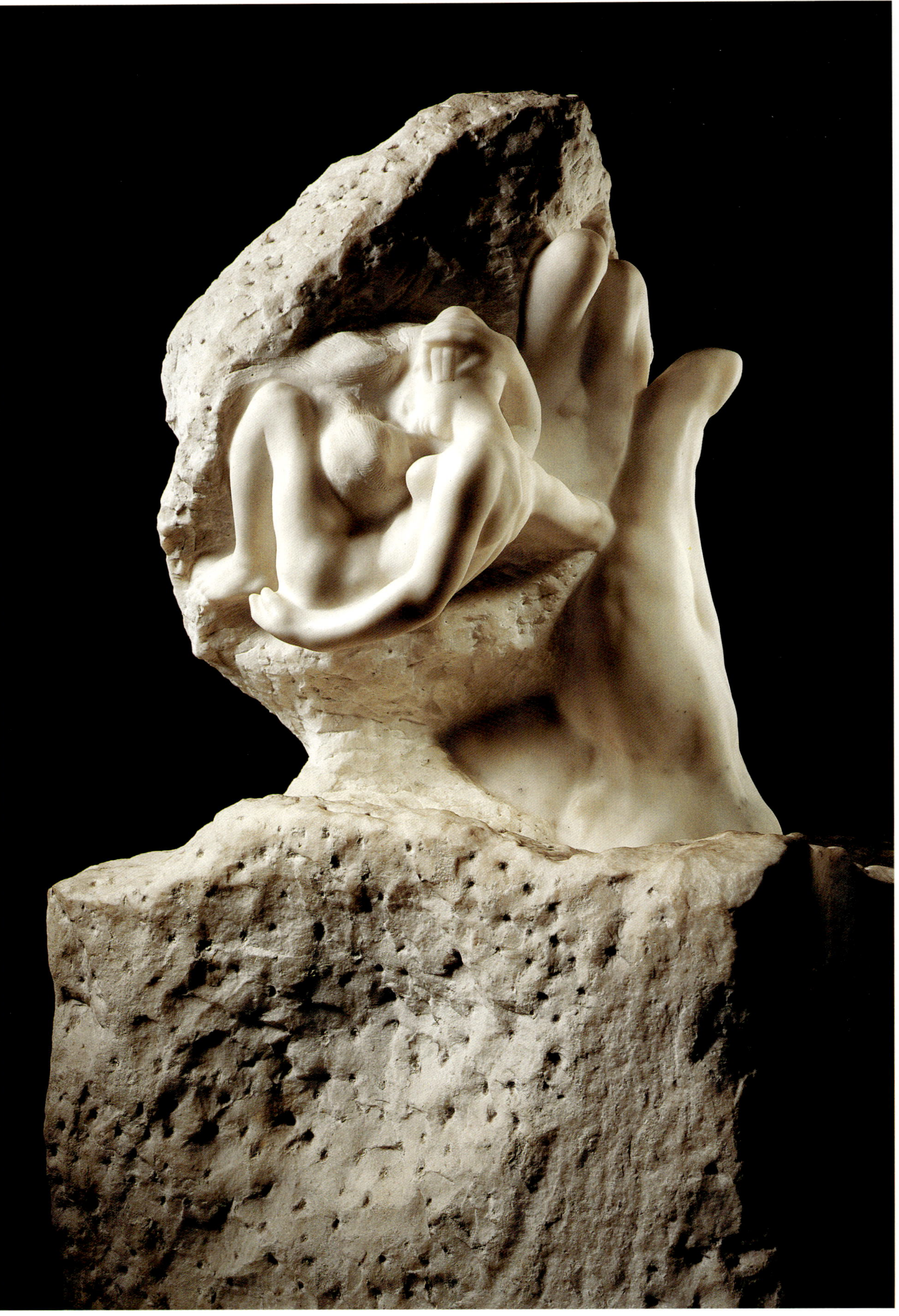

Hands

Hélène Marraud

"Half the size of life, little things, and he never threw one away... They were arranged in drawers, shallow drawers ... which wanted very careful opening so that they didn't stick, and there were all these little tiny hands, and I loved looking at them. And he showed me the hands and we picked out one or two that were particularly good, and I remember him with one little hand in each of his, smiling, and saying, 'How good they are!' " Sir Gerald Kelly recounted.

Hands as "abattis" (see below), hands as studies, hands as monuments, they are always independent works which, though fragmentary, possess amazing expressive power: "small independent hands which without belonging to a body are alive. Hands that rise, irritated and evil, hands which seem to be barking with their five fingers bristling, like the five throats of a dog from hell. Hands that walk, that sleep, and hands that wake up..." (Rilke).

As the body's extremities the hands and feet give the human body all its expressive value: the feet lend stature, poise and grandeur to the figure, the hands lead its gesture and express its thought. Rodin did not hesitate to entrust this work to his pupils, and therefore asked Camille Claudel to make the feet and hands for *The Burghers of Calais* (1884-1889).

The hand is one of the extremities of a figure, and can subsequently be isolated from it like the fragmentary hands in his collection of antiquities, but it is also a point of contact, a passing point between two forms, figures or distinct elements: "A hand placed on the shoulder or thigh of another body no longer belongs completely to the body from which it came: it and the object it touches or clasps together form something new (...) and it is now a question of this special thing which has its own defined limits" (Rilke). With this end in view Rodin had series of small hands moulded which he described as "abattis" (an all-embracing term for hands and feet), meaning feet, legs and arms as well. First of all they had enabled him to complete fragmented, "dissected" figures, thinking only of the plastic effect. Using the same approach, these hands enabled figures to be brought together, making "new juxtapositions." Thus the hand of Pierre de Wissant, one of the Burghers of Calais, also brushes over the face of Camille Claudel.

Enlarged or repeated by turn, as in *The Cathedral* (1908) and *The Secret* (1909), made in stone, marble, bronze or simply plaster and terra cotta, some of these hands are monuments in their own right, hands which concentrate within them the attention of a subject and its allegory (*The Hand of God*, 1896, *The Devil's Hand*, *Lovers' Hands*, 1904, and *Hand Emerging from the Tomb*, 1914).

The hand is also the creator's signature. Thus a small female torso was placed in a moulding of Rodin's hand, made only shortly before the sculptor's death.

The Hand of God,
1896
Marble executed by Soudbinine in 1902.
94 x 82.5 x 54.9
Rodin donation, 1916
Inv. S.988

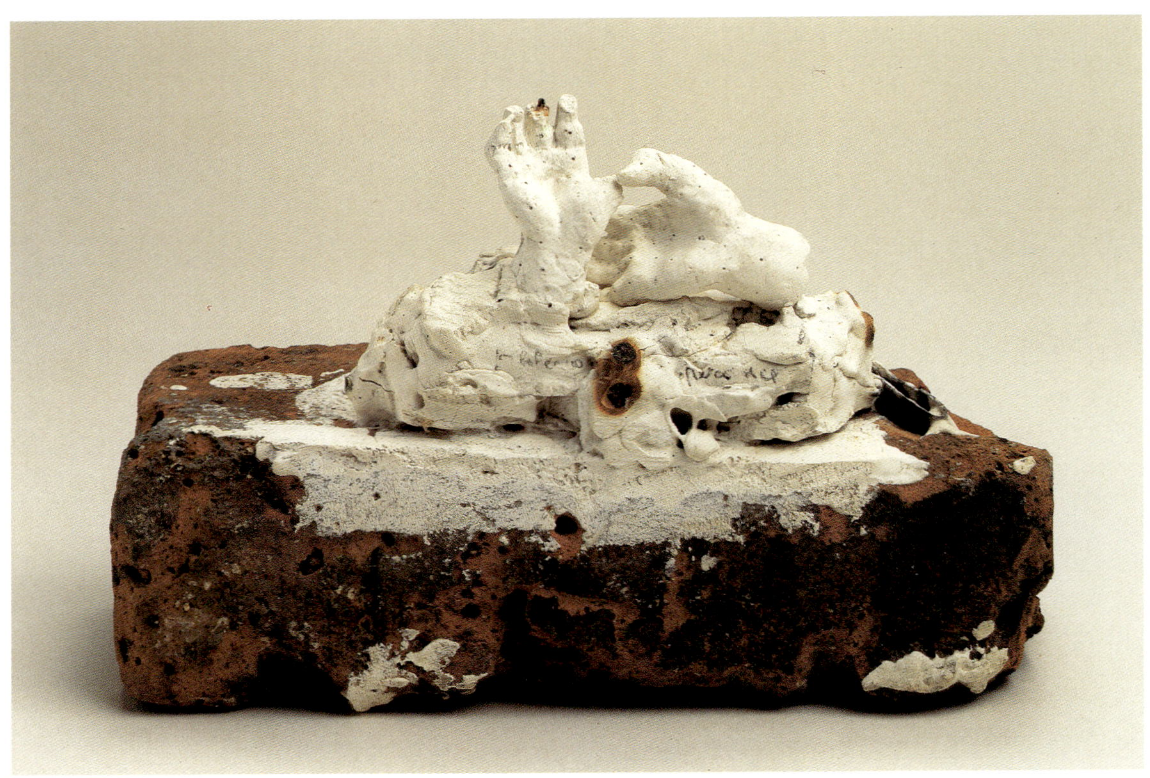

Lovers' Hands,
*c.*1903
Maquette. Plaster on brick.
13 x 21.4 x 10.6
Rodin donation, 1916
Inv. S.2680

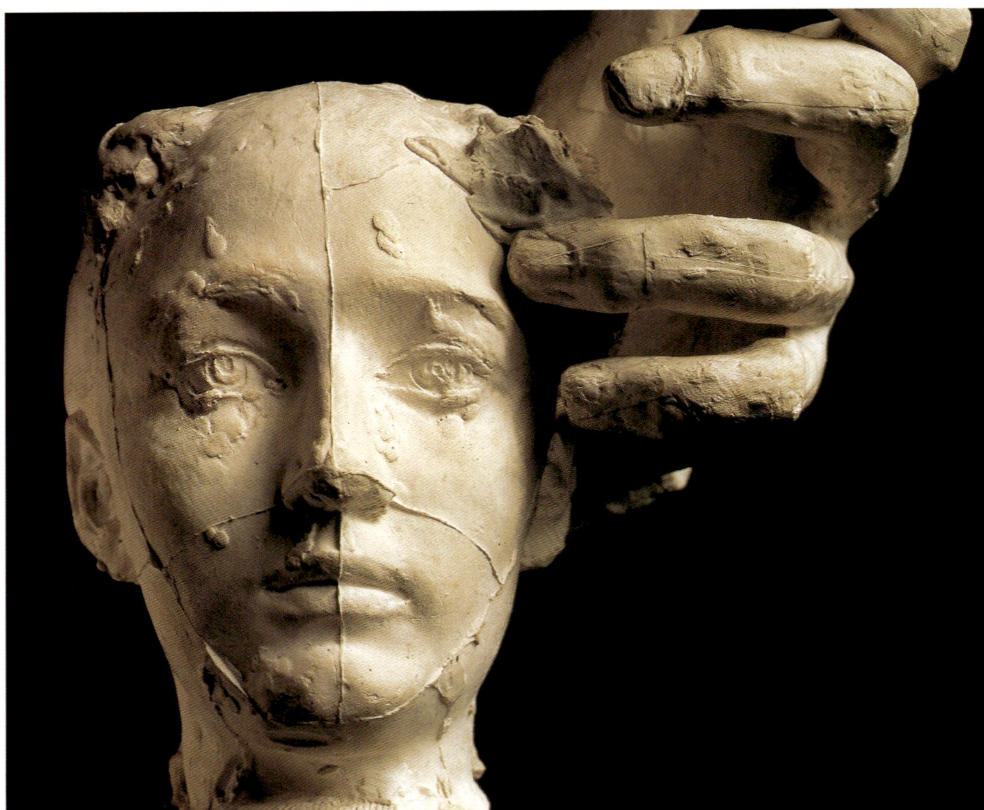

Assemblage:
Left Hand of Pierre de Wissant and Mask of Camille Claudel,
between 1885 and 1895?
Plaster. 32.1 x 26.5 x 27.7
Rodin donation, 1916
Inv. S.349

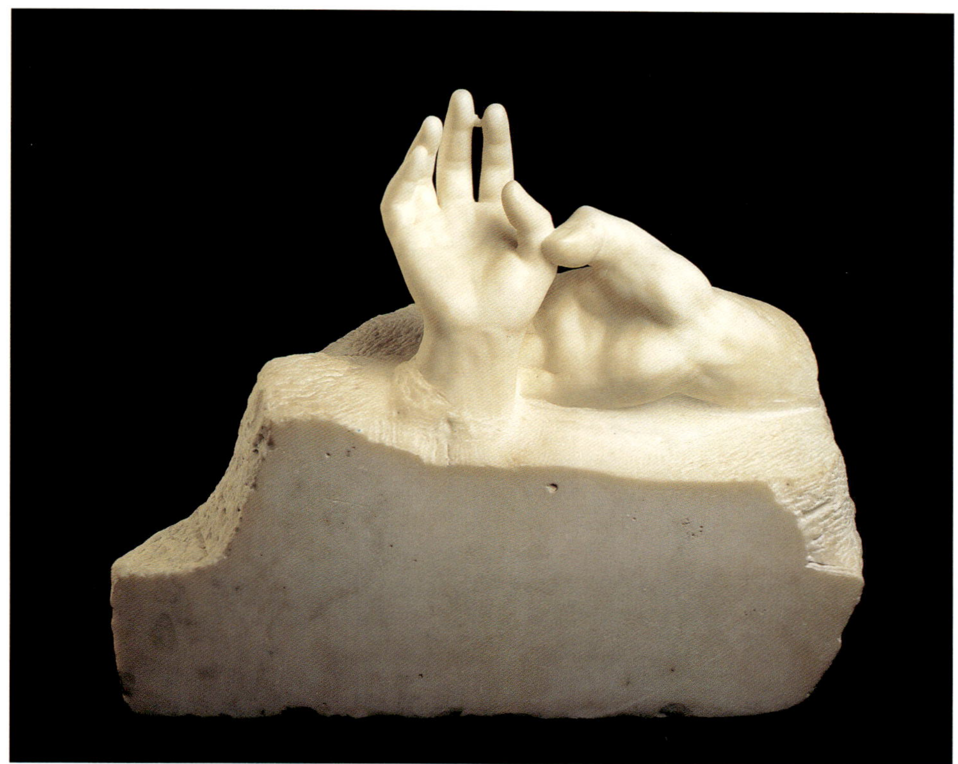

Lovers' Hands,
1904
Marble. 44.3 x 56.9 x 36.5
Rodin donation, 1916
Inv. S.1108

The Secret,
1909
Marble executed by Louis Mathet.
89 x 49.7 x 40.7
Rodin donation, 1916
Inv. S.1000

The Cathedral,
1908
Stone. 64 x 29.5 x 31.8
Rodin donation, 1916
Inv. S.1001

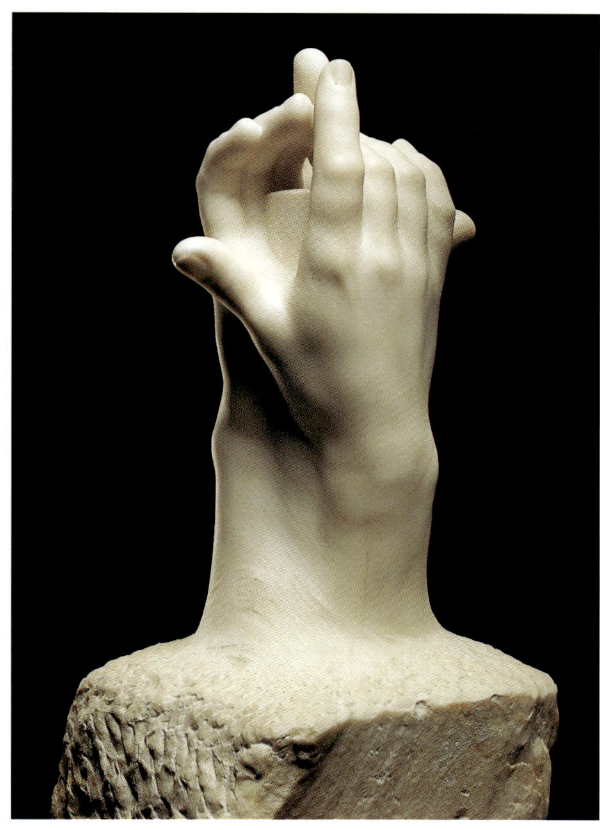

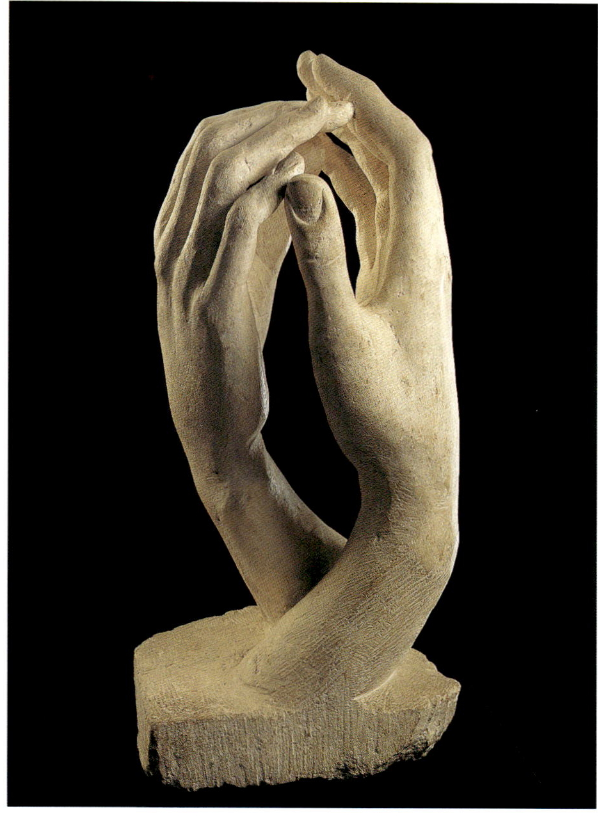

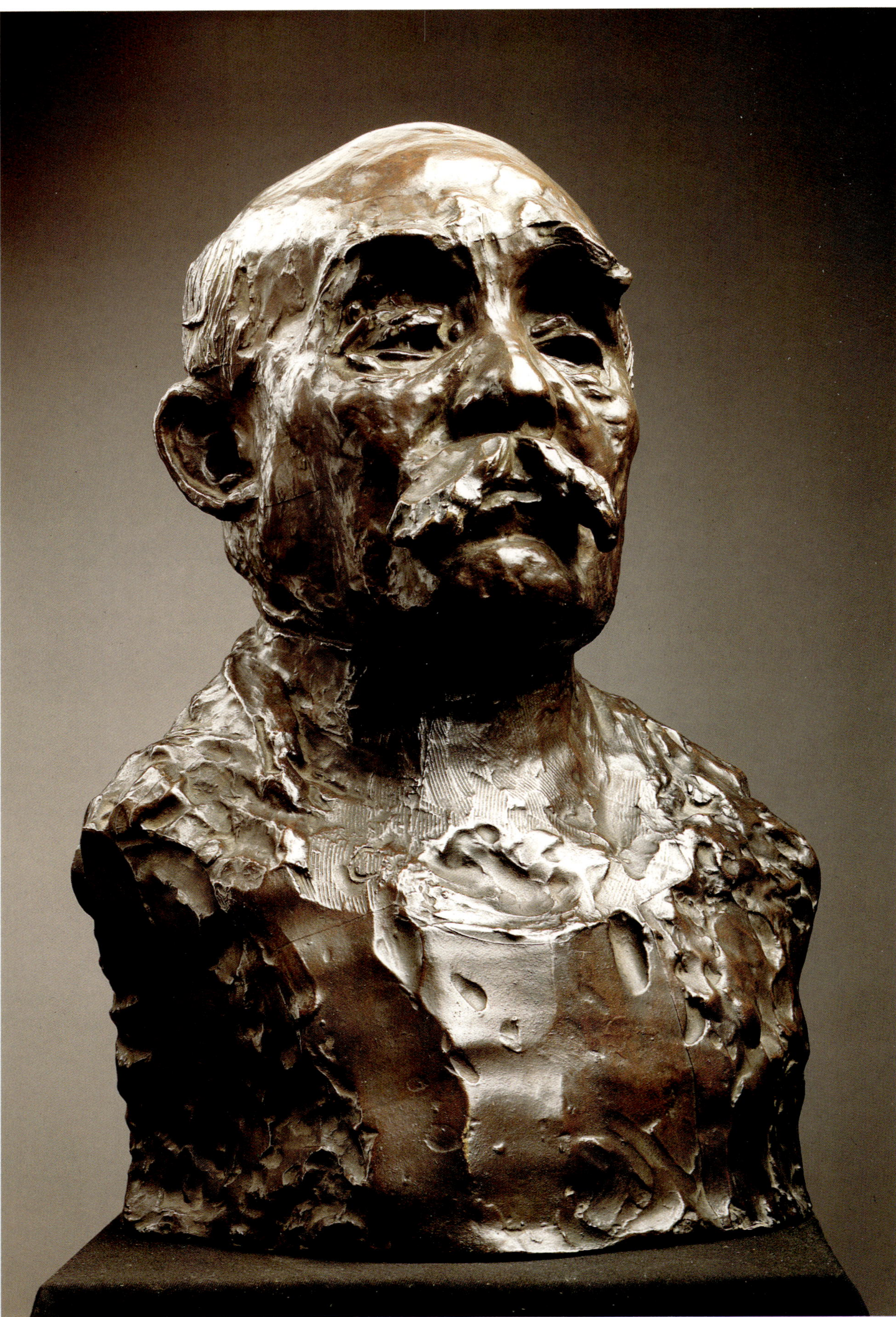

Portraits after 1900

Hélène Marraud

"But the portrait of a woman is another matter; their nature is different and we are far from comprehending it, so we must remain discreet and respectful (...). Even with women, there should always be truth, but not the whole truth. We can sometimes drop a corner of the veil" (Rodin).

After 1900 Rodin's work as a portraitist really took off thanks to the success of the retrospective of his work on show at the Pavillon de l'Alma during the Exposition Universelle. Henceforth working almost solely to order, Rodin saw his clientele constantly growing, and becoming more affluent, international and worldly, which is really demanding for the sculptor who loses some of his freedom, for "the greatest difficulties for the artist modelling a bust or painting a portrait do not come from the actual work he is doing, however. They come ... from the client employing him" (Rodin).

He carried out thirty or so busts, many in marble (40,000 francs for a bust) including many of women, English and American women in particular (Lady Warwick, Mrs Simpson, Mrs Potter-Palmer). Besides more "serious" portraits like that of the poetess *Renée Vivien*, there are busts of women he loved or at least with whom he formed a lasting relationship: *Madame Fenaille*, the wife of an industrialist and art-lover, *Hélène de Nostitz*, *Eve Fairfax*, a young Englishwoman, the famous *Duchesse de Choiseul* who "appropriated" Rodin between 1905 and 1912, and *Lady Sackville*.

Marble was admirably suited to the romantic vision he had of women, giving the subject depicted a certain gentleness, very different from the colder precision of bronze. Chéruy, Rodin's former secretary, related that "For a bust of a man the technique was different. In a man's bust Rodin saw first and foremost character, *Dalou*, *Jean-Paul Laurens*, *Falguière*, therefore he preferred to have his work carried out in bronze. He rarely used marble."

Alongside portraits of poets, musicians and aristocrats such as his *Baudelaire*, *Mahler* or *César Franck* which were cast in bronze Rodin carried out a few busts in marble which are very softly defined: the writer *G.B. Shaw* in 1906, *Mozart*, *Puvis de Chavannes* and *Victor Hugo* which were both commissioned by the State, *Clemenceau* etc. Playing with the material, working it very subtly for the face or leaving it unpolished, in these last effigies he created an unfinished aspect giving the person depicted an eternal dimension. These busts were not always well received. Clemenceau for example, thinking the bust looked like a Mongol, refused to allow his bust to be exhibited in 1912 and, when it was displayed at the Salon the following year, objected to it bearing his name.

"I've done my best," Rodin confided. "I have never lied. I have never flattered my contemporaries. My busts have often not been liked because they were always honest. They certainly have one merit: truthfulness. May that serve as their beauty!"

Clemenceau,
1912
Bronze, cast by Alexis Rudier.
48 x 32.3 x 31.5
Rodin donation, 1916
Inv. S.480

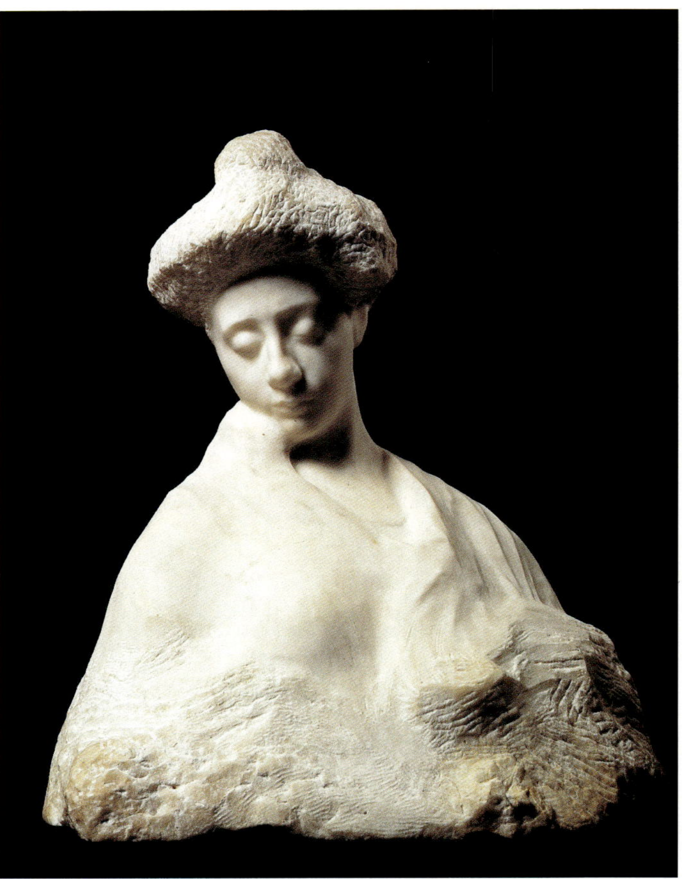

Madame Fenaille,
1900
Marble executed by Raynaud.
64.6 x 59 x 49.5
Acquired by the State, 1907
Musée du Luxembourg, 1908
Deposited by the Musée du Luxembourg, 1927
Inv. S.1043

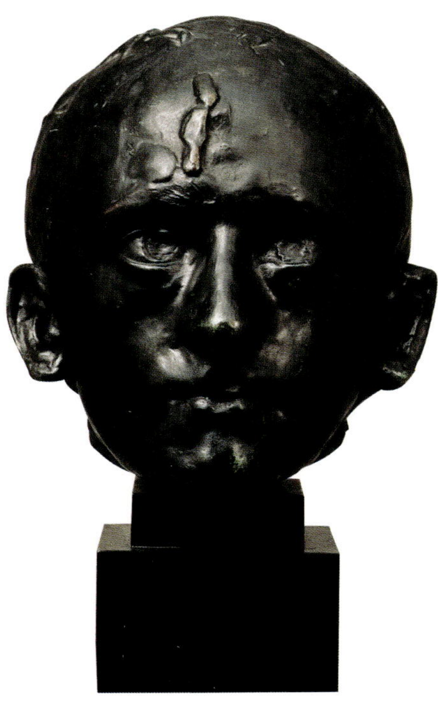

Baudelaire,
1898
Bronze, cast by Georges Rudier.
22.2 x 19 x 21.5
Cast for the Museum's collections in 1969
Inv. S.32

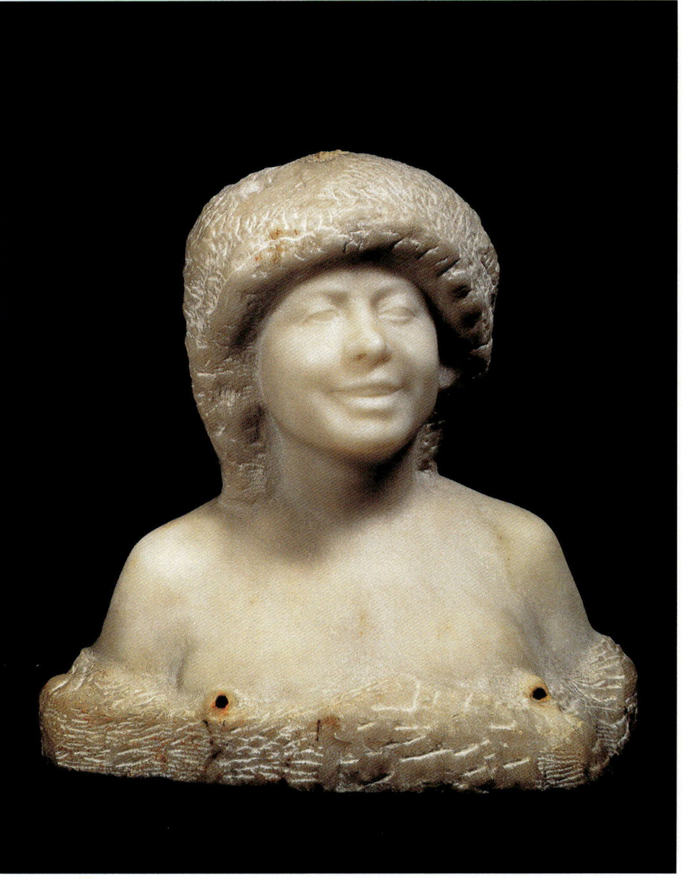

The Duchesse de Choiseul,
1911
Marble executed by Victor Peter.
49 x 50.3 x 31.9
Rodin donation, 1916
Inv. S.1040

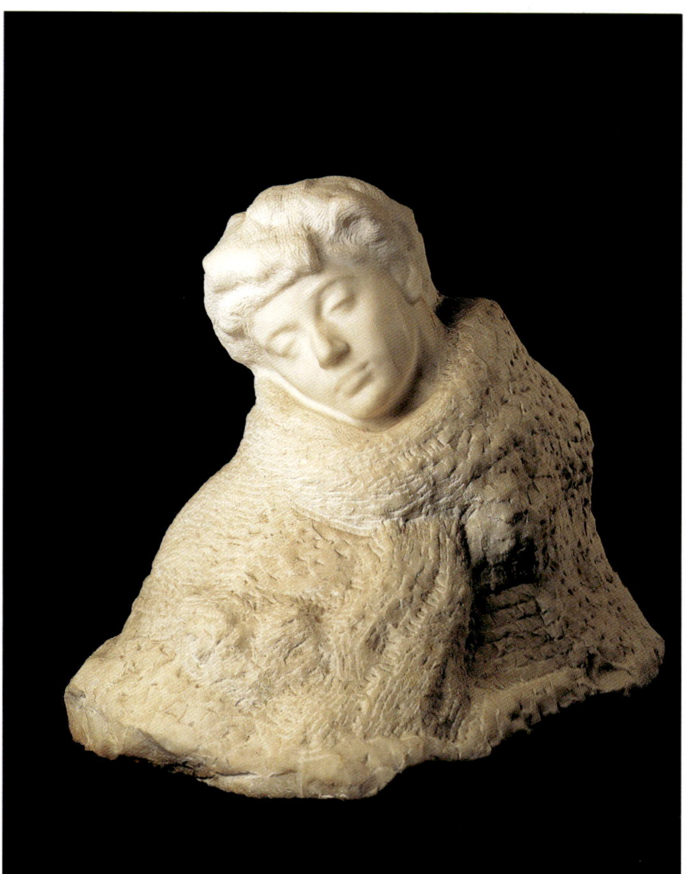

Lady Sackville-West,
1914-1916
Marble executed by Aristide Rousaud.
57 x 75 x 57
Rodin donation, 1916
Inv. S.809

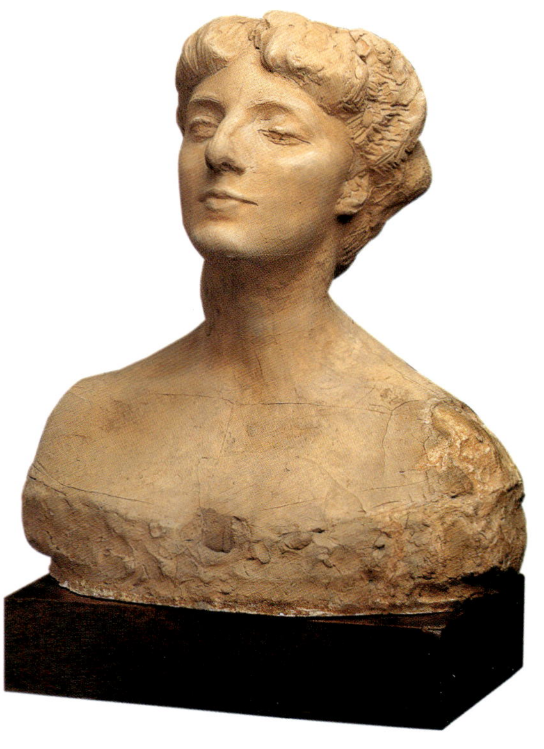

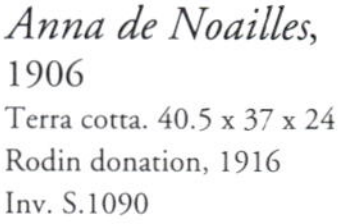

Anna de Noailles,
1906
Terra cotta. 40.5 x 37 x 24
Rodin donation, 1916
Inv. S.1090

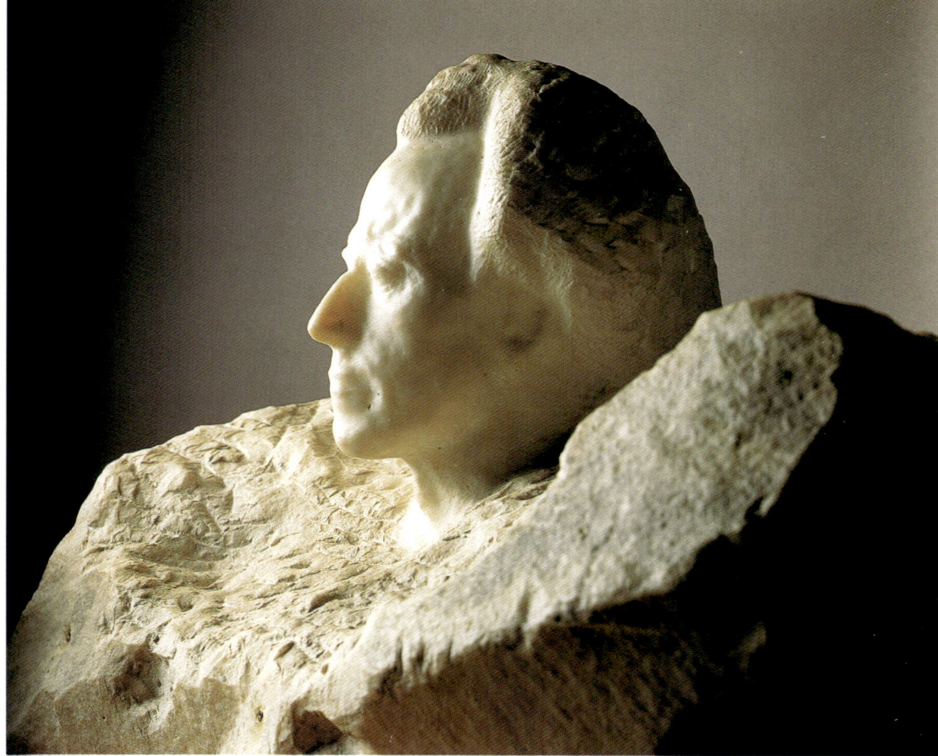

Mozart
(Portrait of Gustav Mahler),
1911
Marble executed by Aristide Rousaud.
50.9 x 99.7 x 58
Exhibited at the 1911 Salon de la Société Nationale des Beaux-Arts
Rodin donation, 1916
Inv. S.1085

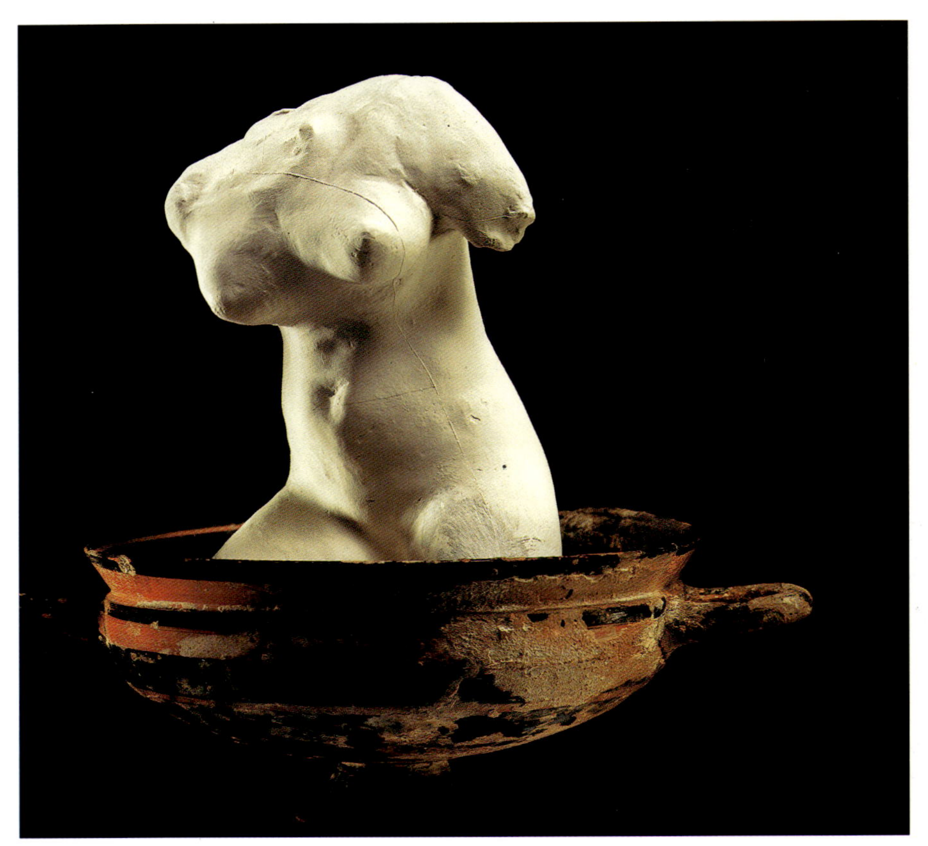

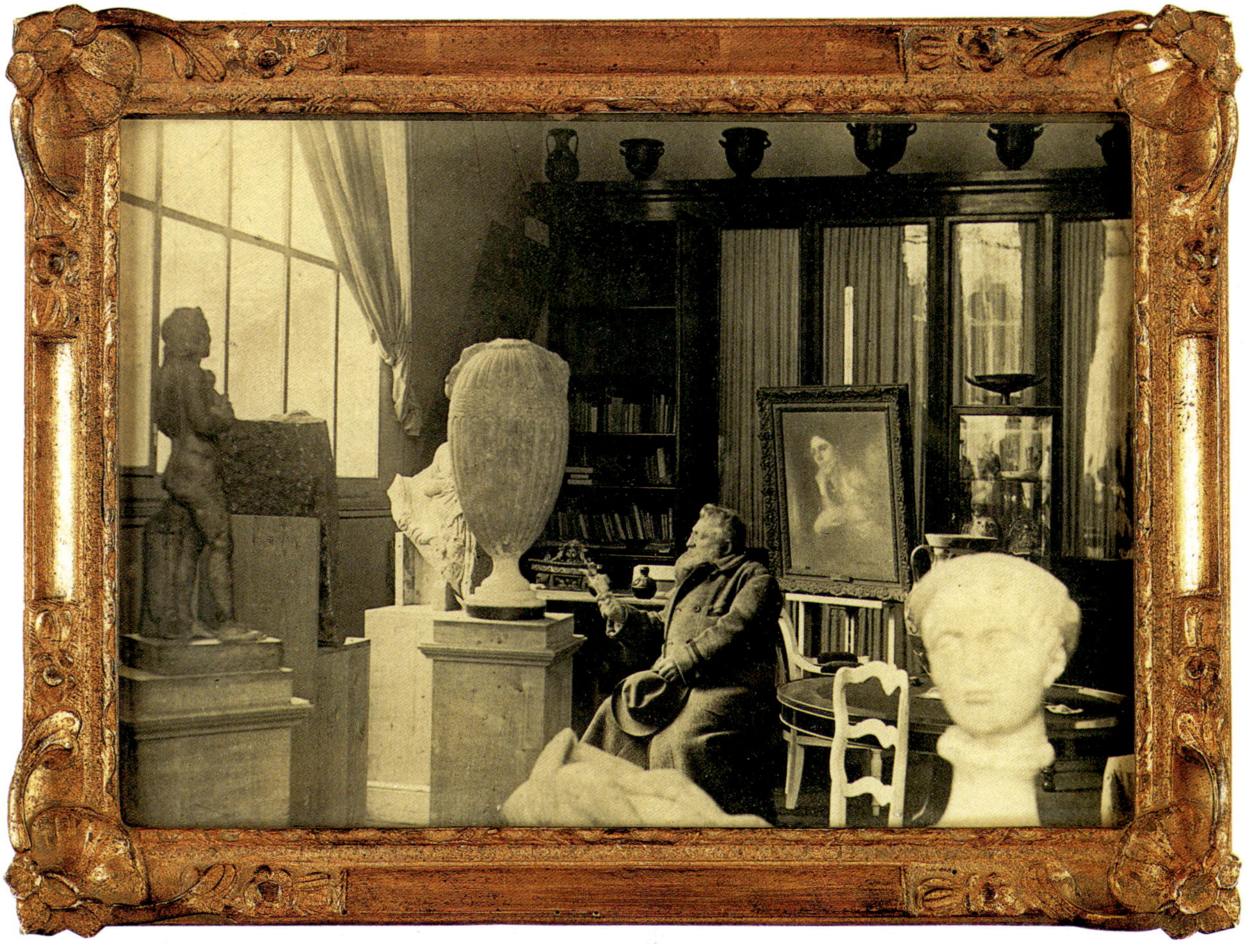

Rodin as collector

Claudie Judrin

An artist's liking for works of art comes into being with his desire to invent. It is through having models beneath his eyes that he finds his own language. At the start of life examples are thrust upon you, and Rodin studied in the studios and at the Louvre. At a later stage when the artist has made his way and success has given him some financial resources and some leisure, he chooses his own surroundings. While the public are sometimes unanimous in recognizing the beauty of these objects, as in the case of Van Gogh's *Père Tanguy*, they may find them disconcerting, for what is involved is a very personal taste, often relating to something the artist was looking for at a given time. We have to be able to decipher the story.

Before moving into the Hôtel Biron Rodin bought the Villa des Brillants in Meudon in 1895. Gradually he furnished his domain with a multitude of objects, virtually doubling the volume of his oeuvre.

His visual curiosity ranged over countries, centuries and genres to such an extent that Ariadne's thread is in danger of breaking. Antique dealers from all over Europe constantly offered him items, and Rodin accepted with varying degrees of felicity as he dabbled in everything.

Setting aside the Far East, Rodin's collection is usually described under the all-embracing term "Antiquities." Rodin saw it as "his museum", whereas today Rodin's own creative work is itself regarded as a museum. The gift made to the State in 1916 included Rodin and his collection. Pharaonic art is fully represented by over 500 items ranging from the Vth to the XXXth Dynasty. We also find a hundred or so Coptic fabrics. Rodin enjoyed describing a certain falcon or cat which he particularly liked.

Greece and Rome in his eyes had a perfection derived from the very fountainhead of nature and life. He accumulated marbles, castings, plasters, bronzes, terra-cottas and hundreds of vases. These Greek vases were so close to the sculptor's heart that he housed his own plaster figurines in them, just as he liked buying columns and capitals and adding his own subjects to them. It was his way of being at one with Antiquity.

The author of *Les Cathédrales de France* did not neglect mediaeval sculpture. A few months before his death he paid 6000 francs for a mourner from the tomb of Jean de Berry at Bourges. He was sometimes given objects as a present. The poet Rainer Maria Rilke who was also his secretary gave him a *St Christopher* when he moved into the Hôtel Biron, seeing him as another Rodin.

Nor did the sculptor fail to take an interest in the painters of his own day. He admired Van Gogh's independence and bought three of his paintings. He

Assemblage:
Kneeling Female Torso in a Greek Cup
Plaster. 23 x 25.7 x 18.5
Rodin donation, 1916
Inv. S.3611

Franck Bal
Rodin Sitting amidst his Collection,
*c.*1905
Gelatin silver print. 19 x 27.8
Acquired in 1994
Inv. Ph.7004

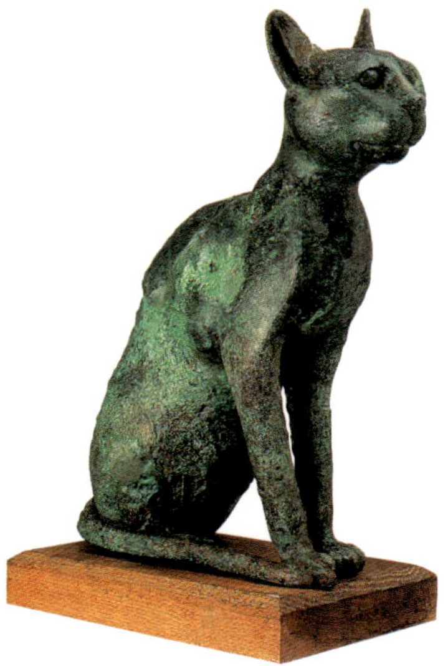

Seated Cat
Egypt, Late Period
Bronze. 32 x 12.5 x 24.3
Rodin donation, 1916
Inv. Co.212

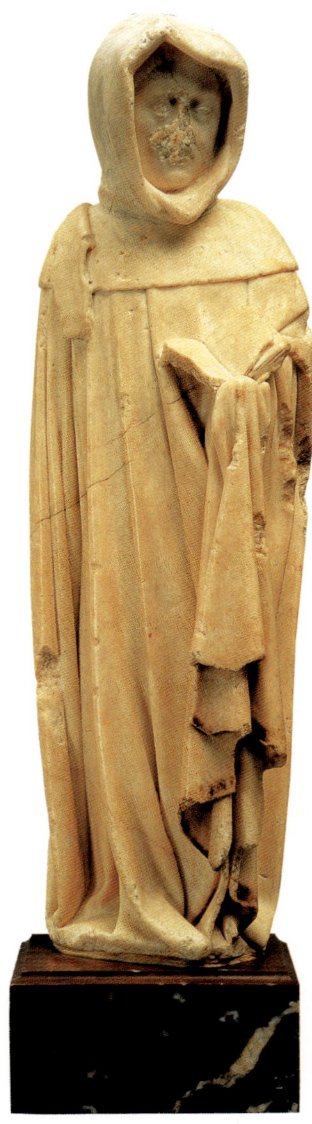

Mourner from the Tomb of Jean de Berry in the Sainte Chapelle in Bourges,
mid-15th c.
Alabaster. 41 x 12.8 x 11.4
Rodin donation, 1916
Inv. Co.914

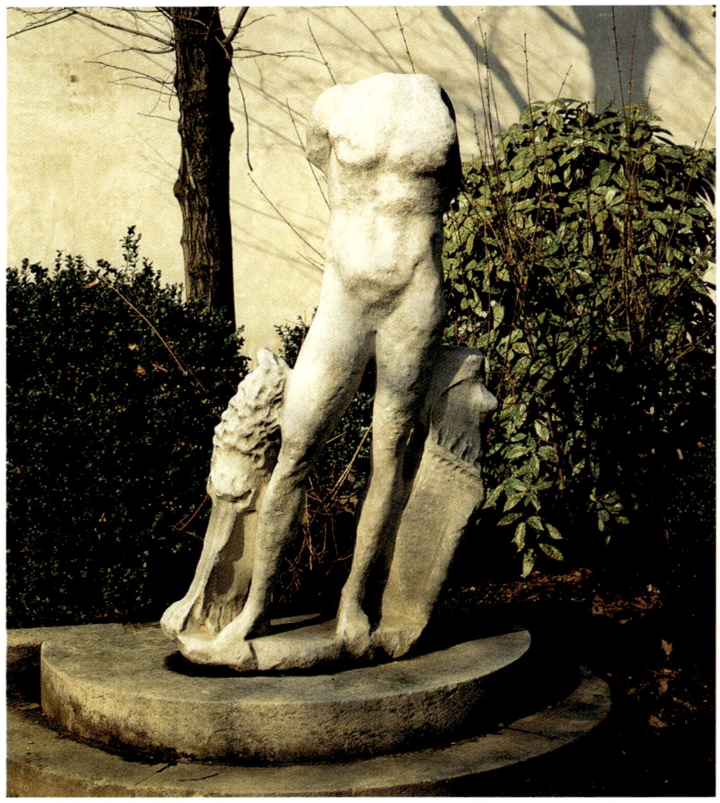

Headless Hercules
Roman copy after a 4th c. BC Greek original
Marble. 183 x 103 x 55
Rodin donation, 1916
Inv. Co.1107

posed for Renoir, buying his *Female Nude* from the Leclanché collection at the Bernheim-jeune gallery for 20,000 francs in 1910. Monet's *Belle-Ile* and the Falguière, the Thaulow and the Zuloaga were acquired in exchange for bronzes, plasters or drawings. A friend he certainly admired profoundly was Eugène Carrière whose *Mother and Child* is reminiscent of the marbles left deliberately rough at the end of Rodin's life.

The presence of a copy of Rembrandt's *Bathsheba* can be accounted for by Rodin's unbounded respect for the Dutch master's mystery. This capacity to marvel at and admire works of art is the privilege of artists and collectors.

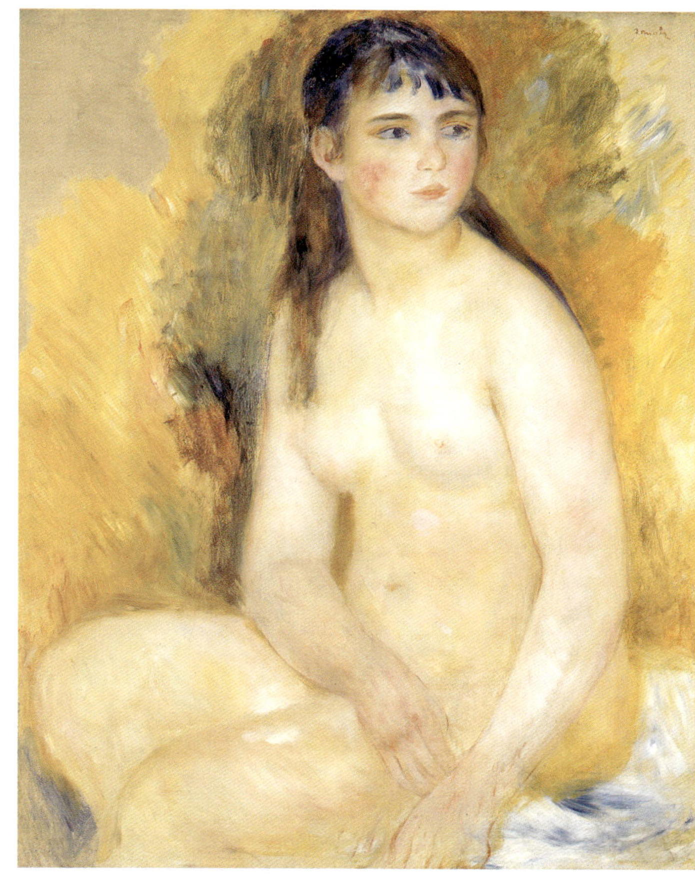

Auguste Renoir
(1841-1919)
Female Nude,
*c.*1880
Oil on canvas. 80.5 x 65
Rodin donation, 1916
Inv. P.7334

Vincent Van Gogh
(1853-1890)
Le Père Tanguy,
late 1887
Oil on canvas. 92 x 73
Rodin donation, 1916
Inv. P.7302

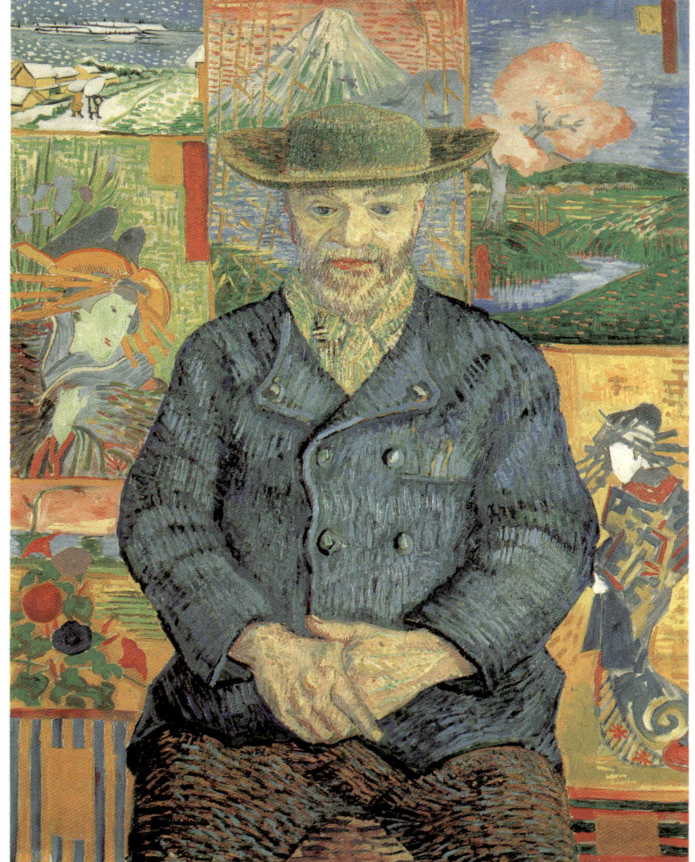

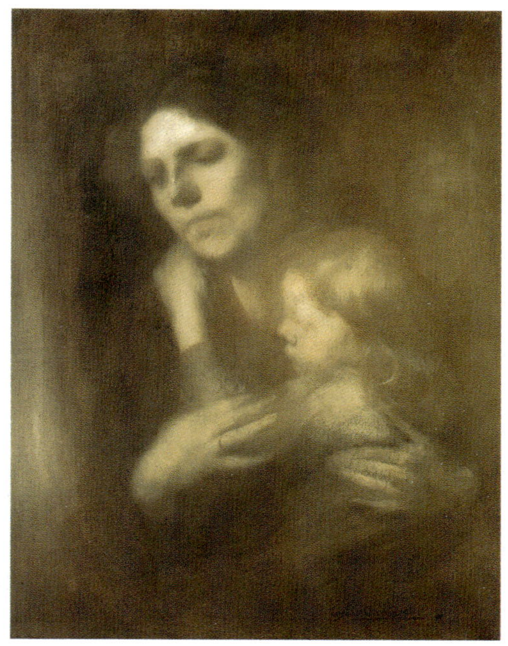

Eugène Carrière
(1849-1906)
Mother and Child,
1891
Oil on canvas. 79 x 62.5
Rodin donation, 1916
Inv. P.7279

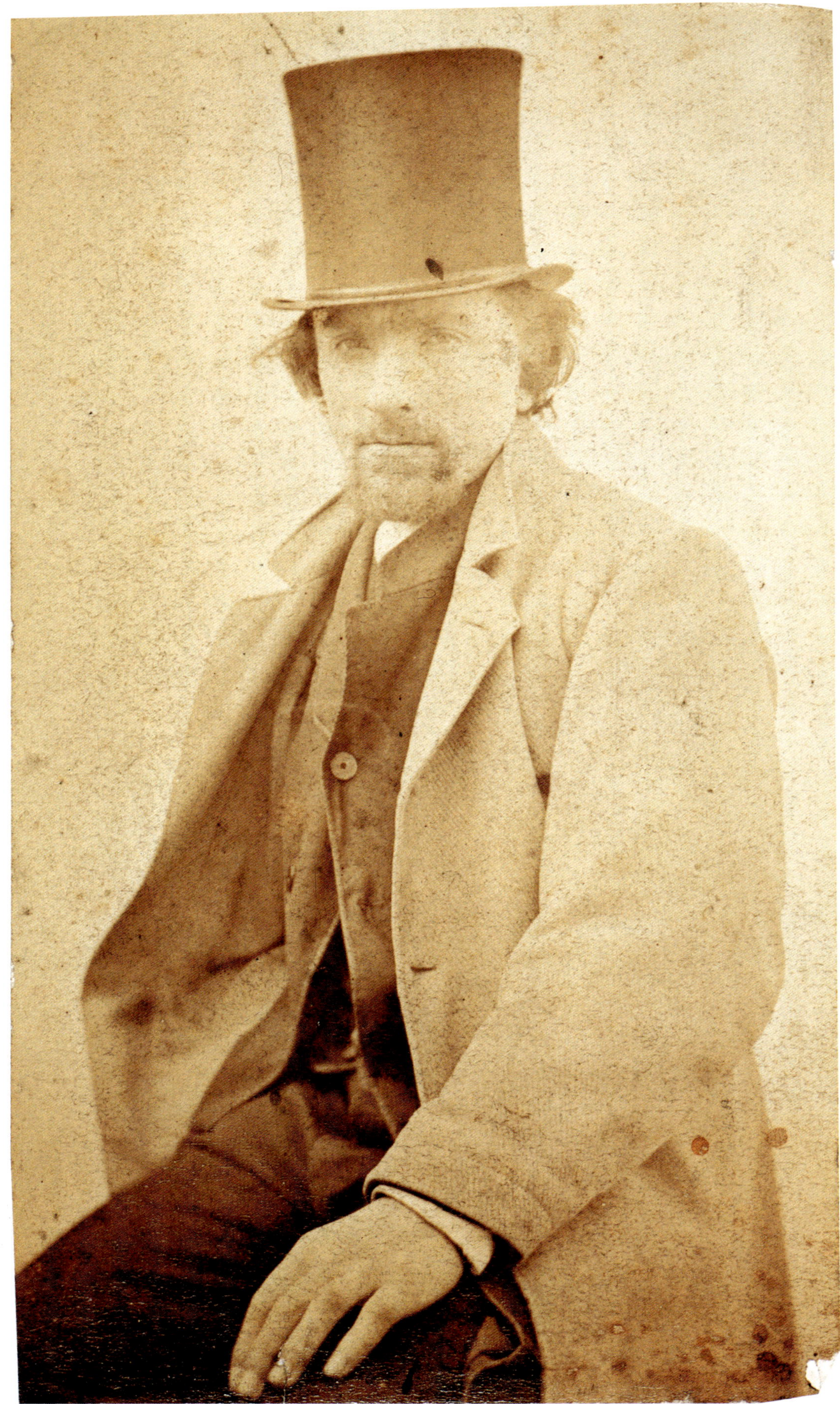

The photograph collections

Hélène Pinet

Because of the quirk of fate that caused Rodin to be born one year after photography was invented he was not immune to the practical and aesthetic attractions of this new technique of reproduction. The 7,000 or so photographs he collected between 1860 and 1917 illustrate his private, public and - especially - professional life. As well as the many official portrait photographs or snaps of Rodin there are portraits of the wide range of notabilities who were crossed his path at one time or another such as Isadora Duncan, Mallarmé or even George Bernard Shaw.

The strong point of the collection is nonetheless the pictures of the sculptures. As he created Rodin built up a tremendous photographic library which enables us to follow his career step by step, to understand his working method and discover the world he lived in, since over and above his work in the round it is the life of the studio which comes out at us from these pictures. They also reflect his desire to control the way observers viewed his work, to enhance the importance of this sculpture or that, to show it at a specific stage of its development and present the viewing angle that to his eyes seemed best.

Yet for a long time the camera remained incidental and photographers were occasional collaborators chosen at random from among people he met or through contacts. The position changed during the 1890s. Once again Rodin was following in the footsteps of Carrier-Belleuse who from 1863 on had exhibited photographs of his works at the same time as the works themselves. Rodin adopted the same procedure for the first time in 1896 at Geneva. From that date on a certain number of photographers followed one another in his studio. Eugène Druet, Jacques-Ernest Bulloz and Adolphe Braun worked each in his own manner but always following Rodin's directions to build up albums of pictures from which anyone and everyone could select illustrations for articles or high-quality prints for exhibitions.

In parallel with this commercial organization Rodin encouraged several artist photographers such as Eduard Steichen, Jean-François Limet, Stephen Haweis and Henry Coles to give a new vision of his work.

It is a tradition which has remained unbroken ever since. The curators of the museum have continued to call on the services of various photographers the most important being Choumoff, Lapina, Bernès and Marouteau, Lacheroy and Adelys. At present we are continuing to enrich and diversify the collections by acquiring early photographs and employing contemporary photographers.

To this collection, exceptional for the variety of techniques employed and points of view chosen, must be added on the one hand the photographic documentation which Léonce Bénédite bequeathed to the museum, including many reproductions of works of architecture and sculptures, and on the other a group of glass plates showing works by Maillol, Bourdelle, Despiau etc in the workshops of the Rudier foundry.

Charles Aubry
(1811-1877)
Rodin in a Top Hat,
*c.*1862
Albumen print. 8.7 x 5.2
Rodin donation, 1916
Inv. Ph.3

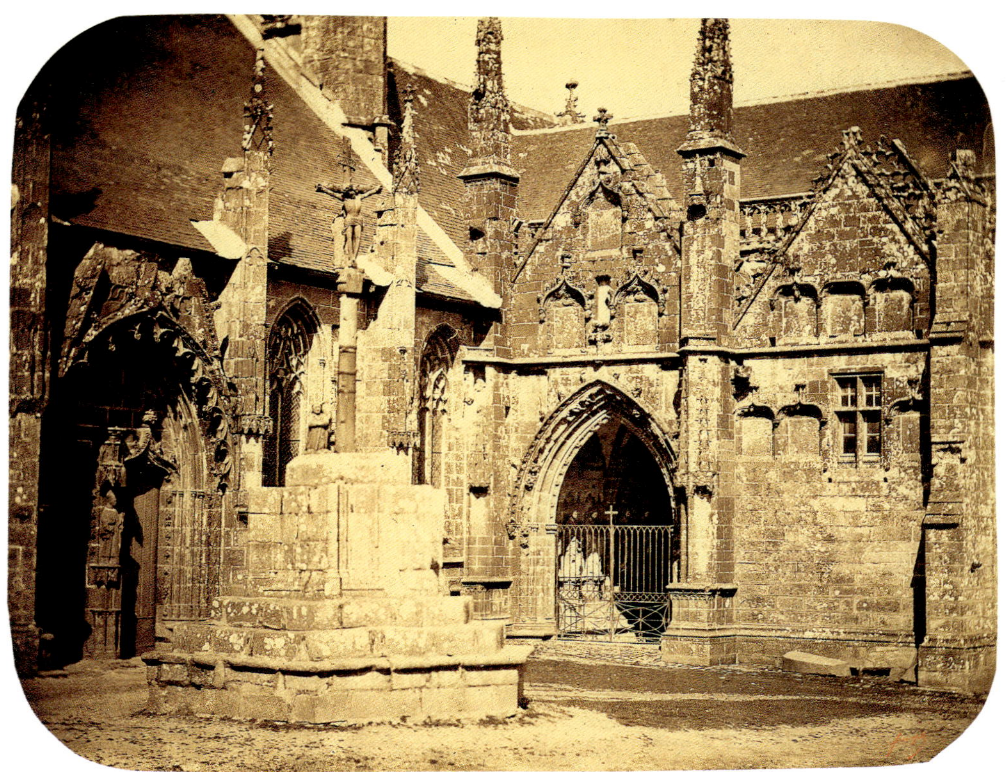

Furne Fils
(active between 1857 and 1861)
Le Folgoet
Albumen print. 20.3 x 26.7
Benedicte Bequest, 1925
Inv. Ph.9108

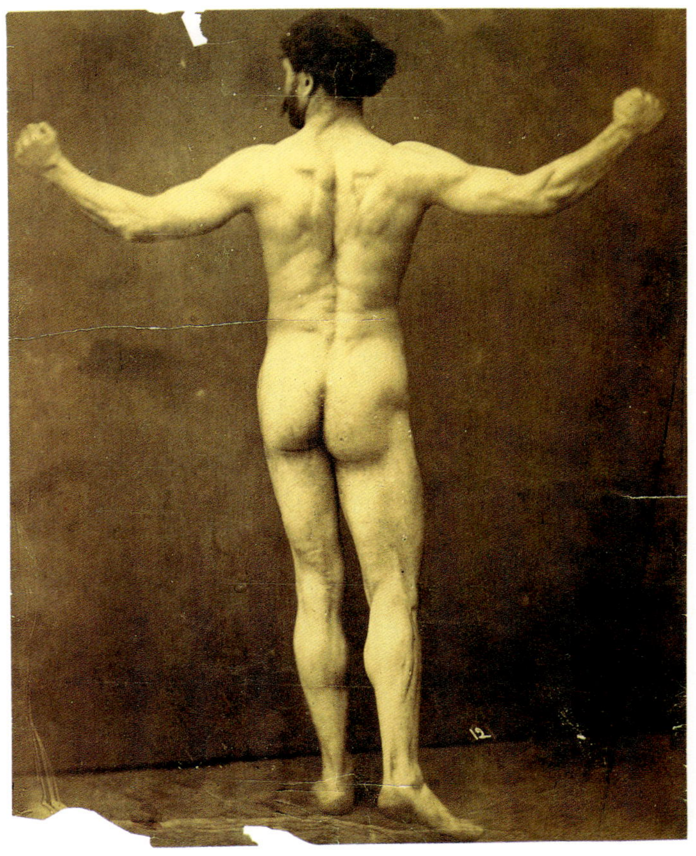

Marconi was one of the most prolific photographers of nude poses for artists of the nineteenth century. His pictures emphasize the transformation or even deformation of the body depending on the pose adopted by the model: the projection of muscles, the hollowing of the back, elongations of the legs.
Rodin bought a few photographs from him which he sometimes stuck into albums, as he had done with this one, mixed up with reproductions of sculptures and architectural works. The sculptor had met Marconi during the 1870s when both were living in Brussels. Accused of having made castings from his model's body, Rodin commissioned him to take shots of *The Age of Bronze* and the model, Auguste Neyt, so that the two could be more easily compared.

Gaudenzio Marconi
(1842-after 1885)
Nude Male Model, Rear View, *c.*1870
Albumen print. 23 x 18.8
Rodin donation, 1916
Inv. Ph.9109

Eduard Steichen
(1879-1963)
Balzac, "Towards the Light at Midnight",
1908
Gum dichromate. 19.3 x 21.2
Rodin donation, 1916
Inv. Ph.226

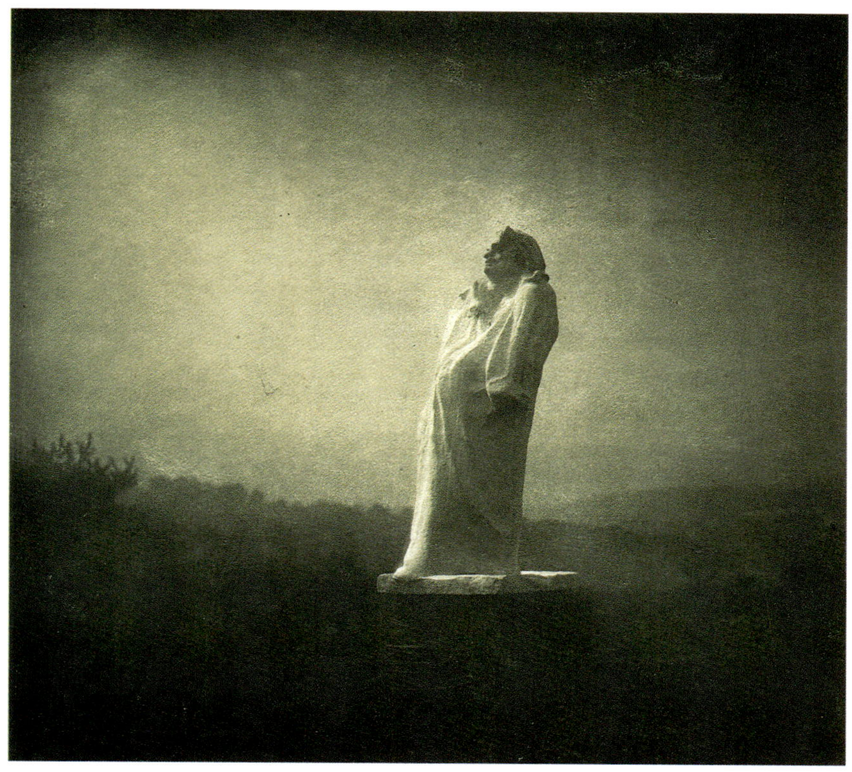

René-Jacques
(b. 1908)
The Three Shades,
1946
Gelatin silver print. 56.1 x 46.1
Acquired in 1995
Inv. 9110

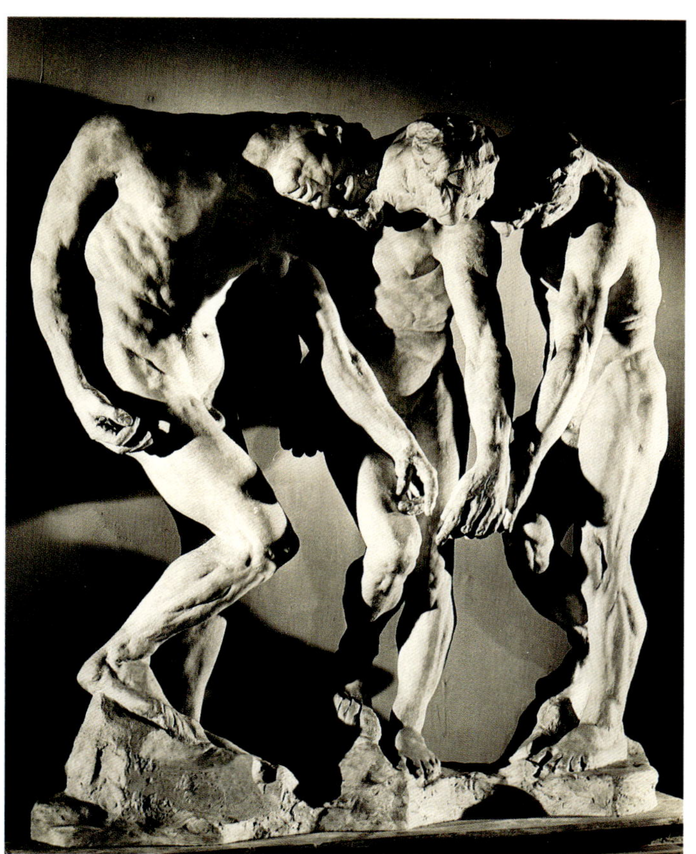

"On a clear, humid summer's day I went up the hill at Meudon and suddenly found myself surrounded by a general commotion. Rodin was having his imposing statue of Balzac brought out of his Meudon studio to have it photographed by his friend, the painter Eduard Steichen." It was Rodin's idea to have the photographs taken at night, which meant that for each shot a posing time of between fifteen minutes and one hour was required. Rodin was so pleased with the results that he said to the photographer: "You will help the whole world understand my Balzac by means of these photographs. They are like Christ walking in the desert."

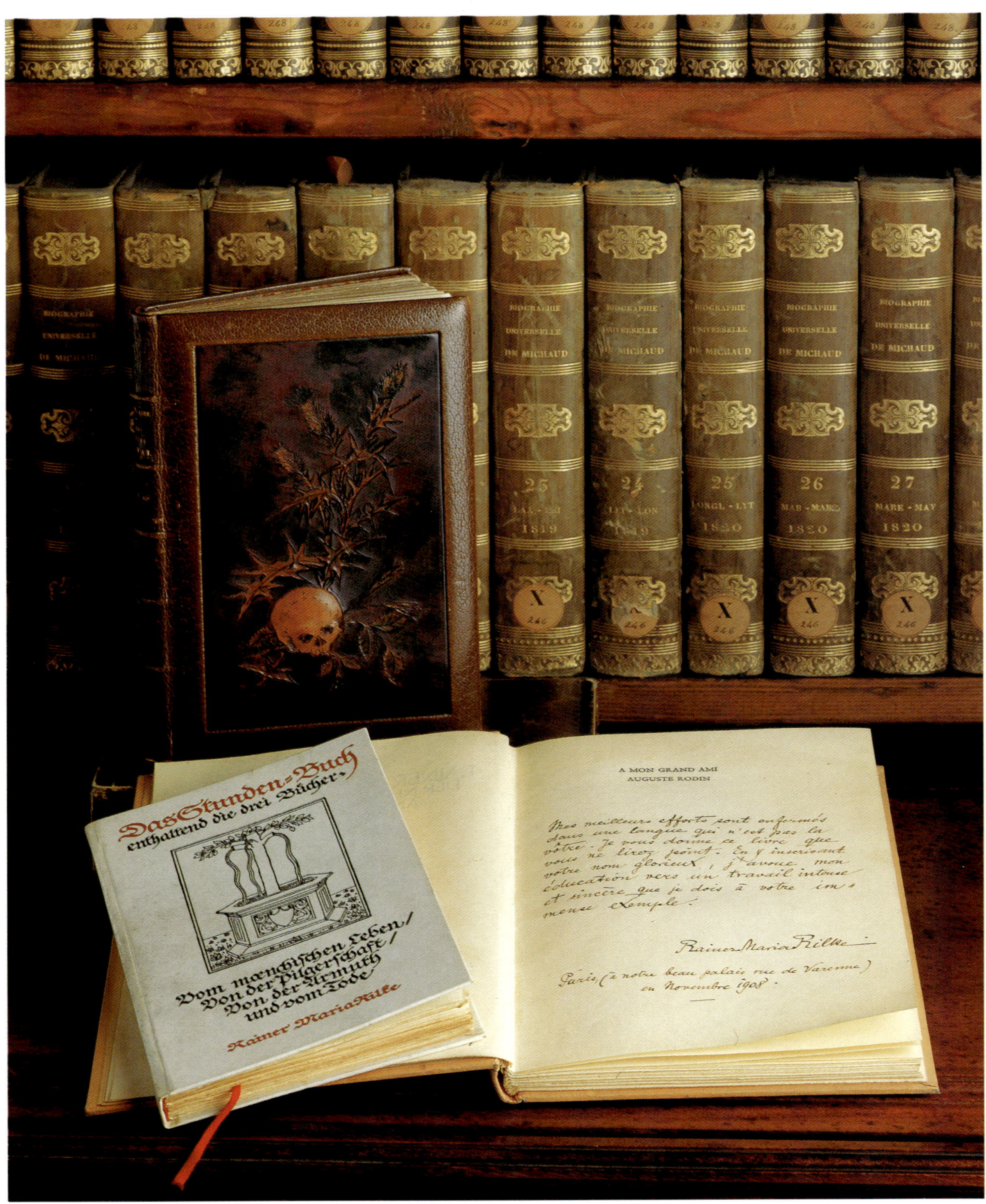
BIOGRAPHIE
UNIVERSELLE
DE MICHAUD
25
LONGL - LYT
1820
26
MAR - MARS
1820
27
MARK - MAY
1820
Das Stunden-Buch
enthaltend die drei Bücher.
Vom mœnchischen Leben /
Von der Pilgerschaft /
Von der Armuth
und vom Tode
Rainer Maria Rilke
A MON GRAND AMI
AUGUSTE RODIN
Mes meilleurs efforts sont enfermés
dans une langue qui n'est pas la
vôtre. Je vous donne ce livre que
vous ne lirez point. En y inscrivant
votre nom glorieux, j'avoue mon
éducation vers un travail intense
et sincère que je dois à votre im-
mense exemple.
Rainer Maria Rilke
Paris, (à notre beau palais rue de Varenne)
en Novembre 1908.

The Musée Rodin's archives

Alain Beausire

COMPLIMENTARY, ENTHUSIASTIC: Rodin got his secretaries to stamp foreign press cuttings from the early twentieth century with these comments: a brief summing up of their reading of them or of an actual translation attached to the documents. This concern for the image of his work and life as seen by the critics was constant.

It was of course only when his first exhibitions were held, i.e. in Belgium, that Rodin could find his name in print; at that time he cut articles out of the newspapers himself and stuck them into notebooks which were unfortunately broken up, probably in the inter-war period, so that they could be classified. As soon as he could afford to do so, i.e. when he was about forty, he subscribed to press-cuttings agencies such as *Je Lis Tout* or the *Argus de la Presse*, and this subscription was carried on by the Musée Rodin after the sculptor's death.

His tendency to hoard things was certainly of longer standing, to judge by the documents kept from his early youth and those coming from family, and was of a dual nature: the sentimental and moral attachment to his roots, maintained in a family held together by the difficulties of life, for whom nothing was superfluous, and his innate feeling for material heritage, whether in the form of individual property or the universal patrimony. He was to provide constant expressions of this feeling from the start of his life to its finish, first of all by preserving everything, from the letters he received to notes scribbled on scraps of paper, from draft accounts to the tiniest press cutting; and secondly by fighting against those who destroyed or damaged the national heritage, whether soldiers or not, all of them wreckers of the popular memory.

For anyone paying a fleeting visit to the Musée Rodin it is hard to have any concept of what its archives and reserve stock were in 1917 and are today. It takes many years of familiarity with the place, tenacity and analysis, one might even say archaeological excavation, to get some measure of the infinite richness of Rodin's donation. Tens of thousands of handwritten and printed documents, books and periodicals counting out over seventy years of the artist's life followed by eighty years of acquisitions by the Museum.

This plenitude of riches is cruelly marred by the absence of most of Rodin's diaries which may have been purloined by his secretaries; the ten or so that have been preserved, from late in life, disparate and partial as they are, reflect their historical importance. Nor are there many posters relating to his exhibitions or

Collection of books from Rodin's library:
Les Fleurs du Mal, by Charles Baudelaire,
Binding by Marius Michel
Copy illustrated with drawings by Rodin
Inv. D.7174
Der Neuen Gedichte anderer Teil, by Rainer Maria Rilke
Dedication to Rodin, 1908
Inv. 11809

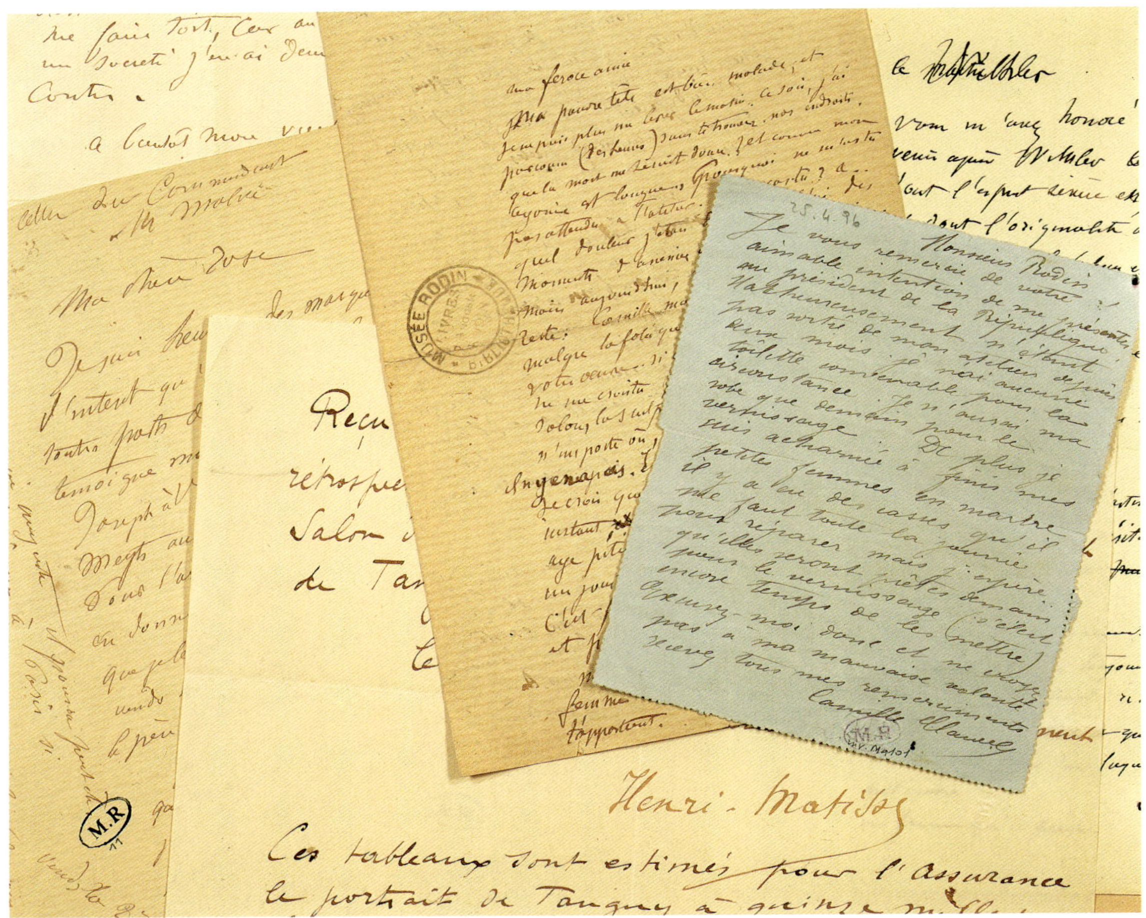

Collection of autograph documents by Rodin, Camille Claudel and Henri Matisse

other events. Apart from these specific gaps, the collection contains rare documents, rare because of the importance of their authors or simply the interest of their content. From the modest receipt to the great stream of letters, warm and friendly or strictly polite, commercial and political or purely administrative, the tens and thousands of handwritten documents preserved by Rodin – he kept everything quite unselectively – all leave some trace of incontrovertible historical signifiance. The whole of society and its workings are concentrated in them, from the doctor to the artist, from the minister to the society lady or mistress, from the workman to the sovereign. As well as letters there are also books, including a number with written dedications which are often valuable.

In this library – containing over 30,000 items dating from the sixteenth century to the present day – Rodin's collection reveals both what he read and what he did not read; for the pages of some works - which we are anxious to preserve as they are - have not been cut, except sometimes for the few pages where the sculptor's name is mentioned. Apart from the evidence thus provided, Rodin was not capable of reading everything, as this dedication by Rainer Maria Rilke in *Der Neuen Gedichte anderer Teil* (Leipzig, 1908) demonstrates: "My finest efforts are enclosed in a language which is not yours. I give you this book which you will not read..."

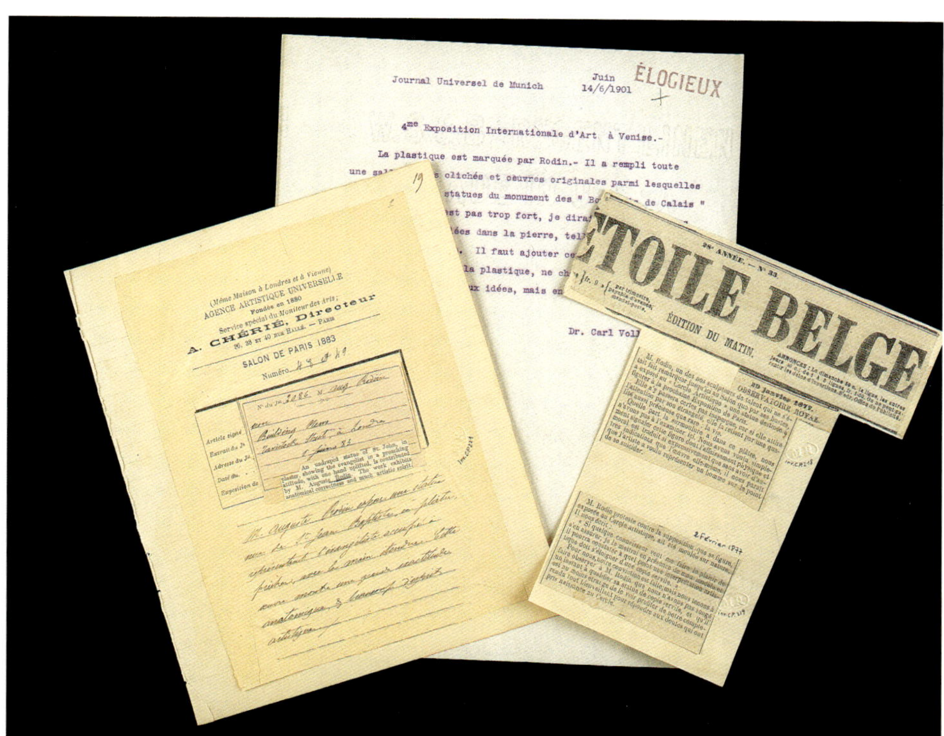

Collection of press cuttings from 1877 to 1901

Louis Malteste
Les Mauvais Bergers - Play in Five Acts by Mr Octave Mirbeau
Poster, lithography. 58 x 42
Rodin donation, 1916
Inv. AF.2

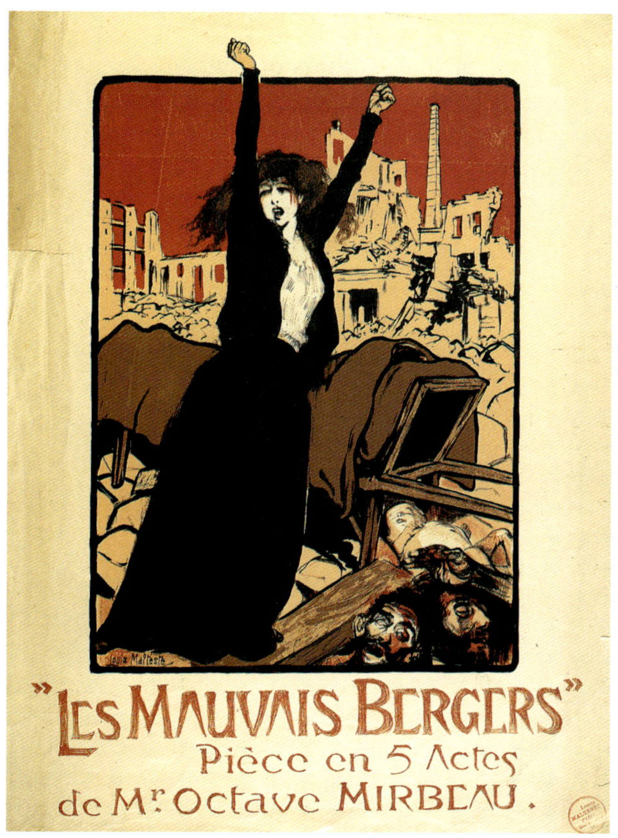

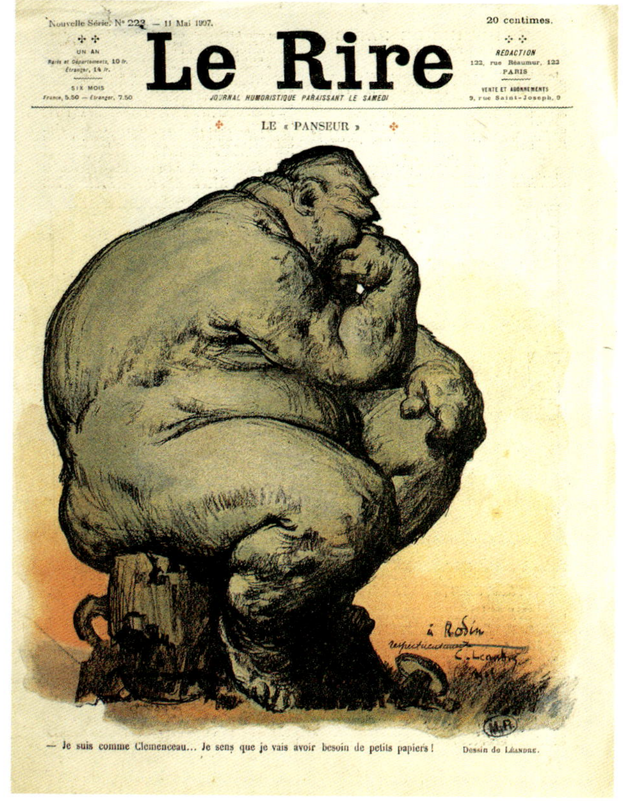

Charles Léandre
(1862-1930)
"Le Panseur" [comic homonym of "Le Penseur", i.e "The Thinker"] in *Le Rire*,
11 May 1907
Cover. 31 x 23.2
Rodin donation, 1916
Inv. CP.224

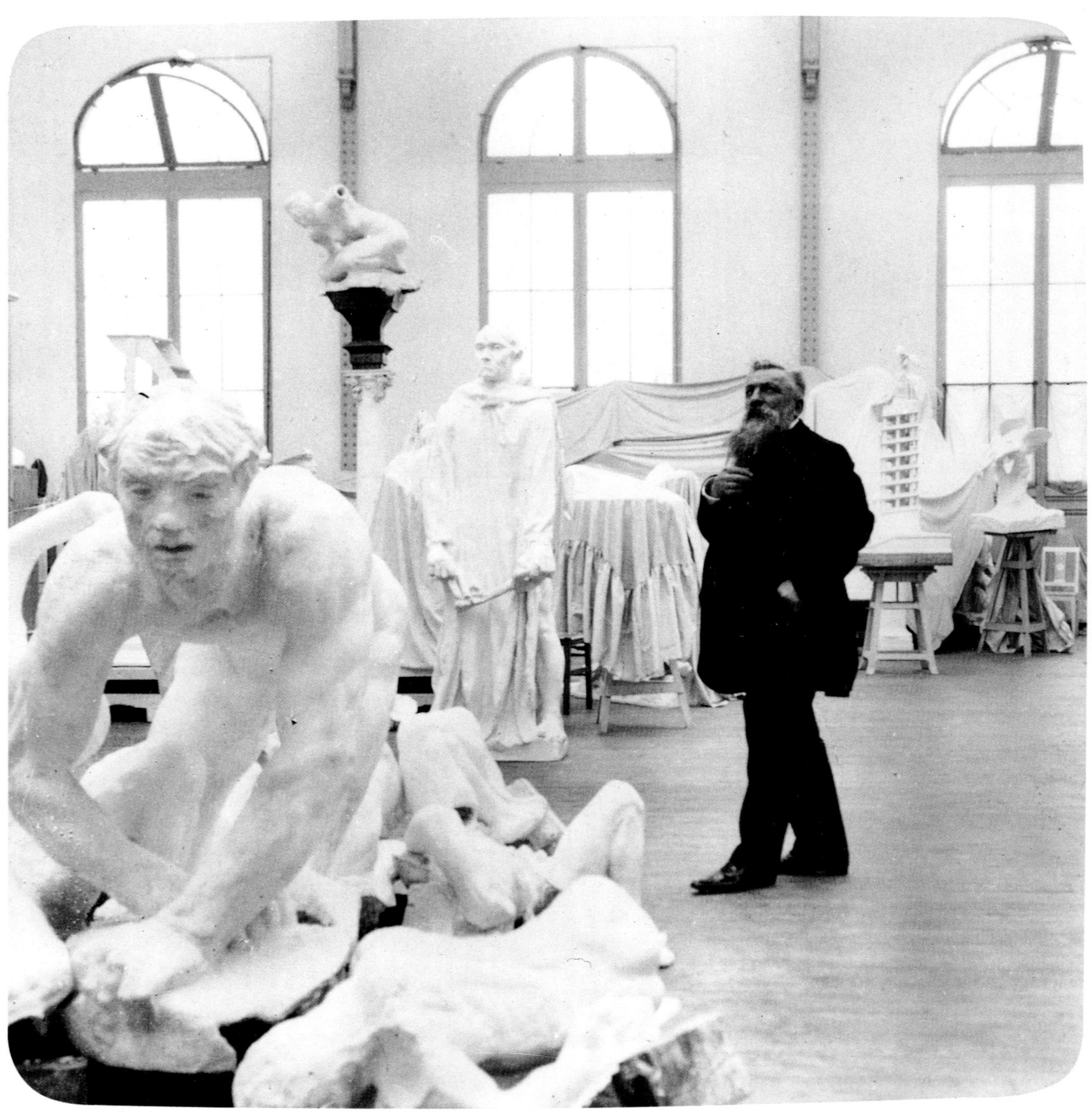

Jules Richard
Rodin in the Pavillon de l'Alma at Meudon,
after 1901
Gelatin silver print. 6,7 x 6,7
Rodin donation, 1916
Inv. Ph.2392

Where Rodin lived and worked

Alain Beausire

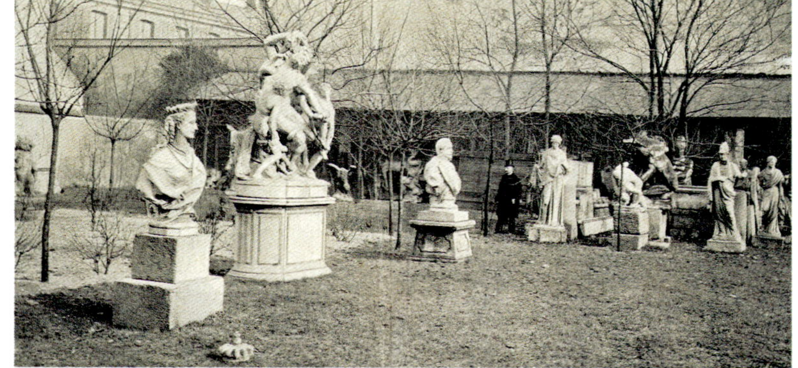

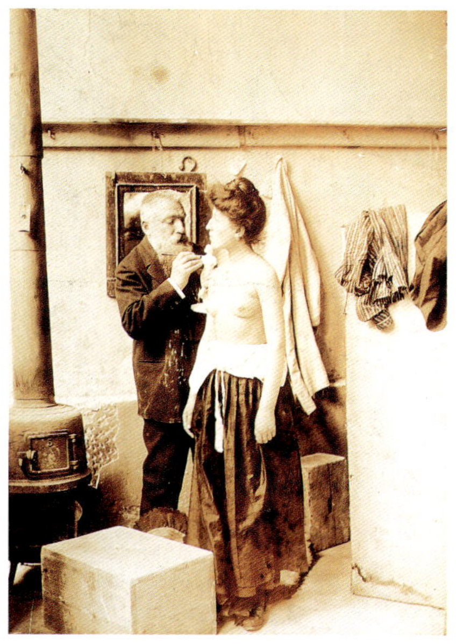

Anonymous
Courtyard at the Dépôt des Marbres, rue de l'Université,
*c.*1900
Photograph in 'Le Depôt des Marbres' by Léon de Montarlot, *Le Monde Illustré*, 2 March 1901. 10 x 21
Rodin donation, 1916
Inv. CP 223

Duchêne
Rodin and a Model in the Boulevard de Vaugirard Studio,
*c.*1895
Albumen print. 22.5 x 16.3
Rodin donation, 1916
Inv. Ph.2005

Even today not a great deal is known about the addresses of Rodin's homes and studios, but the few opportunities for complex, systematic research are gradually producing some hard facts. This is particularly true of his youth when the road system and buildings of Paris were undergoing enormous changes, causing the memory of the city and its people to be obliterated.

Coming soon after the birth of Maria in 1838 that of Auguste at rue de l'Arbalète on 12 November 1840, meant that the family was short of space, even more so when a third child was expected in 1843. By February 1844 at the latest the Rodins moved further down the Montagne Sainte Geneviève to a nearby house at 6 rue des Bourgignons (where the boulevard de Port-Royal now is) between two arms of the river Bièvre; they remained there until 1854.

Apart from ten years or so of travels instigated by Carrier-Belleuse (Montmartre and Belgium), for the first fifty years of his life Rodin remained faithful to the holy triangle bounded by the Place d'Italie, the Panthéon and the Roman road of Saint-Jacques. "Half of these districts in the [old] 12th arrondissement, all of the Montagne Sainte Geneviève and the whole Gobelins neighbourhood, are made up of narrow winding streets where the sun never penetrates, and a carriage could not enter without danger; the sight of a man in a morning-coat walking there would be an event, attracting groups of naked children and women in rags to the doors" (from *L'Ere Nouvelle*, 15 September 1848).

The Rodins next moved to the rue des Fossés-Saint-Jacques on the north side of the Montagne Sainte Geneviève a hundred yards away from the Panthéon (1854-1862); this move seems to have coincided with Auguste's return from Beauvais where he spent a couple of years as a boarder at his Uncle Hippolyte's school (*c.*1851-1854). Despite family problems he enrolled at the Petite Ecole in the rue de l'Ecole-de-Médecine (1854-1857), started sculpting and made three unsuccessful attempts to get into the Ecole des Beaux-Arts. In order to earn his living and help his family he was then forced to do various jobs as an assistant, filling the house with plasters and studies and carrying out the *Bust of Jean-Baptiste Rodin* who then vehemently encouraged him to fight, as did Léon Fourquet, his great friend at the Petite Ecole. Once his father had retired (on 1 August 1861) and become depressed, and after the possible disappointment in love of Maria who became a

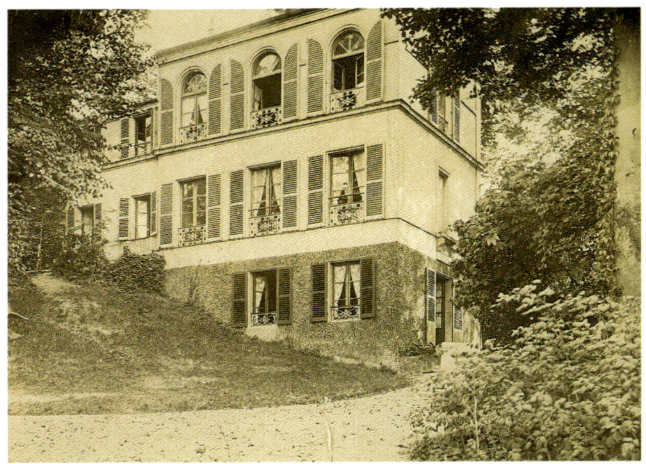

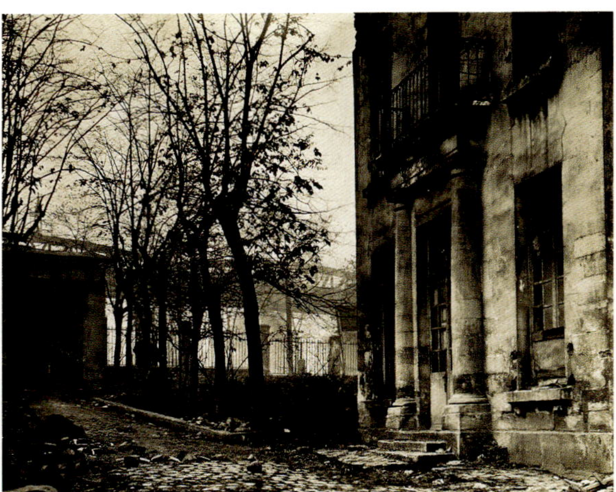

Anonymous
Les Montalets at Meudon,
*c.*1915
Gelatin silver print. 12.1 x 17
Rodin donation, 1916
Inv. Ph.1275

Anonymous
Entrance to the Folie Payen, Boulevard d'Italie,
1910
Gelatin silver print. 12.2 x 17.2
Rodin donation, 1916
Inv. Ph.1187

postulant nun and left home (early 1862), the family went into exile beyond the former city wall constructed [as a toll barrier] by the Fermiers Généraux, moving to the rue de la Tombe-Issoire (mid-1862) in the gloomy districts of the part of Montrouge which became part of the new 14th arrondissement in 1859.

When his sister Maria died in December, Auguste was greatly afflicted and sought refuge with the Pères du Très-Saint-Sacrement at 68 rue du Faubourg-St Jacques, on the selfsame Roman road less than a kilometre from the family home. He was assigned a lean-to in the garden so that he could continue to sculpt; in this first "studio" Brother Augustin produced the *Bust of Father Eymard.*

When he left the community on good terms in May 1963 he at last became completely independent. Jean-Joseph Biès, a "maker of moulds" , owned 20 rue de la Reine-Blanche and it was in his studios opening on to the garden that Rodin carried out a few works of religious art. The photographer Charles Aubry, a friend of Rodin's, also lived there. It may have been him or Biès who found a dilapidated former stable for Rodin in the rue Lebrun. Once again this was the valley of the Bièvre. In this makeshift house and studio Rodin made a home with Rose Beuret. "Oh, my first studio! I'll never forget it; I had some hard times there ... a stable which seemed to me to be sufficiently well lit and where I could stand back far enough to compare nature with my clay... The winter was particularly harsh that year (1863-1864) ... *The Man with the Broken Nose* froze. The back of his head split and fell off. I could save only the mask and sent it to the Salon; it was turned down."

That same year Rodin was introduced to Carrier-Belleuse, his mentor, probably by Aubry, and he had the fine prospect of regular work in Carrier-Belleuse's premises at rue de La Tour d'Auvergne. However Pigalle was a long way from the Gobelins, so Rodin moved to 5 rue Hermel (1865) in Montmartre, then to 175 rue Marcadet, to the north near Clignancourt in those "hideous areas that extend behind the Butte Montmartre" (Zola, *L'Argent,* 1891). Soon after war had been declared (July 1870), Carrier left for Brussels to direct major work being undertaken at the Bourse, and take advantage of the prosperity of Belgium which remained neutral. Rodin was called up in September and released after the armistice of January 1871 in the middle of winter; his son Auguste Beuret was five years old, Rodin had no work and no major personal project. Carrier once again came to his rescue; he

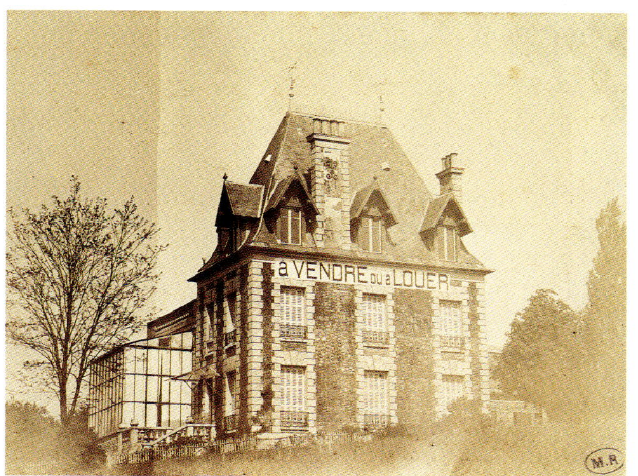

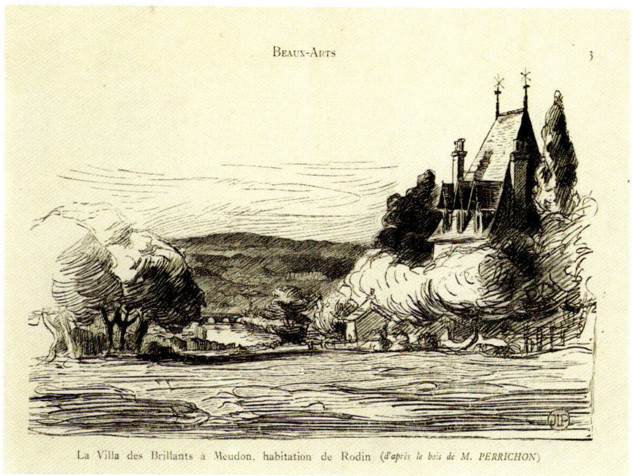

Anonymous
The Villa des Brillants 'For Sale or to Let',
end of 1893
Albumen print. 16.8 x 22.4
Rodin donation, 1916
Inv. Ph.1278

Jules-Léon Perrichon
(1866-1946)
The Villa des Brillants at Meudon
After a wood engraving in *La Revue des Beaux-Arts et des Lettres*, 1 January 1899.
12.5 x 19.7
Rodin donation, 1916
Inv. 1893

needed someone to work for him and asked Rodin to come to Brussels. Rodin lived at 36 rue du Pont-Neuf, then at 348 Chaussée de Wavre and 172 rue du Trône where Rose joined him at the end of 1872, leaving the child with Aunt Thérèse. After signing a contract with Van Rasbourgh in February 1873 he shared his studio at 111 rue Sans-Souci at Ixelles, living at 15 rue du Bourgmestre where he and Rose had a room with a garden. After a three-month tour in Italy (1875-1876) and the *Age of Bronze* affair, Rodin went back to Paris in March 1877 to prepare his exhibition at the Salon, leaving Rose in Brussels. He had to wait for his *Age of Bronze* to be sent from Belgium for the jury of the Paris Salon on 5 or 6 May.

Once back in Paris Rodin made a better job of organizing his studios and homes; these followed one another, becoming more stable with the first large commissions (*Gates of Hell, Burghers of Calais* etc.). From 1877 to 1882 he was at 268 rue St Jacques in the stretch between the Institut de Géographie and the Val-de-Grâce where Zola had also lived in 1864 (at no. 278); from 1882 to 1884 at 39 rue du Faubourg St Jacques and at 71 rue de Bourgogne from 1884 to 1890, not far from the Dépôt des Marbres and quite near to the Hôtel Biron with which he was no doubt unfamiliar at the time. As he needed ever more space, during the same period he occupied a number of different studios, often simultaneously; among these between 1877 and 1889 were 36 rue des Fourneaux (formerly Falguière's studio) which he shared with his friend Fourquet and 182 rue de l'Université, the Dépôt des Marbres, a group of studios and store-rooms belonging to the State. It was founded in 1683 by Colbert to house the blocks of marble that had not been used after the construction of the colonnade at the Louvre was completed, and had come under the Furniture of the Crown until the end of the Second Empire. The Ile des Cygnes was attached to the bank and the small arm of the Seine filled in *c.*1800, so that from the beginning of the nineteenth century the depot could be extended, and it was a staging post for storing items purchased by the State in the provinces (cf. Archives Nationales, series F^{21}); to the east of what used to be the Ile des Cygnes other warehouses were used partly as sculpture studios. At the end of the 1850s new studios intended for the sculptors were completed at rue de l'Université; temporary use of them was granted while State commissions were being carried out, but from the outset there were problems regarding extended

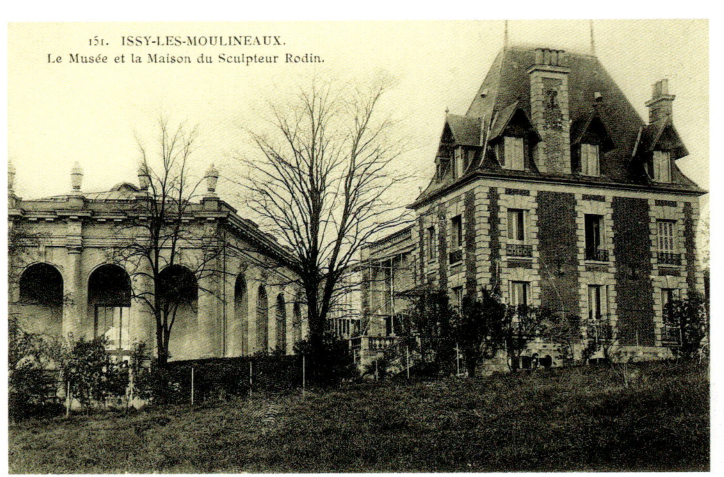

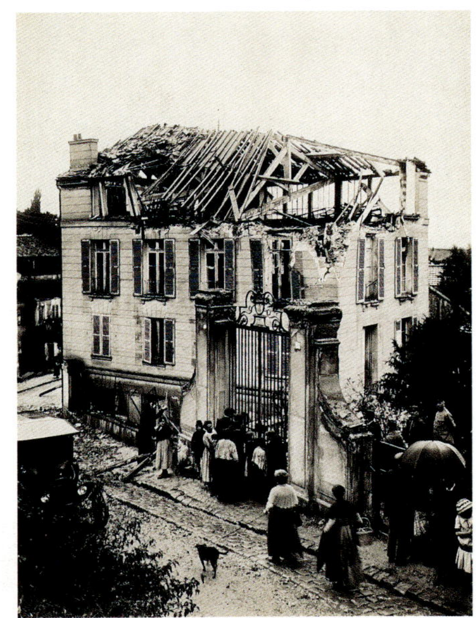

Anonymous
The Villa des Brillants and the Pavillon de l'Alma at Meudon,
after 1901
Photogravure. 9 x 13,8
Rodin donation, 1916
Inv. Ph.1284

Anonymous
La Goulette at Meudon after Bombardment by the Bertha Gun,
1918
Gelatin silver print. 17 x 12.4
Entered the collections in 1918
Inv. Ph.1808

occupancy. There were still traces of the damage caused by the Commune, and restoration work was carried out in 1880; in July Rodin moved into the "M" studios especially for his *Gates of Hell* (the commission was decided on 16 August), the "H" studios (in 1883), and "J" (in 1890); "... the Ile des Cygnes studio is like the dwelling place of poetic human beings straight out of Dante or Hugo" (*Journal des Goncourt,* 17 April 1886, p. 122). In October 1899 permission was granted for electricity to be installed as requested by the sculptor "to carry out the casting for *The Gates of Hell* which will require me to work at night this winter". He was to turn the rue de l'Université into a permanent work-place and a place to receive visitors: "Studios: at Rodin's on Saturday ... a necropolis of official statues no longer in use, this studio is a pilgrimage destination well known to the English and Americans; a cosmopolitan throng of fervent admirers; the kindly giant Thaulow with his yellowish beard; and English ladies and young girls; ... and an art lover from across the Channel turning up specially from London to see, between trains, whether his marble is making progress; between the benches on which the life of the statues palpitates and trembles, among the groups moved by passion and fever, in front of the *Victor Hugo* leaning on his elbows, people move around, talk, go into raptures" ("Un Domino" in *Le Gaulois,* 7 March 1903).
Finally Rodin executed the large figures of *The Burghers of Calais* at 117 boulevard de Vaugirard (1886-1890): "I found the sculptor in his boulevard de Vaugirard studio, his ordinary studio, with its walls splattered with plaster, its miserable cast-iron stove, the cold damp coming from all the big wet-clay machines which are enveloped in rags, and with all those castings of heads, arms and legs amidst which two desiccated cats cut the figure of effigies of fabulous griffons. And in there a model, stripped to the waist and looking like a dock labourer. [...] The rue de Vaugirard studio is full of real human beings..." (Goncourt, ibid.).
In January 1888 Rodin rented a studio at 113 boulevard d'Italie, on the south side of what is now boulevard Auguste-Blanqui, mainly for Camille Claudel. No doubt in order to be nearer his mistress whose studio there was quite small, in March 1890 he rented the Folie Neufbourg in the Clos Payen, a former town house in a state of disrepair at 68 boulevard d'Italie, almost opposite no. 113; he moved out in February 1898 leaving works and other items in store there. Given that Camille

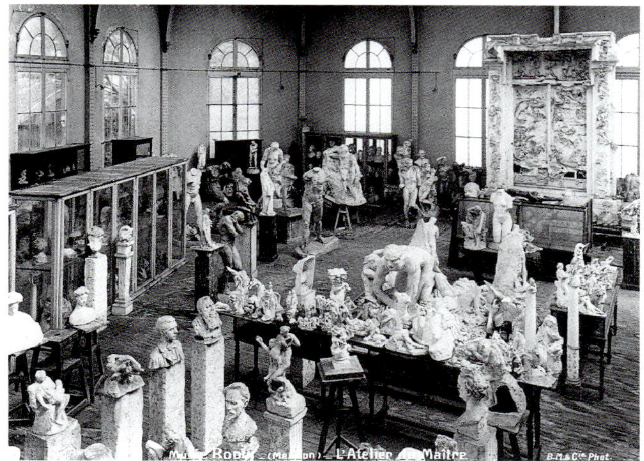

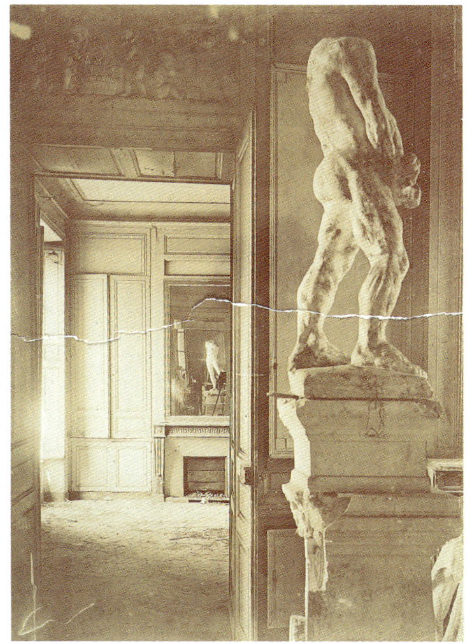

left her studio at almost the same time to move into premises in rue de Turenne, was their final separation which took place at the same period the cause of the move? Probably not, since they had been apart since 1892. Rodin was in fact forced to leave his premises because the new rue Edmond-Gondinet went through the Clos Payen, affecting the west wing of the building; he was to clear out of the premises once and for all in August 1902 and when the building was demolished in 1909 he bought a large number of decorative items. This was still along the course of the Bièvre which travels underground at that point, with both arms under his feet after crossing the boulevard.

In renting a house in Meudon at 8 Chemin Scribe (April 1893-March 1896) was Rodin motivated by a desire to be closer to nature? To cope better with the demands made on him from a distance? To withdraw from the world after his separation with Camille Claudel in 1892, perhaps a painful one? To be better able to prepare his major projects for the turn of the century remote from Paris? At the end of 1893 he also rented a modest suburban house with a large plot of land, still in Meudon at avenue Paul Bert; he bought this house which was called the "Villa des Brillants" in December 1895. He rented or bought various plots of land and premises in the vicinity of the villa to use as stores or studios for castings, such as the "Coulette aux Moines" (known as the "Goulette") at 15 Chemin de Fleury, seriously damaged by a bomb in 1918 but not demolished until 12 August 1983. In March 1901 the pavilion housing his major 1900 exhibition at Place de l'Alma was dismantled and almost totally reconstructed near the Villa des Brillants: "Slender and using light colours, the new Rodin museum [the Pavillon] stands on one of the Meudon hills dominating the valley of the Seine. The elegant arcades of the loggia forming its façade can be seen from afar. From the bottom of the valley where the river follows its peaceful course ... you can see the light building, a temple to great art..." (Anon, n.d.).

In a letter written to Rodin on 31 August 1908, Rainer Maria Rilke, living as a tenant in a room at the Hôtel Biron in the rue de Varenne, extolled the place, the gardens in particular, and suggested that the sculptor should move in, which he did on the following 15 October, making it a home and a place where he received visitors rather than a studio. He was to remain there until his death after making it into a museum.

Bernes & Marouteau
The Pavillon de l'Alma at Meudon,
after 1901
Gelatin silver print. 21 x 29,2
Inv. Ph.9001

Eugène Druet
A Study of Balzac in the Folie Payen,
*c.*1896-1898
Albumen print. 16,8 x 11,9
Rodin donation, 1916
Inv. Ph.1549

Short Biography

by Stéphanie Le Follic

1840
12 November: birth of François-Auguste-René Rodin.

1847-1862
1847-1851: attends the Ecole des Frères elementary school (rue du Val de Grâce).
1852-1854: boarder at a private school run by his uncle, Hippolyte Rodin, in Beauvais.
1855-1857: attends the Ecole Impériale de Dessin et de Mathématiques, known as the Petite Ecole.
1857-1859: leaves the Petite Ecole. Makes three unsuccessful attempts to gain admission to the Ecole Supérieure des Beaux-Arts.
Attends life drawing classes at the Manufacture des Gobelins.
Works at the Museum d'Histoire Naturelle where Barye corrects his proofs.
Takes work with sculptors, decorators, ornamenters and jewellers to earn his living.

1862
Death of his elder sister Maria. Rodin is devastated and enters the order of the Pères du Très-Saint-Sacrement as a novice; makes a bust of Reverend Father Eymard, head of the order.

1863
Return to secular life. Works on the decoration of the Théâtre des Gobelins and the Théâtre de la Gaieté.
Meets Jean-Baptiste Carpeaux.

1864
Works in Carrier-Belleuse's studios.
Meets Rose Beuret, a seamstress, then twenty years old.

1865
The Man with the Broken Nose is turned down by the Salon des Artistes Français.

1866
Contributes towards the decoration of the Hôtel de la Païva, a private town house (Champs-Elysées, Paris).
Restores church sculptures in Strasbourg.
Birth of Auguste Beuret, Rodin's only son, whom he never acknowledged.

1870
Conscripted as a corporal into the 158th Regiment of the Garde Nationale in Paris, then invalided out because of short-sightedness.

1871
Rejoins his employer Carrier-Belleuse who has moved to Brussels. Works on the decoration of the Bourse du Commerce.
Takes part - for the first time - in group exhibitions in Belgium.

1872
End of his collaboration with Carrier-Belleuse.
Rose comes to join him at Ixelles near Brussels.

1873
Goes into partnership with Van Rasbourgh; they work together on the *Monument of Bourgmestre Voos* in Antwerp.

1875-1876
Travels to Italy (Turin, Genoa, Rome, Naples, Sienna and Florence) where he studies the sculpture of Donatello and Michelangelo.

1877
Exhibits *The Age of Bronze* at the Cercle Artistique in Brussels, then back in France at the Salon des Artistes Français in Paris. Accusations that his work is cast from nature provoke a scandal which helps establish the sculptor's name.
In autumn/winter Rodin sets out on his first long odyssey to the centre of France to look at cathedrals.

1877-1878
Finishes *The Walking Man* and *St John the Baptist* preaching.

1879
Works for the Sèvres porcelain factory.
Takes part in the competition for a monument commemorating the defence of Paris in 1870. His *Call to Arms* is not even shortlisted.

1880
The French State, represented by Edmond Turquet, Under-Secretary of State for the Arts, buys *The Age of Bronze* and commissions a *Decorative Doorway* for a planned Museum of Decorative Arts which will come to nothing.

1881
The French State commissions a bronze casting of *St John the Baptist.*

1882
Gives up his job at the Sèvres porcelain factory.
His proposal for a monument to *Lazare Carnot* is turned down.
Executes the figures of *Adam, Eve* and *The Thinker.*

1883
Death of his father.
Meets Camille Claudel, an eighteen-year-old girl, and becomes her teacher.
First exhibition of drawings.

1885
Travels to Italy for the second time.
The town of Calais commissions a monument commemorating *Eustache de Saint-Pierre* which turns into *The Burghers of Calais* (officially unveiled 3 June 1895).
The town of Damvillers commissions a *Monument to Bastien-Lepage* (officially unveiled 29 September 1889).

1886
Prepares the maquette for the *Monument to General Lynch.*
His proposal for the *Bastien-Lepage* monument is accepted.

1887
Is appointed a Chevalier of the Légion d'Honneur.
Illustrates the copy of Baudelaire's *Les Fleurs du Mal* belonging to Gallimard.

1888
The State commissions an enlargement in marble of *The Kiss,* exhibited the previous year, for the 1889 Exposition Universelle.
The State purchases the *Bust of Mme Morla-Vicuna* in marble for the Musée du Luxembourg.

1889
Founding member along with Meissonnier, Puvis de Chavannes, Carolus-Duran, Bracquemond, Dalou, Roll, Besnard etc. of the Société Nationale des Beaux-Arts.
Commission for the *Monument to Claude Lorrain.*
Joint exhibition with Claude Monet at the Galerie Georges Petit.
Commission for the *Monument to Victor Hugo* for the Panthéon.

1890
Rents the Folie Neufbourg at the Clos Payen, 68 Boulevard d'Italie, rejoining Camille Claudel.
15 May-30 June: first Salon of the Société Nationale des Beaux-Arts.

1891
19 June: his proposal for the *Monument to Victor Hugo* having been turned down in 1890, Rodin has to alter the idea proposed for the Panthéon. However, there is a new commission the first project, for the Luxembourg Gardens.
The Société des Gens de Lettres commissions a *Monument to Balzac.*

1892
Is made an Officer of the Légion d'Honneur.

1893
Rodin becomes Vice-President of the Société Nationale des Beaux-Arts and President of its sculpture section.
Rents the Villa des Brillants.
Takes Bourdelle on as an assistant.

1894

28 November: Rodin is invited to visit Monet at Giverny along with Geffroy, Mirbeau, Clemenceau and Cézanne.

Commission for the *Monument to Sarmiento* for Argentina.

1895

Buys the Villa des Brillants in Meudon - now the Musée Rodin in Meudon - where he lives until his death.

1896

First "Rodin - Puvis de Chavannes - Carrière" exhibition abroad, at the Musée Rath in Geneva, made possible by financial backing from Maurice Fenaille. Photographs of Rodin's works are on show for the first time.

1897

Publication of 142 photogravure drawings by Goupil's, with a foreword by Octave Mirbeau.

1898

Final break with Camille Claudel.

The Société des Gens de Lettres turns down the statue of *Balzac* exhibited at the Salon.

1899

Commission for a *Monument to Puvis-de-Chavannes.*

First one-man *Rodin* exhibition (a travelling exhibition: Brussels, Rotterdam, Amsterdam, The Hague).

1900

Creation of an "Institut Rodin" (Rodin is bound contractually to Bourdelle and Desbois).

Rodin is appointed a Chevalier of the Ordre de Léopold of Belgium.

1 June-end of November: major *Rodin* exhibition at the Pavillon de l'Alma, Paris.

1901

The Pavillon de l'Alma is dismantled and reconstructed at Meudon.

Major exhibition of photographs of Rodin's works by Druet at the Galerie des Artistes Modernes.

1902

10 May-10 August: major *Rodin* exhibition in Prague.

1903

Rodin is appointed a Commander of the Légion d'Honneur.

Rodin takes over from Whistler as President of the International Society of Painters, Sculptors and Gravers in London.

1904

The large-format *Thinker* (plaster) is exhibited at the International Society in London, then at the Salon in Paris.

1 May-23 October: major exhibition in Düsseldorf.

Meets the Duchesse de Choiseul, breaks off relations with her in 1912.

1905

Rodin is appointed a member of the Conseil Supérieur des Beaux-Arts.

Rainer Maria Rilke becomes his secretary.

1906

January-March: 14 drawings of female nudes exhibited at Weimar cause a scandal.

21 April: *The Thinker* is installed in front of the Panthéon.

July: Rodin carries out a large number of water colours after Cambodian female dancers appearing at the Exposition coloniale in Marseilles.

Is awarded an honorary doctorate by the University of Glasgow.

Rodin is appointed a full member of the Academy of Fine Arts of Berlin.

1907

Rodin is awarded an honorary doctorate by the University of Oxford.

Major exhibition of drawings (over 300) at the Galerie Bernheim Jeune, Paris.

1908

Important exhibitions of drawings and etchings in Vienna, Leipzig and the Galerie Devambez in Paris.

6 March: King Edward VII visits Meudon.

15 October: Rodin moves into the Hôtel Biron (now the Musée Rodin in Paris).

1909

Major Rodin exhibition at the Galerie Devambez (135 drawings and four photographs of the statue of *Balzac* by Bulloz).

1910

Exhibition of drawings, photographs by Steichen and *The Thinker* at Photo Secession in New York (Gallery 291).

27 April: Mrs Roosevelt visits Rodin at Meudon.

Rodin is made a Grand Officer of the Légion d'Honneur.

1911

March: Royal Fine Arts exhibition in Berlin (Kaiser William II refuses to award Rodin the Order of Merit).

The State commissions a bust of Puvis de Chavannes for the Panthéon.

Grunbaum, Goloubeff, Fenaille and Peytel purchase a large model of *The Walking Man* and present it to the Palazzo Farnese where it is installed on 23 December.

13 October: the State purchases the Hôtel Biron and makes the Beaux-Arts responsible for administering it.

Great Britain buys a *Monument to the Burghers of Calais* for the gardens at Westminster (very simple unveiling ceremony on 19 July 1915).

1912

February: *Rodin* exhibition in Tokyo.

2 May: opening of the *Rodin* collection at the Metropolitan Museum in New York.

11 May-10 June: 222 drawings and photogravure drawings exhibited in Lyons.

1913

17-26 March: the antiquities in the Rodin collection (3) are exhibited for the first time at the Faculté de Médecine in Paris.

Exhibition of drawings and sculptures in Tokyo.

1914

6 March: publication of *Les Cathédrales de France*, published by Armand Colin, with a foreword by Charles Morice, illustrated with 100 facsimile drawings.

September: leaves with Rose for England to escape from the war, accompanied by Judith Cladel and her mother.

1915

8 April-11 May: Rodin is in Rome, visits Pope Benedict XV, and makes a bust of him in a few days.

1916

March: Rodin becomes seriously ill.

9 November: the Senate accepts the Rodin donations with 209 votes in favour and 26 against.

15 December: the Assemblée nationale votes in favour of establishing a Rodin museum at the Hôtel Biron.

26 December: Rodin receives the commission for a monument to the defence of Verdun (fails to materialize; the large version of the *Call to arms* finished in 1920 was not installed at Verdun until 1938).

1917

29 January: marries Rose Beuret at Meudon.

14 February: death of Rose.

25 April: Rodin makes his last will.

17 November: death of Rodin.

24 November: Rodin is buried at Meudon beside Rose. *The Thinker* stands above their grave.

1919

12 March: publication of a decree giving the Musée Rodin the status of a public establishment.

4 August: the Musée Rodin opened to the public.

PHOTOGRAPHIC CREDITS

Harvard University Art Museum - President and Fellows, Harvard College, USA: p. 24 top right
Musée Rodin: pp. 4, 8, 10, 11t, 11 bottom, 12t, 12b, 13 left, 13 right, 36t, 37, 42 l, 54, 61b, 64t, 66b, 68tl, 69, 71, 88tr, 88br, 98tl, 108b, 112, 114t, 114b, 115t, 115b, 119bl, 119br, 120, 121l, 122l, 122r, 123l, 123r, 124l, 124r, 125l, 125r
Musée Rodin - Béatrice Hatala: pp. 20tr, 20tl, 20b, 21t, 38b, 43l, 58, 66t, 68tr, 90br, 99tl, 99b, 106tr, 106b, 110tl, 110tr
Musée Rodin - Erik and Petra Hesmerg: pp. 14, 16t, 25tl, 25tr, 39, 50, 79, 89l, 100, 102b, 103bl
Musée Rodin - Bruno Jarret: pp. 21m, 44, 48b, 67, 83b, 92, 107b, 111t, 111bl, 111br
Musée Rodin - Bruno Jarret / ADAGP: pp. 26t, 75tr, 75b, 87r, 98b, 104
Musée Rodin - Jérôme Manoukian: back cover and pp. 62, 118
Musée Rodin - J. C. Marlaud: p. 94l
Musée Rodin - Adam Rzepka: cover and pp. 16b, 18, 21b, 24tl, 24b, 26b, 27, 28, 30t, 30r, 31t, 35t, 35b, 40t, 41t, 41b, 42r, 43r, 48t, 52t, 53t, 60, 72, 74, 75tl, 76t, 76b, 77t, 78t, 78b, 82tl, 88, 90l, 96, 98tr, 99tr, 102t, 103t, 103br, 107tl, 107tr, 110br, 116, 119t
Musée Rodin - Adam Rzepka / ADAGP: pp. 17t, 32, 34r, 38t, 52b, 53b, 65tl, 65tr, 77b, 84, 87l
Musée Rodin / ADAGP - Bruno Jarret: p. 34l
Musée Rodin / ADAGP - Denis Bernard: p. 49
Musée Rodin / ADAGP - Isabelle Bissière: p. 40b
Musée Rodin / ADAGP - Béatrice Hatala: p. 94br
Musée Rodin / ADAGP - Erik and Petra Hesmerg: pp. 17b, 108t
Musée Rodin / ADAGP - Bruno Jarret: pp. 30bl, 31bl, 31br, 46t, 46b, 80, 82tr, 83tl, 83tr, 95b
Musée Rodin / ADAGP - Bruno Jarret / ADAGP: p. 56r
Musée Rodin / ADAGP - Adam Rzepka: pp. 22, 36b, 57tl, 57tr, 61tl, 64b, 70, 90tr, 91b, 94tr, 95tl, 95r
Musée Rodin / ADAGP - Adam Rzepka / ADAGP: pp. 56l, 57b, 61tr, 91t, 106tr
Musée Rodin / ADAGP - Philippe Sebert: p. 47

Printed in Italy by Editoriale, Trieste
Colour separation by Daiichi Process, Singapore
Dépôt légal: October 1996